T0331646

Goal-Based Reasoning for Argumentation

This book provides an argumentation model for means-end reasoning, a distinctive type of reasoning used for problem-solving and decision-making. Means-end reasoning is modeled as goal-directed argumentation from an agent's goals and known circumstances, and from an action selected as a means, to a decision to carry out the action.

Goal-Based Reasoning for Argumentation provides an argumentation model for this kind of reasoning, showing how it is employed in settings of intelligent deliberation where agents try to collectively arrive at a conclusion on what they should do to move forward in a set of circumstances. The book explains how this argumentation model can help build more realistic computational systems of deliberation and decision-making and shows how such systems can be applied to solve problems posed by goal-based reasoning in numerous fields, from social psychology and sociology, to law, political science, anthropology, cognitive science, artificial intelligence, multi-agent systems, and robotics.

DOUGLAS WALTON is a Canadian academic and author, well known for his many widely published books and papers on argumentation and logic. He is Distinguished Research Fellow of the Centre for Research in Reasoning, Argumentation, and Rhetoric at the University of Windsor, Canada. Walton's work has been used to better prepare legal arguments and in helping to develop artificial intelligence. His books have been translated worldwide, and he attracts students from many countries to study with him.

Goal-Based Reasoning for Argumentation

DOUGLAS WALTON
University of Windsor

CAMBRIDGE
UNIVERSITY PRESS

CAMBRIDGE
UNIVERSITY PRESS

Shaftesbury Road, Cambridge CB2 8EA, United Kingdom

One Liberty Plaza, 20th Floor, New York, NY 10006, USA

477 Williamstown Road, Port Melbourne, VIC 3207, Australia

314–321, 3rd Floor, Plot 3, Splendor Forum, Jasola District Centre, New Delhi – 110025, India

103 Penang Road, #05–06/07, Visioncrest Commercial, Singapore 238467

Cambridge University Press is part of Cambridge University Press & Assessment, a department of the University of Cambridge.

We share the University's mission to contribute to society through the pursuit of education, learning and research at the highest international levels of excellence.

www.cambridge.org
Information on this title: www.cambridge.org/9781107119048

First published 2015

A catalogue record for this publication is available from the British Library

ISBN   978-1-107-11904-8   Hardback
ISBN   978-1-107-54509-0   Paperback

For Karen, with love

Contents

Acknowledgments

All of the chapters in this book have benefited enormously from many discussions and collaborative research projects with colleagues working in the field of artificial intelligence in computer science, and with my fellow members of CRRAR (the Centre for Research in Reasoning, Argumentation, and Rhetoric) at the University of Windsor. Without the support and inspiration provided by these colleagues over the last decade, my continuing research over this period, which culminated in this book, would not have been possible. It will be readily evident to the reader how much the theory of practical reasoning put forward in the book owes to my collaborative work with Tom Gordon. Work and discussions over the past years with Henry Prakken and Chris Reed on argumentation models of artificial intelligence have also influentially guided my views, helped to solve many problems, and shown ways forward.

For discussions on the subject of value-based practical reasoning during our collaborative work on subjects treated in Chapter 1, I would like to thank Katie Atkinson and Trevor Bench-Capon. For discussions on material in Chapter 2 presented at a CRRAR meeting on this subject, I would especially like to thank Tony Blair, Marcello Guarini, Hans Hansen, Cate Hundleby, Ralph Johnson, Steven Patterson, Bob Pinto, Phil Rose, and Chris Tindale. Chapter 2 is a substantially revised version of an article, "Practical Reasoning in Health Product Ads," originally published in the journal *Argument and Computation* (1(3), 2010, 179–198). I would like to thank Taylor and Francis for permission to reprint the material in this article.

I would like to thank Floris Bex, Tom Gordon, Henry Prakken, and Bart Verheij for many helpful discussions on the subjects treated in Chapter 3. My work with Floris Bex on uses of scripts and stories in artificial intelligence greatly helped to refine and improve my treatment of this subject in Chapters 4 and 5. My collaborative research with Tim Norman and Alice Toniolo on building formal models of deliberation dialogue for realistic applications in artificial intelligence has provided the computational foundations for my treatment of these matters in Chapters 6 and 7. The theory of practical rationality put forward in Chapter 8 was helped and inspired by my collaborative research work with Fabrizio Macagno and Giovanni Sartor.

I would like to thank Giovanni Sartor for making it possible to work with him on a joint project on argumentation and artificial intelligence at the European University Institute in Florence in 2012 (funded by a Fernand Braudel Research Fellowship). I would also like to thank Eddo Rigotti and Andrea Rocci for organizing The Thematic School on Practical Reasoning, held at the University of Lugano, November 28–30, 2012. Additionally, I would like to thank Thomas Roth-Berghofer, Nava Tintarev, and David B. Leake for organizing the ExaCt 2009 Workshop on Explanation-Aware Computing, which took place at the 2009 International Joint Conference on Artificial Intelligence (IJCAI 2009) Workshop in Pasadena, July 11–12, 2009. My thanks are also due to Thomas Roth-Berghofer, David B. Leake, and Jörg Cassens for organizing the ExaCt 2011 Workshop on Explanation-Aware Computing, which took place at the 20th European Conference on Artificial Intelligence (ECAI 2012) in Montpellier on July 28, 2012. For helpful discussions I would like to thank Marcin Koszowy, Erik Krabbe, Henry Prakken, Chris Reed, Bart Verheij, and Simon Wells.

I would like to thank the Social Sciences and Humanities Research Council of Canada for support of the research in this book by Insight Grant 435-2012-0104 on the Carneades Argumentation System (held jointly with Tom Gordon). Finally, I would like to thank Rita Campbell for composing the index and helping with proofreading.

1

Introduction to Practical Reasoning

Practical reasoning of the kind described by philosophers since Aristotle (384–322 BC) is identified as goal-based reasoning that works by finding a sequence of actions that leads toward or reaches an agent's goal. Practical reasoning, as described in this book, is used by an agent to select an action from a set of available alternative actions the agent sees as open in its given circumstances. A practical reasoning agent can be a human or an artificial agent – for example, software, a robot, or an animal. Once the action is selected as the best or most practical means of achieving the goal in the given situation, the agent draws a conclusion that it should go ahead and carry out this action. Such an inference is fallible, as long as the agent's knowledge base is open to new information. It is an important aspect of goal-based practical reasoning that if an agent learns that its circumstances or its goals have changed and a different action might now become the best one available, it can (and perhaps should) "change its mind."

In computer science, practical reasoning is more likely to be known as means-end reasoning (where an end is taken to mean a goal), goal-based reasoning, or goal-directed reasoning (Russell and Norvig, 1995, 259). Practical reasoning is fundamental to artificial intelligence (Reed and Norman, 2003), where it is called means-end analysis (Simon, 1981). In goal-based problem-solving, a search for a solution to a problem is carried out by finding a sequence of actions from available means of solving a problem. An intelligent goal-seeking agent needs to receive information about its external circumstances by means of sensors, and store it in its memory. There are differences of opinion about how practical goal-based reasoning should be modeled. One issue is whether it should be seen as merely an instrumental form of reasoning, or whether it should be also based on values. Many automated systems of practical reasoning for

1

multi-agent deliberation (Gordon and Richter, 2002; Atkinson et al., 2004a, 2004b; Rahwan and Amgoud, 2006) take values into account.

Chapter 1 introduces the reader to current research on modeling goal-based means-end reasoning and identifies the direction the rest of the book will take in order to build and implement one model. Section 1 explains the simplest forms of practical reasoning. Section 2 explains the two different approaches to practical reasoning in philosophy and artificial intelligence: the belief-desire-intention (BDI) model and the commitment model. Section 3 defines the notion of an autonomous, rational, intelligent agent – the entity, whether human mechanical or animal, that carries out practical reasoning. Section 4 contrasts the practical reasoning of an agent acting alone with that of multi-agent practical reasoning. Sections 5, 6, and 7 show how the simplest form of practical reasoning is the basis of several more complex forms that take into account consideration of alternative actions, chaining of actions, multiple goals, and side effects. These sections show that in addition to instrumental practical reasoning there is also a value-based variant that has proved to be important in computing, especially in artificial intelligence. Section 8 shows how trying to account for all the steps in a complex sequence of practical reasoning results in a state space explosion. Section 9 shows how the various complexities can be accounted for by using an argumentation model with a set of critical questions matching an argumentation scheme for practical reasoning. Section 10, on practical reasoning in multi-agent systems, sums up the findings of Chapter 1 and shows how they lead forward to the work of the subsequent chapters.

1.1 The Basic Form of Practical Reasoning

There are three basic components of a practical inference in the simplest kind of case. One premise describes an agent's goal. A second premise describes an action that the agent could carry out that would be a means to accomplish the goal. The third component is the conclusion of the inference telling us that this action should be carried out. The simplest and most basic kind of practical inference that is readily familiar to all of us can be represented in the following scheme. The first-person pronoun 'I' represents an agent. More correctly, it could be called a rational agent of the kind described by Woodridge (2000), an entity that has goals, some (though possibly incomplete) knowledge of its circumstances, and the capability of acting to alter those circumstances and to perceive (some of) the consequences of so acting.

Basic Form of Practical Inference:
I have a goal, G.
Carrying out this action A is a means to realize G.
Therefore, I ought (practically speaking) to carry out this action A.

This basic form of practical inference is very simple, yet we all recognize its importance as a kind of reasoning we use in daily life, and especially in technology of all sorts.

Of course, as we will see, this form of inference is much too simple to represent all of the complications that arise in everyday cases of practical reasoning and that need to be taken into account in any reconstruction of this form of argument. An agent may have many goals, and there may be many ways to carry out a goal. Also, practical reasoning is used in explanations as well as arguments, and thus contexts of use can vary. Still, it is best to start with the simple form of inference given above as representing the most basic kind of practical reasoning. The reason is that this simple form of inference has the most explanatory power. After explaining all the complicating factors that make the basic form too simplistic to work on its own, in the end we will return to something like it.

The basic form of practical inference can be represented as a process of rational deliberation in which an agent reasons from a goal to an action. One way to represent practical reasoning is as a sequence from one state to another in an activity diagram. A diamond-shaped node represents a choice point where an agent needs to make a decision. The basic form of practical reasoning can be represented as a sequence of reasoning in a structure of this kind. The sequence shown in Figure 1.1 has an agent asking at the first choice point whether he has a goal. If not, the sequence of reasoning stops. If so, the agent goes on to ask the question of whether there is a means available to carry out the goal. If not, the sequence of reasoning stops. If so, the agent takes the action that is the means. That is all there is to the procedure. At that point it stops. The activity structure of this simplest form of practical reasoning is displayed in Figure 1.1. In this figure and subsequent activity diagrams, rectangles with rounded corners represent actions the agent needs to carry out. The diamond-shaped node represents a decision point. The black dot means 'start' and the black dot with the white border means 'stop.'

It is easy to see that this most basic form of practical reasoning is too simplistic to represent even the most ordinary kinds of cases that admit of some complexity. The following example of practical inference from Aristotle (*De Motu Animalium* 701 a 18) illustrates the simplistic nature of the basic form. The use of the word 'good' indicates that the reasoning is based on values as well as purely instrumental goals.

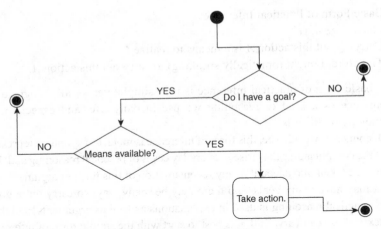

Figure 1.1: The Basic Structure of Simple Practical Reasoning

I should make something good.
A house is something good.
At once I make a house.

The reasoning in this example could be described as "breathless," because the agent immediately leaps to the conclusion to take action. It could even be seen as leaping to a conclusion too quickly, a kind of fallacious reasoning. The fallacy is one of leaping to action immediately without carefully considering the options and costs. This example shows that the basic form, on its own, is inadequate as an argumentation scheme that can be used to represent practical reasoning.

A more complex form of practical reasoning is achieved by chaining together a sequence of practical inferences. The sequence leads toward an ultimate goal, and concludes with a practical directive recommending a course of action to take in a given initial situation, as an agent sees that situation. For example, my goal may be to get to Arnhem this afternoon. The means to get there is for me to take the train that leaves the station at 3:00. The way to get to the train station by 3:00 clock is to take the number 9 bus that leaves the university at 2:30. But in order to take this bus, it may be necessary for me to leave my house by 2:15. It may also be best to get a train ticket. To get the train ticket, I may have to pay some money. Thus, there is a lengthy sequence of actions that I have to carry out in order to fulfill my goal of getting to Arnhem this afternoon. At first, the practical reasoning looks simple, but once I begin to examine it carefully, it breaks down into a complex sequence of connected actions that have to be performed in a particular order. The whole sequence aims at the goal state.

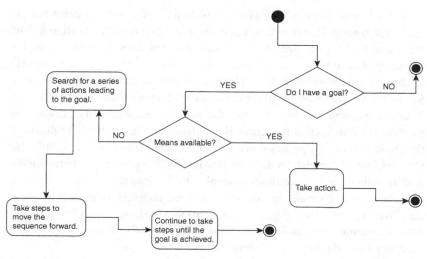

Figure 1.2: Chaining of Practical Inferences.

An example from Aristotle represents a kind of chaining of practical inferences with two steps. The first inference postulates an agent stating a need as a
premise, and then finding a means that fulfills the need. In the second step, the
agent sees that attaining this means is itself something that requires an action
(*De Motu Animalium* 701 a 19).

> I need covering.
> A cloak is a covering.
> Therefore, I need a cloak.
> But, what I need I have to make.
> And [as concluded above], I need a cloak.
> Therefore, I have to make a cloak.

In this case, two practical inferences are joined together to make a chain of
practical reasoning. The conclusion of the first inference becomes a premise in
the second one.

This kind of case can be generalized. In a sequence of practical reasoning, a
series of practical inferences are connected one to the other, as shown in
Figure 1.2.

Practical reasoning as represented in Figure 1.2 represents the typical kind of
forward chaining that takes place when an agent looks forward in deliberation
to try to achieve a goal in the future by carrying out an action now, or before
the realization of the future event is contemplated. This could be called the
projective use of practical reasoning.

A simple example has been given in Walton (1990a, 89). An agent has the goal of balancing his budget, and decides to try to reduce his heating bill by cutting some firewood with his chainsaw. He thus goes through a complex sequence of actions. He gets the chainsaw and puts it in the trunk of his car. He hitches his trailer to the car. He gets in the car and reaches the woods. Once he has gotten the chainsaw out of the car in the spot he has chosen, he starts it up. The long sequence of how to start the saw is described in the instruction manual. He follows this sequence. He switches on the ignition. He pulls out the choke control. He pushes down the safety catch. He opens the throttle. He puts his foot on the plate behind the rear handle. He grasps the starter handle with the other hand. An ordinary example like this one shows how complex a chain of practical reasoning can be in even the simplest and most everyday case. We all know now that the early attempts in AI to model everyday common sense reasoning were confounded by the realization of how complex the most everyday kind of practical reasoning can be.

In addition to the forward or projective kind of practical reasoning illustrated in the chainsaw case, there is also an abductive or backward use of practical reasoning. In this use, a set of data describing the actions of one agent is known to a second agent or observer. The second agent then concludes to a best explanation of the data, using practical reasoning (Walton, 2004). Typically, the second agent uses a sequence of practical reasoning to connect the first agent's observed actions and presumed goals, putting the whole thing together in what could be called an account. The account serves as the basis of an explanation. There can be several competing explanations that are possible or plausible, and the second agent tries to pick out the best or most plausible one. This is the retrospective or abductive use of practical reasoning. It is very common in law and history. This use of practical reasoning will be studied in Chapter 3.

What has been shown so far is that it is necessary to have more complex forms of practical reasoning in which other relevant considerations are taken into account before drawing a conclusion and closing the case. We now go on to consider these more complex forms of practical reasoning.

1.2 The BDI and Commitment Models

The structure of the practical inference can be brought out in a more useful way if we represent the outcomes of actions as propositions – A, B, C, ..., so that carrying out an action can be described as bringing about a proposition, or "making it true." Using this way of speaking, the structure of the practical inference can be represented by the following scheme, a variant on the basic form cited above:

My goal is to bring about A.
Bringing about B is the way to bring about A.
Therefore, I should bring about B.

It is controversial whether this model represents the right approach. According to one theory of action, an action may be analyzed as the bringing about of an event or state of affairs, something like a proposition that is made true or false by an agent (Horty and Belnap, 1995). As shown in an overview of formal action systems (Segerberg, 1984), some have argued for an opposed approach that sees actions as a species of events.

There are two more specific ways of representing practical inferences, depending on what is meant by the expression 'means' when it is said that an action is a means to achieve a goal. Typically what is referred to is a necessary condition for bringing about something, but in some cases what is referred to is a sufficient condition for bringing about something. For example, paying tuition is a means of graduating, in the sense that it is a necessary – but not a sufficient – condition of graduating. My swatting a mosquito may be a sufficient condition of the mosquito's being dead. But it is not a necessary condition, assuming that the mosquito could have died in some other way.

Audi (1989, 86) recognized the distinction between necessary condition schemes and sufficient conditions schemes for practical reasoning. He offered the following example of a sufficient condition scheme (87).

> I really need a peaceful visit in the country. Accepting their invitation for a weekend in the Catskills would be a good way to have such a visit, so I'll accept it.

The assumption made in this example is that accepting the invitation for a weekend in the Catskills would provide a sufficient condition for having a peaceful visit in the country.

The train to Arnhem example given above, however, suggests that in many common cases of practical reasoning, the means refers to a necessary condition. Von Wright (1963, 161) used the following variant on this sort of example.

X wants to reach the train on time.
Unless X runs he will not reach the train on time.
Therefore, X must run.

In another early essay (1972, 41), von Wright, describing practical reasoning as using the means mentioned in the second premise in order to attain the end mentioned in the first premise, offered this example.

> I want to make the hut habitable.
> Unless I heat the hut, it will not become habitable.
> Therefore, I must heat the hut.

This example, like the train example, suggests that the means being described is meant to be a necessary condition of achieving the goal.

The formulation of the goal premise has been a longstanding controversy. One group of theorists holds that the goal premise should be an expression of the agent's intentions, wants, or desires. For example, Clarke (1985, 17) offered this kind of formulation in which E is an end (goal), M is the means (an action), and C is the set of circumstances beyond the control of the agent.

> I want E.
> My doing M is a means to attaining E if C obtains.
> _____
> I should (ought to) do M.

He cited the following example (p. 3): I want to keep dry. Taking this umbrella is a means of keeping dry if it rains. It will rain. I may conclude then that I should take the umbrella. This version, which expresses the major premise as a want, fits the BDI model. Audi (1989, 87) presented a version of the sufficient condition scheme for practical reasoning that also fits the BDI model:

> I want this goal.
> Carrying out this action is a way for me to bring about this goal under these circumstances.
> There is no other way to bring about this goal now, which is as preferable to me, or more preferable to me, than carrying out this action.
> There is no sufficient reason for me not to bring about this action under these circumstances.
> Therefore, let me carry out this action.

Others have expressed the view that the first premise should express the agent's goal as a commitment. Walton (1990a) based the analysis of practical reasoning on a commitment model. Von Wright, in different places, seemed to accept both models. In his first paper (1963), he used the term "want" predominantly. However, in his 1972 paper he started out using "want" as the key word, but then (1972, 45) described an intention to pursue an end as being "resolved" to go after something in the future. This usage seems more like the language of commitment.

Von Wright did not appear to see practical reasoning as a deductive form of inference, given that he wrote (1972, 59) that the premises do not entail the behavior stated in the conclusion. Instead, as he put it, the agent is logically bound to his intention "within the teleological frame . . . for his prospective action." But what does that mean? It seems to imply that the binding nature of practical inference is something other than deductive validity. Perhaps it suggests that a prudent agent should adopt a consistent plan of action. But what sort of consistency is that? This question has led to a lot of philosophical theorizing about weakness of will. Suppose the agent has the goal of doing his homework, and has the means to do it, but is just too lazy? Does that mean the agent is inconsistent, in some sense? This problem remains unsolved (Walton, 1997), relating to problems of retraction of commitments in plans.

There are two different philosophical theories about how practical reasoning should be modeled. The commitment-based argumentation approach (Walton and Krabbe, 1995) can be contrasted with the BDI (belief-desire-intention) theory (Bratman, 1987; Bratman, Israel, and Pollack, 1988; Paglieri and Castelfranchi, 2005; Wooldridge, 2002). In argumentation theory, two agents (in the simplest case) interact with each other in a dialogue in which each contributes speech acts. Each has a commitment set, and as the one asks questions that the other answers, commitments are inserted into or retracted from each set, depending on the type of move (speech act) each speaker makes. A commitment is a proposition that an agent has gone on record as accepting. One type of speech act is the putting forward of an argument. When the one agent puts forward an argument, the other can reply, either by asking critical questions or by putting forward a counter-argument.

According to BDI theory, an agent has a set of beliefs that are constantly being altered by sensory input from its environment that continually updates its previous beliefs. From these beliefs, the agent builds up desires (wants) that are then evaluated by desirability and achievability to form intentions. An intention is a persistent goal that is not easily given up. The two models are different because a commitment is not necessarily a belief. Belief implies commitment, but not vice versa. Belief is a psychological notion whereas commitment is a procedural notion based on dialogue rules (Engel, 2000).

An outline of the main features of the BDI model and the thematic variations in the approaches of its chief exponents has been given by Hitchcock (2002). According to Hitchcock, the BDI model was first articulated by Aristotle (*Nicomachean Ethics* III.31112b15-20), who wrote that good deliberation begins with a wish for some end and follows through with a means for attaining it, and with other means that may be needed to carry out the first means.

The conclusion of this process, according to Aristotle, is a decision to take action. In Bratman's (1987) variation of the BDI model, to form an intention to do something is to adopt a plan, and thus intentions, as well as desires (wants) and beliefs, need to be added to the model. Pollock (1995) added what he called "likings," as well as desires, which need to work in combination with beliefs and intentions. Hitchcock argued that although Pollock's system has many advantages, it is incomplete in three important respects:

1. it is solipsistic, in that it does not allow for back-and-forth discussion between agents;
2. it is egoistic, in that it does not take community values or likings into account; and
3. it is unsocial, in that it does not take groups of agents with a governance structure into account.

Searle (2001) also advocated the BDI model of practical reasoning, but, like Bratman, often shifts to the language of commitment. The problem for the BDI model is that it is hard to model practical inference because beliefs are not transferred from the premises to the conclusion of a practical inference. If I believe that proposition A, and proposition B is a logical consequence of A, it need not follow that I believe that B. Searle (2001, 241) poses the problem as one of seeking patterns of practical validity such that acceptance of the premises of the valid practical argument commits one to acceptance of the conclusion. However, acceptance – another word for commitment – does not equate with, or necessarily imply, belief. Bratman, who often expresses his view of practical reasoning in terms of commitment (1987, chapter 7), is, however, also seen as an advocate of the BDI model. Bratman, Israel, and Pollack (1988, 347) wrote, "The fundamental observation of our approach is that a rational agent is committed to doing what she plans." Perhaps what is shown is that commitment is associated with planning.

Planning – also called automated planning and scheduling – is a technology used in artificial intelligence, based on an intelligent agent having a set of goals and being able to generate a sequence of actions that leads to the fulfillment of one or more of these goals. Solutions, which often resort to trial and error strategies, are found and evaluated prior to the execution point at which the agent carries out the action. Problem-solving is another area of computing, but problem-solving is similar to planning and both technologies are based on a practical reasoning framework in which an agent concludes to an action based on its goals and what it takes to be the means to lead to fulfillment of a particular goal. Although planning and problem-solving are considered different subjects, and represent goals and actions in somewhat different ways, the underlying structure of reasoning from goals to actions shared by both technologies is structurally similar (Russell and Norvig, 1995, 338). In both technologies, an agent has a goal and uses a search algorithm to try to find a solution in the form of an action sequence that leads to realization of the goal (Russell and Norvig, 1995, 56).

Bratman's theory of shared agency, he claims (Bratman, 2014, Preface, ix) "departs in important ways" from the BDI model, now that he has offered "the planning theory of intention and our agency." But the fact that he continues to use the word "intention" to describe his theory suggests that it is still a BDI model. It can perhaps be described as a planning model that still contains important elements of the BDI model.

An important problem for the BDI model of practical reasoning is that of weakness of will, often described in the literature using the Greek expression *akrasia*. An agent exhibits weakness of will where the agent has a goal, and determines what is the best means to carry out that goal, but cannot marshal sufficient strength of purpose to actually carry out the goal. This is a problem for the BDI model because this model equates goals with states of mind of an agent, such as the agent's intentions or desires, and views practical reasoning as proceeding from these internal psychological goals to the agent's actions. Hence, for the BDI model, if the agent decides to do something else, or actually does something that is different from what is required by its goals and its accepted account of the means required to carry out these goals, that is a problem because what the agent actually does has deviated from what it should do.

Searle (2001, 42) describes this problem as the experience of a gap in a decision situation between our reasons and our actions. However, this kind of situation is not a problem for the commitment model (by itself). In this model there is no gap in the decision situation. The commitment model only presents a normative structure of practical reasoning that links a rational agent's goals, along with its knowledge about the means to carry out these goals, to a conclusion that, practically speaking, it should carry out the actions that it takes to be the best means for carrying out its goals. Hence, in the commitment model there is no such gap. It is only when we try to extend the commitment model to the much richer BDI model that this kind of problem arises. It arises when using the combined model to try to explain the behavior of agents in cases where the agent appears to be using practical reasoning but where there is a gap of the kind described above between the agent's reasons and actions. A solution to this problem will be proposed in Chapter 5.

1.3 Autonomous Agents

In some cases, practical reasoning can be quite complex, and the literature has shown that there are borderline cases where it is hard to decide from the data in a given case whether the agent was using practical reasoning or not. Indeed, there are philosophical questions on whether animals, machines, and other entities can engage in practical reasoning at all, and, if they do so, whether it is a kind of practical reasoning different from what humans do. Borderline cases of apparently intelligent behavior by animals, and by electrical, chemical, and physical systems that interact with an environment, are controversial. Do they exhibit goal-directed practical reasoning of some kind or not? Other controversial cases are reflexive and habitual human actions, and actions of a person judged to be mentally ill. To make sense of practical reasoning it is necessary to begin with the notion of a rational agent as an entity that is capable of goal-directed action based on its capability to have limited knowledge of its circumstances. This notion is now widely accepted in distributed computing (Wooldridge, 2000). Such an agent is assumed to be capable of carrying out actions based on how it is programmed with goals. Agents are now being widely used to carry out a variety of tasks that involve not only knowledge of circumstances, but also capability for communication with other agents (Wooldridge, 2002). Multi-agent systems are primarily systems for the inter-action of software agents, although the agents can also be robots, humans, or combinations of software agents, robots and humans, which carry out actions in an environment that they can be aware of and collect information from. Such agents in a multi-agent system have the capability to search for information both from the environment and from the other agents. Hence, the agents must communicate with each other.

Practical reasoning is most visible in paradigm cases of intelligent deliberative goal-directed action by an autonomous agent exhibiting characteristic properties. The following fourteen characteristics of an intelligent agent (expanded from the list in Walton, 1990a, 142–143) provide guidance for understanding practical reasoning.

1. Goals. An agent has goals and can also set goals that become commitments as it moves forward through a set of changing circumstances and decides what to do.
2. Perception. An intelligent agent can view or otherwise find out about some aspects of its current circumstances.
3. Actions. The agent is capable of carrying out actions that can change its external circumstances.

4. Common Knowledge. The agent has at least some common-sense knowledge about the normal way it can expect things to happen in its external circumstances.
5. Foresight. An intelligent agent needs to be aware of the normal and expected consequences of its actions.
6. Feedback. The intelligent agent can not only monitor the consequences of its actions, but also has the ability to make error corrections if consequences are contrary to its goals.
7. Complexity of the Act-Sequence. An autonomous agent is capable of carrying out a sequence of different kinds of actions – for example, through a list of instructions.
8. Hierarchy of Act-Descriptions. The agent has the ability to organize the sequence of actions into a hierarchy with levels of abstraction, fitting general goals to specific actions.
9. Conditional Projections. An intelligent agent can project possible future consequences of contemplated lines of action and plan ahead on what to do in the future.
10. Plasticity. An agent can use a search procedure to look over different possible alternative lines of action in flexible decision-making and can adapt to new information.
11. Persistence. This characteristic means that if one action fails to lead to a goal, the agent will try another. As some alternative actions are blocked, others will be tried.
12. Memory. An intelligent agent needs to keep track of its commitments and retain knowledge of its factual circumstances and goals. See also characteristic 14 ("Memory of Consequences of Past Actions").
13. An autonomous agent needs not only to add new commitments to its commitment store when required, but also to retract commitments when that is required.
14. Memory of Consequences of Past Actions. A rational agent must be able to keep track of its experiences concerning the effects of its actions in the past. It must be able to "direct future reasoning by relying upon generalizations it has formed about the efficacy of certain kinds of reasoning in the past." (Sartor, 2005, Section 4.4.4)

As characteristic 3 indicates, any model of practical reasoning presupposes a theory of action. There is no space for further comment on theories of action in Chapter 1, except to say that the model of practical reasoning put forward here analyzes an action as the bringing about of a state of affairs (proposition-like entity) by an agent (Horty and Belnap, 1995). In addition to these fourteen characteristics, an autonomous agent in a multi-agent setting will have other characteristics (listed in Section 10). An autonomous agent using practical reasoning in a multi-agent system will have to communicate and collaborate with other agents. To do this, such an agent has to be able to identify goals of other agents and to share goals with them, and to discuss goals with them.

1.4 Shared Intentions

The traditional literature in analytical philosophy portrayed practical reasoning using a solitary model. In this model a self-motivated autonomous agent has a goal and, based on its beliefs about its external circumstances, determines that a particular action would be an appropriate means for achieving this goal. The more recent literature in both philosophy and artificial intelligence (Tuomela, 2007; Panzarasa et al., 2002) has swung to the opposite extreme, portraying practical reasoning as a procedure of social decision-making in which cooperating agents deliberate collectively to decide on a course of action in which a group of agents needs to move from a problem confronting the group to an intelligent response based on their shared intentions. This book brings these two approaches closer by building an argumentation model of practical reasoning that situates the simpler solitary model within collective argumentation frameworks in which a group of agents can not only formulate and act on their collective goals, but can also discuss them intelligently, collect and assess information in a set of circumstances that is constantly changing, and use practical reasoning in their deliberations. The argumentation model is shown to be applicable to cases of individual problem-solving, but also to more common multi-agent applications where one agent employs practical reasoning to persuade another to do something, and also to conduct rational deliberation of the kind used in collective decision-making where more than two agents are involved.

Analytical philosophers have attempted to adapt the solitary notion of practical reasoning to cases where groups of agents practically reason together by transferring the concept of intention to represent practical reasoning in group activities. An example of collective intentionality would be a case where a group of individuals work together to carry a heavy object up a flight of stairs, wherein all individuals in the group are required to collectively undertake the task in order to fulfill their goal of getting the object up the stairs to the desired location. Showing how practical reasoning is displayed in such a case presumes that it is only the collective intention of the group that makes it possible for the agents to collectively achieve their goal. This notion in turn presumes that the intention that is involved is more than just a summing up of the individual intentions of each of the agents (Tuomela, 2013). It is a collective notion that assumes that the agents can arrive at the intention – for example, by discussing the problem and agreeing on a way to solve it.

Tuomela and Miller (1988) first formulated this notion of collective intentionality by setting down several requirements on an agent who is a member of the collective group contemplating the carrying out of an action. First, the agent must intend to do his/her part of accomplishing the group action. Second, the agent must believe that carrying out the action is possible. Third, the agent must believe that all the members of the group intend to do their parts toward carrying out the action together. Fourth, the agent must believe that all the members of the group believe that carrying out the action is possible. Searle (1990) objected to this definition of collective intention by bringing forward a counterexample. In this counterexample, each individual in a group of business school graduates intends to pursue his/her selfish interests, even though they believe that by pursuing this course of action, the collective outcome of their individual group efforts will be to serve humanity. Searle argued that this example fulfills all four requirements for collective intentionality, but that collective intentionality does not actually exist in the case described unless the business school graduates have formed an explicit agreement with each other to serve humanity through their self-interested actions. Searle argued that collective intentionality is a primitive notion in its own right that cannot be reduced to the individual intentions of the members of the group.

Bratman (1992) argued, contrary to Searle, that shared cooperative activities could be reduced to the individual intentions of the members of the group who shared these activities. For Bratman, there are three requirements that something has to meet to be shared cooperative activity. First, each of the agents in the group must be responsive to the intentions and actions of the others. Second, each of the agents must be committed to the activity. Third, each of the agents must be committed to supporting the efforts of the other agents. Bratman used the example of two agents who intend to paint a house by working together, but who disagree about the color. One wants to paint it red, while the other wants to paint it blue. In such a case, the two agents cannot have a shared cooperative activity because the plan of one is in conflict with the plan of the other.

Gilbert (1990) set four requirements on collective intentionality. First, the agents must be aware that they are entering into an agreement by communicating clearly what the agreement is to each other. Second, the agreement arrived at by the members of the group commits each of them to achieving the final goal they are working toward. Third, this commitment creates a right to rebuke any one of the agents who fails to do his/her part toward achieving the goal. Fourth, an agent can retract this commitment only if all members of the group agree to break the agreement. Gilbert's account is noteworthy for emphasizing three aspects: the communicative aspect of collective intentionality, the incurring of commitment that can hold on all members of the group as a result of a collective intention, and the possibility of retracting commitment under certain conditions. As shown in Section 10, her view of practical reasoning comes closest to the argumentation approach.

The argumentation approach stresses the communicative activities that are necessary for reaching agreement on how to proceed through a procedure of practical reasoning whereby the members of a group of agents make and retract commitments.

1.5 Complex Practical Reasoning

The next complication to be considered is that an agent can often have a choice between two or more different actions, each of which could by itself be a means to obtaining the goal. For example Walton (1990a, 96) supposes the agent wants to be healthy, and sees that he needs to engage in some athletic form of physical activity in order to achieve this goal. A wide range of such activities is available. He narrows the choice down to jogging, judo, and badminton. How can he choose the best means? He can refine his goals a bit better by looking into related goals like costs and time available, and he can look at how each of these activities would contribute to his health in ways that might differ, and so forth. The complication is that there is no single way that the agent can immediately fix on what would achieve his goal. Instead, he must compare a number of alternative means and try to decide which would best or most efficiently do the job.

To take the possibility of several alternative means into account, a more complex model of practical reasoning called practical reasoning with several alternative actions needs to be considered. In this kind of reasoning, the agent must search to find a set of alternative actions to the one initially being considered, and then pick the best of these as the action to carry out. Obviously, such a model of practical reasoning presupposes some criterion by which the alternative means can be compared on a scale from worst to better to best. Such

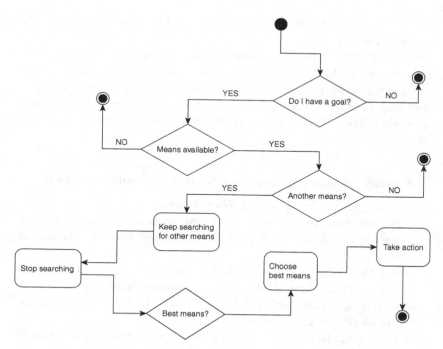

Figure 1.3: Practical Reasoning with Several Alternative Actions

a criterion in turn presupposes some notion of value whereby the actions can be ranked in this way. The structure of this richer notion of practical reasoning is displayed in Figure 1.3.

The problem with this kind of practical reasoning is similar to the problem of abductive reasoning modeled as inference to the best explanation. The agent must choose among several possibilities to select the best one. Different criteria – some purely instrumental, and some more frankly ethical – could be used to define what 'best' means. But 'best' does not always refer to the best possible means. In maximizing, the agent seeks to choose the one action that is better than all the others. In what is called satisficing (not a spelling error), the agent keeps trying to find a means to achieve the goal, and stops and selects one as soon as it finds one that is good enough to realize the goal.

Some other complications of practical reasoning were studied in Walton (1990a). In some cases, multiple goals have to be considered. In some cases, one goal might conflict with another and so the agent has a problem of trying to resolve inconsistent goals. These are all serious problems. Suffice it to say that the simple model of the previous section has to be made more complex in various dimensions before an adequate account of the structure of practical reasoning can be built up.

Walton (1990a) set out an argumentation scheme for a form of goal-directed, knowledge-based reasoning that concludes in an action, called practical reasoning. In this analysis, two argumentation schemes for practical reasoning were postulated: a necessary condition scheme and a sufficient condition scheme. The necessary condition scheme is as follows (Walton, 1990a, 48).

Practical Reasoning: The 1990 Necessary Condition Scheme

(*N1*) My goal is to bring about *A (**Goal Premise**)*.

(*N2*) I reasonably consider on the given information that bringing about at least one of $[B_0, B_1, \ldots, B_n]$ *is* necessary to bring about *A (**Alternatives Premise**)*.

(*N3*) I have selected one member B_i as an acceptable, or as the most acceptable, necessary condition for *A (**Selection Premise**)*.

(*N4*) Nothing unchangeable prevents me from bringing about B_i as far as I know *(**Practicality Premise**)*.

(*N5*) Bringing about *A* is more acceptable to me than not bringing about *Bi (**Side Effects Premise**)*.

Therefore, it is required that I bring about B_i *(**Conclusion**)*.

The sufficient condition scheme (1990a) is the same, except that in its premises (N2) and (N3), the expression 'sufficient condition' must be substituted for 'necessary condition.'

The 1990 scheme is quite useful because it enables us to identify the characteristic premises and conclusion of an argument that is an instance of practical reasoning, but there are some problems with it. One is that it makes practical reasoning look quite complex, and while it is true that practical reasoning is generally quite complex, a simpler model would have more explanatory power. That is why the procedure above was to start with a simpler basic model, and then work by step to more complex models. Another problem is that we need a way of evaluating the scheme in relation to the data and context of use in a given case. Conditions for evaluation may be simpler if the database is closed and all the information the agent can find has been collected. But in the typical case, practical reasoning is a defeasible form of argument. Not all the relevant data has been collected yet, and the agent needs to act under uncertainty instead of collecting more data.

Another problem is that the 1990 scheme does not deal explicitly with cases where an agent has several goals that need to be considered – goals that may even be in conflict. However, there are extensive studies (Walton, 1990a, 64–83) of incompatible goals and practical conflicts arising from them, including a case study (64–68).[1] But there needs to be more work on this problem, since cases where an agent, or a group of agents, have conflicting goals requires that they communicate by reasoning together. They need both to recognize inconsistencies and to deal with them, perhaps even by engaging in negotiation or persuasion to solve the problem.

Still another problem is that values enter into the 1990 scheme at various points, but no distinction was made between goals and values. In premise (N3), one of the means is described as the best or most acceptable one. In premise (N5), bad side effects are taken as a reason not to carry out an action by valuing some consequences as more acceptable (or less acceptable) than others. Aristotle's famous example of making a house (cited in Section 1) has already made it evident that values can sometimes be central to practical reasoning in an explicit way. To move forward, it is necessary to go beyond purely instrumental practical reasoning and investigate resources for modeling value-based practical reasoning.

1.6 Values and Goals

An issue that is of concern, especially in the context of ethical and political deliberation, is whether practical reasoning is purely instrumental or takes values into account. Rescher (1966, 121) pointed out that throughout the discussions of practical reasoning in the early literature on this subject in analytical philosophy, there was a failure to recognize the central role that should be given to values in theories of practical reasoning. In Rescher's view (133), when deciding on the best course of action, especially when confronted with practical conflicts, the decision-making agent must deal with values when, at the point of decision, a choice must be made between incompatible alternatives. In his view, the rational process of decision-making proceeds from a comparative assessment of alternatives to a decision on what is the best thing to do, and this decision inevitably involves the values of the agent making the decision.

---

[1] This third problem is also dealt with in the critical questions that supplement the revised schemes introduced in Section 9.

It is a widely accepted principle in philosophy, sometimes called Hume's law, that an 'ought' cannot be derived from 'is.' This principle claims that a conclusion about what you should do can never be logically derived from premises made up of propositions that describe facts about the circumstances of your decision. Searle (2001, 44) has famously denied this principle, based on his theory that institutional facts can be included as facts about the circumstances in which an agent arrives at a decision about what to do.

The model of practical reasoning developed in this book will not only accept Searle's rejection of Hume's law, but will broaden the basis for rejecting it even further. In this model, the agent's taking into account the circumstances of the decision-making situation will be shown to be vitally important in practical reasoning. On this account, practical reasoning needs to be seen generally as a form of argument from an 'is' (along with premises about an agent goals) to an 'ought.' Part of the defense of the reasonableness of arguing from an 'is' to an 'ought' is the inclusion of value-based practical reasoning alongside instrumental practical reasoning so that both kinds of practical reasoning can be combined in the model. This broadening of practical reasoning to accommodate value-based practical reasoning should be acceptable to Searle, because part of his criticism of what he calls the classical model of rationality (Searle, 2001, 44) is its failure to take values into account in rational deliberation. On Searle's theory, this failure is a primary weakness of the classical model of rationality. The model of practical reasoning built in this book will provide a way of both supporting Searle's rejection of Hume's principle and combining value-based practical reasoning with instrumental practical reasoning. This way forward will be built on the model of value-based practical reasoning developed by Trevor Bench-Capon and his associates.

In purely instrumental practical reasoning an agent carries out an action as a means to fulfilling a designated goal. Based on such a sequence of reasoning, the agent's having carried out that action can be said to be practically reasonable. This conclusion seems like a positive form of endorsement for carrying out the action. But what if the agent's goal is antisocial, or represents something we would consider morally wrong. Can the action be positively evaluated as practically reasonable in such a case? Some might say not, on the grounds that carrying out such an action would conflict with worthy goals that should be taken into account. Generally speaking, an agent has a plurality of goals. Some of these goals might conflict with others. Some goals might be deemed more worthy or more socially productive than others. In such cases, values play a role.

Atkinson, Bench-Capon, and McBurney (2004a, 88) cited two comparable examples of practical reasoning. In the first example the goal stated in the first premise is a specific event or state:

> I want to be in London before 4:30.
> The 2:30 train arrives in London at 4:15.
> So, I shall catch the 2:30 train.

But consider another instance of practical reasoning, where the goal stated in the first premise is more general:

> Friendship requires that I see John before he leaves London.
> The 2:30 train arrives in London at 4:15.
> So, I shall catch the 2:30 train.

As Atkinson, Bench-Capon, and McBurney (2004a, 88) pointed out, the action in the conclusion is justified in the second case not in terms of its consequences or results, but in terms of an underlying general social value: friendship. On their account (Atkinson, Bench-Capon, and McBurney, 2004a), three elements need to be considered as the result of performing an action: the state of affairs brought about by carrying out the action, the subset of this set that forms the desired features (the goal), and the reason why the goal is desired (the value). They do not describe values as states of the world that are desirable, but as social interests that explain why goals are desirable.

Atkinson, Bench-Capon, and McBurney (2006, 166) formulated their model of value-based practical reasoning – said to be an extension of Walton's instrumental practical reasoning scheme – as follows:

> In the circumstances R
> we should perform action A
> to achieve new circumstances S
> which will realize some goal G
> which will promote some value V

Here is a simple example of value-based practical reasoning. In this case, I have been having problems with my car, and as a way of solving the problem I decide to look for a new one. My goal is to buy a new car. This task is not that simple. I will not just go into the nearest dealership and buy the first car I find there for sale. I need to collect a lot of data to make an intelligent decision. Cost is involved, and I have certain requirements in mind, based on my situation. Nearly all of my driving is in the city, and so I am looking for a car that will fit these circumstances and do the job at the least cost. I also have factors like style and comfort in mind. Another factor that is very important for me is concern for the environment. All these factors narrow down the search to a car that will not use too much fuel, and so I concentrate on small cars. As I discuss matters with a salesperson in a showroom, she argues, "The Smart Car uses less fuel than the other cars you are considering. Also, it has style and comfort." Let's call this case the Smart Car example. The argumentation in the case can be structured as an application of value-based practical reasoning.

In the example there are three instances of value-based practical reasoning. In the first instance, one premise is that my goal is to buy a car, and another premise is that the Smart Car uses less fuel than the other cars I am considering. A third premise is that any car that uses less fuel than the other cars I am considering is less harmful to the environment. The value of concern for the environment supports this third premise. The second instance of practical reasoning is the goal statement that I want to buy a car that has style. The other premise that goes along with this one in practical reasoning is the statement that the Smart Car has style. Backing up the goal premise is the statement that style is of value for me. Similarly, there is a third practical reasoning argument where my goal is to buy a car that has comfort, and the other premise is the assertion that the Smart Car has comfort. Finally, the statement that comfort is of value for me backs up the first premise, the statement that my goal is to buy a car that has comfort. So, in this example there are three instances of the application of the scheme for value-based practical reasoning. In each instance the goal statement is backed up by a value statement.

Examples such as this one suggest that there are two notions of practical reasoning that ought to be considered. One is a narrower and simpler instrumental notion of practical reasoning. The other, a broader conception, takes values into account (Bench-Capon and Atkinson, 2009). It could be seen as an ethical notion of practical reasoning, or at least a notion of practical reasoning that takes values into account. The instrumental account is simpler, because it views values as a species of goals. It does not see anything special about values as kinds of goals, and simply evaluates them in the same way that other goals would be evaluated. On the broader conception, however, values are defined separately from goals. There are several reasons for this approach. One is that in ethical and political deliberations, ethical goals tend to be implicit and in the background, yet they are vitally important in evaluating actions and in persuading other agents to undertake a course of action as the conclusion of the deliberation dialogue. In political deliberation, an arguer is typically trying to persuade an audience to see a course of action as practically reasonable for the group to adopt. Implicit in such a discussion is the assumption that both the group and the arguer share some broad social values. In this kind of context it may be important to take values into account, even if they are not clearly articulated as goals that can be precisely specified.

1.7 Taking Consequences into Account

Practical reasoning is commonly used in advertising – for example, in health product ads, as shown in Chapter 2. Ads for medications now typically also present a long list of side effects along with the argument that the medication will fulfill some goal, such as relieving pain. For example, an ad for the pain reliever medication Cymbalta (*Newsweek*, December 31, 2012, 12–14) presents the message that Cymbalta can help to significantly reduce chronic lower back pain. This positive outcome is taken to be the goal of someone who is considering buying Cymbalta. However, the ad also cites a list of side effects, including itching, headache, feeling unsteady, confusion, problems in concentrating, high fever, muscle twitching, racing heart rate, abnormal mood (mania), and convulsions. These bad consequences could be reasons for hesitating to buy or take the drug.

Typically in cases of practical reasoning, the argumentation needs to be evaluated by weighing the negative value of the side effects against the positive value of the goal. The general pattern of this kind of reasoning is shown in Figure 1.4.

However, once we examine Figure 1.4 it is easy to see that this way of modeling an instance of practical reasoning involves the asking of questions. The contents of the diamond-shaped nodes are questions. It suggests that we should be interested not only in how practical reasoning is to be modeled as a type of inference from premises to a conclusion, but also whether it could be modeled as a series of choice points where the agent has to ask questions that pose choices on what to do next.

If we take a look at the Cymbalta advertisement, it certainly represents a case where the person who is viewing the ad is concerned about the negative consequences of taking Cymbalta. So, we could model the practical reasoning in the ad after the fashion of Figure 1.4. The person is an agent, he has the goal of relieving his pain, and he might be convinced that this medication will achieve this goal. However, he has to consider the potential negative consequences of taking the medication. To this point, the problem-solving activity of the reader of the ad can be seen as an instance of value-based practical reasoning, assuming that the consequences cited are negative for him. But there is more to the example than meets the eye. The ad is a message

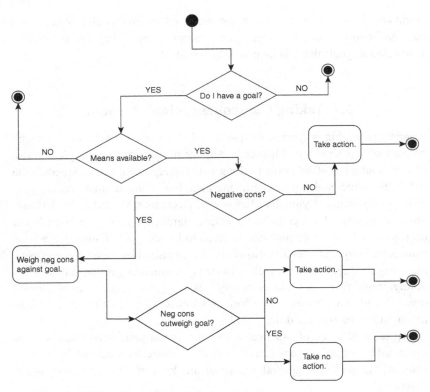

Figure 1.4: Taking Consequences into Account

directed to many readers, and the ad agency that crafted it has sent it to them hoping that it will persuade them to buy Cymbalta. The ad agency has used practical reasoning to craft the ad, but to do that they had to enter into the practical reasoning of the supposed target: the person who will read the ad and be persuaded to buy the medication. They opted for the strategy of stating the potential side effects right in the text of the ad. The framework of the use of practical reasoning in this example is rather complex. The side effects listed certainly function as reasons for the reader of the ad not to take the medication if the reader thinks he/she might suffer from any of them. But the precise relationship of the stating of the side effects to the practical reasoning in the case is far from straightforward.

Another approach to modeling practical reasoning would be to see it as a defeasible form of argument that is evaluated by testing it to judge how well it responds to critical questioning. On this approach, practical reasoning could be modeled as a defeasible argumentation scheme that is subject to critical questioning and counter-arguments. The argumentation proceeds in three steps. The first step is to identify the argument by determining its premises and its conclusion in a given case. Helpful for this purpose is to see how the argument fits an argumentation scheme. The second step is to analyze the argument, standardly by filling in any implicit premises and using an argument diagram to represent the structure of the argument as a set of premises and conclusions chaining toward some ultimate claim to be proved or disputed. The third step is to evaluate the argument by applying a formal system of argument evaluation – for example, one of the formal systems currently being developed in artificial intelligence. Each argumentation scheme has a set of basic appropriate critical questions attached to it, and it is these critical questions that are helpful in determining weak points in the argument that are open to criticism or counterattack. A case in point is the relationship between practical reasoning and argument from consequences.

The side effects critical question is so important for evaluating practical reasoning that it is sometimes put forward as an attacking argument in its own right. This form of argument is so common it is called *argumentum ad consequentiam*, or argument from consequences. This form of reasoning is used in a negative way, as an argument to attack a proposal previously selected as representing the best course of action in a situation. However, it has a positive counterpart as well. In argument from positive consequences, a policy or course of action can be supported by citing favorable consequences of carrying it out. These two forms of argument are (respectively) argument from negative consequences and argument from positive consequences (Walton, 1995, 155–156):

Major Premise: If A is brought about, then consequences C will occur.
Minor Premise: Consequences C are bad.
Conclusion: Therefore A should not be brought about.

Major Premise: If A is brought about, then consequences C will occur.
Minor Premise: Consequences C are good.
Conclusion: Therefore A should be brought about.

Both forms of argument from consequences can be attacked by the asking of the same set of critical questions (Walton, 1995, 155–156):

CQ$_1$: How strong is the likelihood that the cited consequences will (may, must) occur?

CQ$_2$: What evidence supports the claim that the cited consequences will (may, must) occur, and is it sufficient to support the strength of the claim adequately?

CQ$_3$: Are there other opposite consequences (bad as opposed to good, for example) that should be taken into account?

In the case of the Cymbalta ad described above, each side effect in the list may be taken as an instance of a negative side effects critical question. But should any of these side effects actually be experienced by the person taking the drug, the critical question is transformed into an argument from negative consequences. Now it is an argument against continuing to take the drug. To come to a conclusion on what to do using practical reasoning, the person will have to weigh the negative consequences against the positive benefits of the drug in helping with back pain. It is a question of balancing the negative side effect of how bad the side effects are against the worth of relieving the back pain.

One can also see that both variants of argument from consequences are based on the assumption that consequences of an action can be designated as having positive or negative value. However, arguments from positive or negative values can also operate as individual arguments in their own right (Bench-Capon, 2003a) independently of argument from consequences. The first argumentation scheme represents the argument from positive value:

Major Premise: If value V is positive, it supports commitment to goal G.
Minor Premise: Value V is positive as judged by agent a.
Conclusion: V is a reason for a to commit to goal G.

The negative counterpart is called argument from negative value:

Major Premise: If value V is negative, it supports retracting commitment from goal G.
Minor Premise: Value V is negative as judged by agent a.
Conclusion: V is a reason for a to retract commitment to goal G.

But now a number of controversies about how to evaluate practical reasoning arise. In order to refute an argument based on practical reasoning, is it enough to ask one of the critical questions in the list fitting the scheme for practical reasoning? Or should it be required to mount a counter-argument – for example, an argument from negative consequences? On which side should the burden of proof lie, when an argument based on practical reasoning is being evaluated as weak or strong, reasonable or fallacious? These issues will be taken up in Chapter 2.

1.8 The State Space Explosion

Some examples were given to illustrate how to formulate four models of practical reasoning as sequences of decision-making, including a basic model

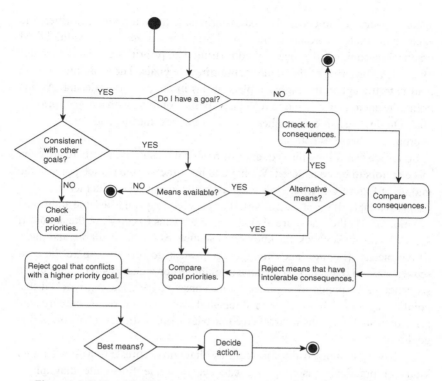

Figure 1.5: Taking All Critical Questions into Account

and three more complex models. Clearly, however, using four separate models of the activity structure of reasoning characteristic of practical reasoning as a method of decision-making is a piecemeal approach. The next step is to try to put all four models together into one larger model that encompasses all the aspects of practical reasoning covered in the first four models. It turns out that this is not an easy task to accomplish. The result of a provisional attempt to carry it out is shown in the activity diagram in Figure 1.5.

The activity diagram in Figure 1.5 starts the same way as the others. The agent asks whether it has a goal, and if so, it proceeds to the next choice point. At this point the agent asks whether this goal is consistent with its other goals. If so, the agent goes on to the next choice point, where the question of whether there is a means available to carry out the goal is asked. If not, the decision-making stops there. If so, the agent goes on to consider the next choice point, where the question is asked whether there is an alternative means to carry out the goal. Now, backtrack to the choice point where the agent asked whether its goal is consistent with its other goals. If there is an inconsistency of goals, the agent is instructed to check for goal priorities. If there are goal priorities, the agent is instructed to compare these goal priorities. In the case of value-based practical reasoning this process of comparing goal priorities can be carried out by using an ordering of the values supporting the goals. The more important a goal is to the agent, the higher a place it has in the priority ordering. At this point, the agent is instructed to reject a goal that conflicts with a higher priority goal. On this basis it can go ahead to select the best means, and decide on the appropriate course of action.

So far we can follow the sequence of practical reasoning, but there are even more factors to be considered. We have to backtrack to the choice point in the middle of Figure 1.5, where the agent asked the question of whether there is a means available. If the answer is yes, the agent has to go on to ask the additional question of whether there are also alternative means to carry out the action. If so, the agent must check for known consequences of the available and alternative means. Having done this, the agent must go on to compare the consequences, and reject those that have intolerable consequences. This part of the sequence corresponds to argument from consequences. Having reached that point the agent reaches the rounded rectangle where he needs to compare goal priorities. So, both paths we tracked come back to the same action of comparing goal priorities.

By having combined the four activity diagrams representing four simpler kinds of practical reasoning, we can see how the fifth state diagram in Figure 1.5 takes the various considerations into account. But the diagram has become quite complex, and it is by no means clear that all the bugs have been worked out. Suppose, for example, that the agent has reached the "means available" diamond. According to the sequence shown in Figure 1.5, it must stop if no means is available. But in a realistic case, even though there is no immediate means available, the agent may be able to carry out some sequence of actions that create such a means. This possibility is not allowed in the activity diagram shown in Figure 1.5. The only way to provide it is to incorporate some of the alternative sequences of actions available in the previous activity diagrams. To cite another problem, what if the agent has reached the "alternative means" diamond, but there are no alternative means available. Should the agent stop, or should it seek out some line of actions that might move forward to providing such an alternative means? This possibility is not represented in Figure 1.5, and to provide it we must go back to one of the previous activity diagrams and factor sequences of actions available there into the sequence shown in Figure 1.5. There are other complications that need to be taken into account, suggested by the critical questions matching the two schemes for practical reasoning, especially the scheme for value-based practical reasoning, where the list of critical questions needed to evaluate an instance of practical reasoning is lengthy.

We can sum up these problems by saying that we have reached a state space explosion. We have gone as far as we can go in Figure 5.1 in representing all the relevant aspects of practical reasoning that need to be checked in order to completely evaluate a given instance of this type of reasoning. If we go any further, it will make the activity diagram so complex that it will be more confusing than enlightening.

1.9 Critical Questions for Practical Reasoning

Practical reasoning is defeasible, as noted right at the beginning of this chapter. An intelligent agent must have the capability to not only see errors, but also to correct them when it is required in order to achieve its goal. It must also profit from its experience to criticize ways the practical reasoning in its planned actions might fail. Hence, the fourteen characteristics of an intelligent rational agent listed in Section 3 need to be supplemented with other characteristics that support a capability for self-criticism. A higher-order rational agent carrying out its goals by practical reasoning needs to have the ability to criticize short-comings in its own actions and plans. An important task of criticism is to uncover practical inconsistencies in a plan – for example, in cases where projected action sequences in the plan run counter to themselves, tending to block or hinder achievement of the goal.

In order to be able to engage in the kind of self-criticism needed to ask critical questions about its own actions, a higher-order agent needs to possess this characteristic, called capability for criticism. An agent of this kind needs not only to construct a chain of defeasible reasoning into a plan that links actions together into a projected sequence that moves toward its goals, it must also be able to find the weaknesses in such a projection. This capability means that it must be able not only to formulate a plan of action, but also to criticize it. A fully rational autonomous agent is not only able to use reasoning to pursue its goals, but is able to look critically at its own goals and values, and to weigh its goals against the consequences of achieving them, based on the data of its past experiences about how things can generally be expected to go. If a plan is going wrong, an autonomous agent needs to be able to modify it or move to a different plan. This kind of practical rationality will be further elaborated in Chapter 7.

There are three basic ways (methods) of criticizing practical reasoning. The first is to question support for one of the premises of the argumentation scheme by arguing that the premise has not been adequately justified. The second is to attempt to undercut the argument by questioning the defeasible inferential link between the premises and the conclusion – for example, by asking critical questions. The third is to mount a counter-argument designed to rebut (refute) the original argument from practical reasoning. The distinction between the second and third methods corresponds to one already widely known in the AI literature. Pollock (1995) drew an influential distinction between two ways of attacking an argument, called undercutters and rebuttals. A rebuttal is a strong form of defeat of a given argument utilizing a stronger opposed argument, one that has the negation (opposite) of the original conclusion as its conclusion. An undercutter is a weaker, or more temporary, form of defeat of an original argument that attacks the inferential link of the original argument to derive the conclusion from the premises.

The second method of attack on an instance of practical reasoning is to ask critical questions that pinpoint weak points in the scheme. The key device for evaluating practical reasoning in this manner (Walton, 1990a) is a set of basic critical questions matching the scheme.

Critical Questions for Practical Reasoning

CQ_1: Are there alternative means of realizing A, other than B? [*Alternative Means Question*]

CQ_2: Is B an acceptable (or the best) alternative? [*Acceptable/Best Option Question*]

CQ_3: Is it possible for agent a to do B? [*Possibility Question*]

CQ_4: Are there negative side effects of a's bringing about B that ought to be considered? [*Negative Side Effects Question*]

CQ_5: Does a have goals other than A, which have the potential to conflict with a's realizing A? [*Conflicting Goals Question*]

Each of the critical questions acts as an undercutter that, when asked, defeats the inferential link between the premises and conclusion of an argument based on practical reasoning. It is a general method of argumentation theory that each scheme has a distinct set of matching critical questions attached to it. The solution to the problem of how to evaluate a given case in which practical reasoning occurs set out in 1990 was to study the text of the case to see (1) whether the requirements for the practical reasoning scheme are met by the given argument, and (2) to judge how adequately the critical questions were asked and answered according to the evidence in the given case. There does appear to be agreement that practical reasoning is a defeasible form of argument in most typical cases of the kind we want to model, as opposed to being deductive or inductive. It would seem that the right way to evaluate it would be through the use of critical questions. But here there has been some divergence of opinions.

The set of critical questions above was devised for a commitment model, while a different set has been adopted in a recent computing system using a BDI model. Atkinson, Bench-Capon, and McBurney (2004a, 89) devised the following set of sixteen critical questions for the argumentation scheme for the sufficient condition value-based practical reasoning scheme for use in an e-democracy system.

1. Disagree with the description of the current situation.
2. Disagree with the consequences of the proposed action.
3. Disagree that the desired features are part of the consequences.
4. Disagree that these features promote the desired value.
5. Believe the consequences can be realized by some alternative action.
6. Believe the desired features can be realized through some alternative action.
7. Believe that the desired value can be realized in an alternative way.
8. Believe the action has undesirable side effects which demote the desired value.
9. Believe the action has undesirable side effects which demote some other value.
10. Agree that the action should be performed but for different reasons.
11. Believe that the action will preclude some more desirable action.
12. Believe that the circumstances as described are not possible.
13. Believe that the action is impossible.
14. Believe that the consequences as described are not possible.
15. Believe that the desired features cannot be realized.
16. Disagree that the desired value is a legitimate value.

This list fits the prior set of critical questions above very well, but one can see differences. For one thing, these critical questions appear to represent ways of attacking an argument that fits the scheme of practical reasoning by mounting counter-arguments. Such a system raises some questions about the function of critical questions as tools that can be used to evaluate practical reasoning. We return to these evaluation questions below, and, based on these considerations, a different argumentation scheme for practical reasoning will be proposed. What will change is the relationship between the scheme and the critical questions.

The third way to attack practical reasoning is to mount a counter-argument that has the opposite conclusion of the original argument from practical reasoning. It can be hard to separate a rebuttal attempt from questioning that is merely skeptical, in some instances, because opposed forms of argument are related to some of the critical questions appropriate for criticizing practical reasoning. Practical reasoning is about taking some course of action in the future, but, in complex situations of economics, politics, ethics and business, there is uncertainty about what will happen in the future. Thus, one common and important critical question for many cases of practical reasoning is that pertaining to known or possible side effects of the action selected.

1.10 Communicative Agents in Multi-agent Systems

Evaluating real instances of practical reasoning in cases where it has been used in natural language discourse can be a lengthy and complex task in many instances. Indeed, there is even a completeness problem, because there can be critical sub-questions to each critical question. Thus, in theory, the process of questioning could go on without terminating, as long as there are more critical questions to be asked. Hence, the problem of epistemic closure – the problem of knowing when the closed world assumption can be applied in a given case – can reappear in any given case. In Chapter 2, it will be shown how each critical question matching the scheme for practical reasoning needs to be classified as either being a presumption or an exception. By this means an argument based on practical reasoning can be structured as a set of premises and a conclusion, represented by an argument diagram. So analyzed, it can be evaluated by assessing the strength of the evidential links between the premises and the conclusion, and weighing it against the attacking counter-arguments that can also be diagrammed in the case.

What is needed is a method of solving the problem of evaluating such arguments by fitting the critical questions onto a diagram structure in a way that permits one agent to communicate with another. Multi-agent systems are primarily systems for the interaction of software agents – although the agents can also be robots, humans, or combinations of software agents, robots, or humans – that carry out actions in an environment that they can be aware of and collect information from. Such agents in a multi-agent system have the capability to search for information both from the environment and from the other agent. Hence, the agents must communicate with each other.

In multi-agent systems, argumentation is seen as an approach that supports communication between agents and among groups of agents. The argumentation approach adopts the view that communication is based on the kind of argumentation that takes place between agents in a dialogue structure. In such a structure one agent makes a move, such as putting forward an argument, and the other agent takes its turn responding to that move, such as criticizing the argument. In this approach, six types of dialogue were initially recognized (Walton and Krabbe, 1995): information-seeking, inquiry, persuasion, negotiation, deliberation, and eristic dialogue. Such dialogues each have an individual formal structure, defined by the initial conditions of the dialogue, the participants' goals, and the collective dialogue goals fitting the type of dialogue the participants are supposed to be engaged in. It is assumed that both agents have a commitment store: a set of propositions representing public information that each of the parties has gone on record in the dialogue as accepting. In the argumentation approach, arguments correspond to structures called argumentation schemes – for example, the scheme for practical reasoning.

In the argumentation approach, goals are identified by means of the public commitments that the agents in the dialogue have gone on record as accepting, and by propositions that can be derived from them as implicit premises or conclusions by means of inferences fitting argumentation schemes. In the BDI approach, goals are equated with an agent's intentions, identified as the agent's internal mental states that represent the motivations of its actions. It is a problem to determine what an agent's intentions are or might be, however, especially in multi-agent settings where one agent has to try to figure out what the intentions of other agents might be. In Chapter 5, a theory will be put forward that combines the argumentation approach with a modified version of the BDI approach. In this theory, the problem for the BDI approach as it is represented in multi-agent systems arises when one agent has to try to elicit the intentionality of another agent by examining the evidence of the public record contained in the knowledge base consisting of the other agents own actions and its commitments. This theory is based on an argumentation scheme for abductive reasoning that equates abductive reasoning with inference to the best explanation. The theory requires an analysis of the concept of explanation showing both how arguments and explanations are different, and how they fit together in abductive reasoning.

The argumentation model of practical reasoning built in this book should be compatible with Searle's (2001, 103) theory of reasons for actions. In his account, reasons are proposition-only structured entities that can be of three types: facts about the world describing circumstances of the decision to be made; what he calls propositional intentional states such as desires or intentions, or they can fit a third category that contains obligations, commitments, requirements and needs. The computational model of practical reasoning put forward in this book appears to conform to the requirements of Searle's theory in general outline. The main difference would appear to be that for Searle the propositional intentional states are the desires or intentions of an agent, where these entities represent the mental states of a human agent. Even though Searle includes commitments and obligations in this category as well, in the model presented in this book a careful distinction needs to be drawn between the commitment model and the BDI model that Searle apparently takes to be the only model of practical reasoning

In Searle's theory, it is important that the set of statements making up an agent's reasons in a given case are not causally sufficient for the performance of the action (Searle, 2001, 133). This approach appears to be compatible with the model of practical reasoning built in this book, because the defeasibility of practical reasoning is the central feature of this model.

An autonomous agent in a multi-agent setting will need to have other characteristics in addition to the fourteen listed in Section 3. In many cases, multi-agent practical reasoning requires agents that can communicate information to each other and collaborate in carrying out goals that require teamwork. For example, it may need to obtain information from other agents to find out about its circumstances, to formulate shared intentions, to deliberate by cooperating with these other agents to achieve shared goals, or even to negotiate with them on who should undertake which subtasks. In such cases, agents need to deliberate collectively on how to achieve a goal by asking and answering questions about ways and means.

At the beginning of Section 7, it was shown that a higher-order rational agent needs to possess the characteristic called capability for criticism. It needs not only to build a plan of action, but also to be able to probe it to find the weaknesses in it. In a multi-agent system, exercising this capability requires the rational agent not only to look critically at its own goals and values, but also to find conflicts between them and the goals and values of other agents it is collaborating with. For these reasons, an autonomous intelligent rational agent capable of practical reasoning in a multi-agent environment must have seven other characteristics:

15. The agent must be able to coordinate its plans with other agents so that it can effectively collaborate with them in group planning, decision-making, and problem-solving.
16. The agent must be able to not only identify its own goals and values, but also those of the other agents with whom it is interacting.

17. The agent must be able to identify conflicts between its goals and values, on the one hand, and the collective goal supposedly to be achieved by collaborating.
18. The agent must be able to not only identify conflicts among its own goals and values, but also conflicts between these and the goals and values of the other agents.
19. The agent must be able to use practical reasoning to resolve conflicts between its own goals and actions derived by practical reasoning proposed for collective acceptance.
20. The agent must also have the capability of retracting or suspending its own goals for the sake of reaching agreement.
21. The agent must have the capability to resolve these three kinds of conflicts by discussing them in a rational manner with the other agents.

The last requirement is one of compromise and flexibility. In some instances the intelligent agent may need to be assisted by negotiation, but shifts of this sort will not be taken up until later in the book (see Chapter 7).

In the argumentation approach, the way to move forward is to situate practical reasoning within a context of use in a formal dialogue structure where arguments are being put forward and critical questions are asked, as well as counter-arguments posed, to evaluate the given argument. In this approach, the two devices – the scheme and the matching critical questions – need to be fitted into a dialogue framework representing a multi-agent context of use. In such a context, practical reasoning is used by one agent to argue for a conclusion to take a specified action. The argument is then communicated to another agent with the capability of asking critical questions that might undercut or even defeat the argument. There are four requirements that need to be met by this model that will turn out to be vitally important. First, the dialogue structure in which the agents communicate with each other must have a collective goal. Second, each of the agents must have individual goals. Third, as noted above, these goals can conflict with each other. Fourth, some way for the agents to communicate in order to resolve these conflicts, or at least overcome them moving forward, is necessary for the sequence of practical reasoning to come to a conclusion on what to do. The way to meet these requirements, it will be argued, is to frame practical reasoning in a multi-agent argumentation system.

In applying argumentation methods of evaluation to cases of practical reasoning, the critical questions need to be seen as posed in a dialogue in which it is assumed that there is a global burden of proof, and standards are set on how strong an argument has to be in order to successfully collect enough knowledge about the agent's circumstances, the likely consequences, and so forth, before arriving at a decision to act. As will be shown in Chapter 5, even in cases of solitary decision-making, the agent needs to ask the right critical questions and consider relevant counter-arguments (pros and cons). The role of the questioner is to probe into weaknesses or implicit assumptions of the argument that the agent might not have thought of at first glance, or properly taken into account. Thus, for example, the first question is not meant to be a simple yes–no question that the arguer can answer by replying, "Yes, I have another goal," and then get off the hook. The arguer has to satisfy the questioner that she has thought about this – that is, she has searched around in her goal set and not found any conflicting or competing goals that might override G in the given circumstances. Formulating these notions as part of the evaluation method will take us, in Chapter 3, toward considering burdens of proof for critical questions and how such burdens need to be framed in rational delibera- tion. Before getting to that point, it will help the reader to examine some short and relatively simple examples of the use of practical reasoning of a kind that everyone can easily understand and appreciate.

The BDI model and the argumentation model are working along parallel but independent lines, and formulating the precise difference between them is a recurring problem. The commitment model uses argumentation schemes, based on a dialogue format. Its best asset is that it accounts for communication between agents. Because commitments are part of the dialogue framework, perhaps they are best seen as essentially involving orderly communicative relations between rational agents or in groups of them. Whatever the advan- tages of each theory are, the problem at present is that of clarifying the relationship between them more clearly and precisely. Girle, Hitchcock, McBurney, and Verheij (2003) considered some tentative ways of bringing these two theories together. One of these is to extend the narrowly instru- mental models of practical reasoning that dominated the early literature. This agenda has already been moved forward by the advent of multi-agents systems that can take into account interactive settings in which practical reasoning can take place.

The state space explosion shown in Figure 1.5 suggests that the best way to move forward is to see practical reasoning as being carried out in a multi-agent framework of dialogue in which a rational agent (or group of them) decides what is the best course of action by considering the pro and con arguments furnished by the circumstances of the given case and the agent's goals and values. Having shown how to identify and analyze practical reasoning as a defeasible form of rational argument, this chapter discussed the problem of how to evaluate it as a strong or weak form of argument in a given case.

The method proposed in this chapter (and elaborated in the rest of the book) builds on the technique of using critical questions as ways of attacking or defeating an argument fitting the scheme. The conclusion reached is that earlier versions of the scheme, and accompanying sets of critical questions, need to be revised. These are replaced by two new schemes with a new matching set of critical questions for each. One scheme, called the basic scheme, represents a simpler model of instrumental practical reasoning while the other, called the value-based scheme, represents a richer model that takes values into account. In Chapter 2 it will be shown how real cases of practical reasoning can be identified and analyzed by using both schemes along with argument diagramming tools to represent instances of these two types of practical reasoning in argumentation systems of multi-agent dialogue.

2

Practical Reasoning in Health Product Ads

The conclusion of Chapter 1 was that even though practical reasoning can sometimes be a solitary form of reasoning – for example, where an agent needs to figure out how to fix a flat tire on his car – there are many other cases where a rational agent needs to communicate with other agents in order to move forward with intelligent practical reasoning. As noted in the conclusion of Chapter 1, in such cases an intelligent agent may need to deliberate with other agents on how to achieve shared goals. It may also need to collect information from them, or even to negotiate with them on how to divide up responsibility for the actions needed for them to reason together to achieve their common goal. In the subsequent chapters we will examine some complex cases of group deliberations by agents collaboratively using practical reasoning. In Chapter 2 we will start with some simpler cases in which one agent is interacting with another and is using practical reasoning to try to persuade the other to carry out a designated action.

In this chapter, several illustrative examples of direct-to-consumer health product advertisements that exemplify practical reasoning are analyzed using argumentation methods, and some conclusions about the analyses are drawn. The ads studied include commercials for pharmaceuticals, as well as ads for other medications, including health foods, and treatments and devices that purport to have health benefits. It is shown that they use arguments of a kind that fit the argumentation scheme for practical reasoning. The findings are interesting for many reasons. They can be applied both to the crafting of the ads and to the enhancement of critical thinking skills for intelligent consumers. They are also applicable to recent efforts to use computational techniques to assist consumer health informatics to inform consumers and improve health care. Most interestingly, they suggest that the central persuasion structure of the argumentation in health care ads is that of practical reasoning. Use of practical reasoning of this sort as argumentation is commonly called the problem-solution strategy in advertising. This chapter will use the technique of representing the structure of each case using an argument diagram (sometimes called an argument map) as a step toward grasping how practical reasoning is used.

This chapter shows how to apply argumentation tools, especially argumentation schemes, argument visualization tools, and dialogue frameworks, to model the structure of persuasive communication messages as practical reasoning. The way the arguments are configured using these tools provides a base of examples so that the exploration of the structure of practical reasoning in the rest of the book has at least some relatively short and familiar examples as a jumping-off point. The ads are shown to be centrally based on the argumentation scheme for practical reasoning, chained with other kinds of arguments that can be represented by argumentation schemes. Practical reasoning is defined, as described in Chapter 1, as goal-directed reasoning, where an agent concludes that a course of action should be carried out for the reason that it will contribute to the fulfillment of goals it is committed to. It is shown how practical reasoning and its critical questions are key components in the dialogue structure of these communicative health messages. The hypothesis put forward is that in such ads practical reasoning is used in a framework of persuasion dialogue in which the seller of the product aims a message at the audience (prospective buyer) to take the action of buying the product. The approach taken in Chapter 2 is that of the commitment model, as opposed to the BDI model. Subsequent chapters will study connections between the two models.

2.1 The Dialectical Structure of the Ads in the Examples

In this section the reader is introduced to the argumentation tools that will be applied in the rest of the chapter, including argumentation schemes, enthymemes, and argument mapping tools. Argumentation schemes are standardized forms of reasoning of the kind explained in Chapter 1. Enthymemes are arguments with implicit premises or conclusions (Walton and Reed, 2005; Walton, 2008). Argument mapping tools are devices used to visualize the premises and conclusions of arguments in a tree structure, and to display a sequence of connected arguments chained together to support an ultimate conclusion. More than forty such tools are described by Scheuer et al. (2009). The one used in this chapter, *Araucaria* (Reed and Rowe, 2004), was the first to use argumentation schemes, and can be downloaded at http://araucaria.computing.dundee.ac.uk/.

The most interesting schemes in current research are defeasible ones that represent plausible reasoning, rather than deductive or inductive reasoning. Each scheme has a special set of critical questions matching it. An argument is evaluated using the critical questions in relation to the scheme. The argument holds as plausible unless critically questioned or attacked by an opposing argument, or by the asking of a critical question.

An example of an enthymeme is: 'All men are mortal, therefore Socrates is mortal', where the implicit premise 'Socrates is a man' was not stated. But there is a problem (Ennis, 1982; Burke, 1985; Gough and Tindale, 1985; Hitchcock, 1985). If the analyst is allowed to fill in any proposition needed to make such an inference valid, he or she may be inserting assumptions into the text of a discourse that the speaker did not mean to be part of his or her argument. There is even the danger of committing the straw man fallacy – the fallacy of attributing an implicit premise or conclusion to an opponent's argument that exaggerates or distorts the argument in order to make it easier to refute (Scriven, 1976, 85–86). However, new methods of reconstructing enthymemes (Walton, 2008) have been shown to be useful in contending with this danger.

An important tool needed for the analysis of the examples of the health product ads that follow is the specification of the context of dialogue. Each model of dialogue is defined by its initial situation, the participants' individual goals, and the collective goal of the dialogue as a whole (Walton and Krabbe, 1995). Six basic types of dialogue previously recognized in the argumentation literature are persuasion dialogue, inquiry, negotiation dialogue, information-seeking dialogue, deliberation, and eristic dialogue. These dialogues are normative models, meaning that they do not necessarily correspond exactly to real instances of persuasion, and so forth, that may occur in a real conversational exchange. There is a formal model of persuasion dialogue (Prakken, 2006).

In Walton (1990a) it was argued that a process of deliberation should be seen as a dialogue procedure in which knowledge of an agent's circumstances can be used as evidence to support or undermine the agent's practical reasoning as argumentation. In a dialogue one agent asks questions, and another agent responds with the answers that are supplied from a knowledge base they partly share. As noted above, commitment is a procedural notion based on a framework of dialogue in which two parties take turns making moves that have the form of speech acts. In this model, deliberation is seen as a form of dialogue that is related to other types of dialogue containing argumentation and reasoning. A classification of seven such basic types of dialogue is presented in Table 2.1. Each type of dialogue has four stages, and each has

Table 2.1: *Dialogue Typology*

Type of Dialogue	Initial Situation	Participant's Goal	Goal of Dialogue
Persuasion	Conflict of opinions	Persuade other party	Resolve issue
Inquiry	Need to have proof	Verify evidence	Prove hypothesis
Discovery	Need an explanation	Find a hypothesis	Support hypothesis
Negotiation	Conflict of interests	Get what you want	Settle issue
Information	Need information	Acquire information	Exchange information
Deliberation	Practical choice	Fit goals and actions	Decide what to do
Eristic	Personal conflict	Hit out at opponent	Reveal deep conflict

a distinctive goal that can normatively be used to judge whether a move, or series of moves, contributes to the dialogue or not. In a critical discussion, for example, a sequence of argumentation can be judged fallacious if it seriously interferes with or blocks the progress of the dialogue toward its goal.

Practical reasoning can be used in all seven types of dialogue, but it needs to be evaluated differently, depending on the type of dialogue in which it was used in a given case. For example, the conditions for closure, affecting the closed world assumption, can be different. Also, there can be shifts from one dialogue to another that may need to be taken into account. For example, a parliament may be deliberating on whether to pass legislation to fund a dam project. But there may be a shift to information-seeking dialogue as engineers and other experts give advice on the cost of the dam, what its requirements should be, and how it should be built. There may then be a shift to a persuasion dialogue as the elected representatives debate whether the project should be funded or not. Party politics may enter, and they may start to attack each other and quarrel. If they cannot agree, they may begin to negotiate some way of moving forward to a compromise. If a big problem – or even a scandal – ensues about mismanagement of government funds, an official inquiry may be launched.

Hitchcock, McBurney, and Parsons (2001) formulated a formal model of deliberation dialogue in which two participants make proposals and counter-proposals to solve a common problem. In their model, deliberation is set in motion by the asking of what they call a governing question, such as, "How should we respond to the prospect of global warming?" First, there is an opening stage, and as the dialogue proceeds (Hitchcock, McBurney, and Parsons, 2001, 7) an "inform" stage is reached, where goals and constraints on actions are considered. Second, at a proposal formulation stage, possible action-options appropriate to the governing question are formulated as proposals. Third, proposals can be revised, in light of information-gathering and fact-checking. Fourth, there is a stage where each option for action is recommended for acceptance or non-acceptance. Fifth, at the closure stage, all participants must confirm their acceptance of a recommended option for normal termination of the deliberation dialogue. There are dialogue rules for the speech acts that can be made at each move, and unanimity is required at the closure stage for a decision on a course of action to be made. This formal model of deliberation dialogue will be discussed further in Chapter 6.

Practical reasoning in deliberation dialogue can vary in strength, depending on the stage the dialogue has reached. In some cases, practical reasoning has to be conducted under conditions of uncertainty in which conditions are changing fast. Here, a weak argument could be a reasonable basis for arriving at a decision on what to do now. The plan can always be revised later as new data come in, but too much collecting of data could mean that the decision to act is useless because too much time has lapsed without any action. In other cases, we might want to be very sure before taking action. For example, if the cost of taking a wrong action is very high, it may be best to study the situation and examine the consequences very carefully before rushing into an action. The problem is when the deliberation should be closed so that the premises of a practical inference can be evaluated as providing enough support for the conclusion.

2.2 The Yogurt Example

The advertising campaign called "In Soviet Georgia," designed by the Burson ad agency, was run in various media. From 1975 through to 1978, these commercials were broadcast on American television, and print ads were run in magazines such as *Time* and *Newsweek*. The commercial – called "Son of Russia," and written by Steve Kasloff – won the Clio award in 1978. The commercial presented shots of elderly Georgian farmers and the announcer said, "In Soviet Georgia, where they eat a lot of yogurt, a lot of people live past 100." *Advertising Age* ranked "In Soviet Georgia" as number 89 on its list of the 100 greatest advertising campaigns.

The text of the example to be analyzed is the statement "In Soviet Georgia, where they eat a lot of yogurt, a lot of people live past 100." Two premises are explicitly expressed:

Explicit Premise: In Soviet Georgia, they eat a lot of yogurt.
Explicit Premise: In Soviet Georgia, a lot of people live past 100.

Similar to the previous example, it would seem that in this case the conclusion is a prudential statement: 'You should eat yogurt.' However, the chain of reasoning in this case is a little more complex. We can analyze it by inserting some other implicit premises, and a secondary conclusion that links these premises to the ultimate conclusion:

Implicit premise: The eating of the yogurt is causing the people in Soviet Georgia to live past 100.
Implicit conclusion: If you want to live longer, you should eat yogurt.
Implicit premise: You want to live longer.
Implicit Conclusion: You should eat yogurt.

We can put all these elements together into an analysis by applying the argumentation scheme for argument from correlation to cause (Walton, Reed, and Macagno, 2008, 328):

PREMISE: There is a positive correlation between A and B.
CONCLUSION: Therefore A causes B.

The following are three critical questions for argument from correlation to cause:

CQ$_1$: Is there really a correlation between A and B?
CQ$_2$: Is there any reason to think that the correlation is any more than a coincidence?
CQ$_3$: Could there be some third factor, C, that is causing both A and B?

This scheme is shown in the screenshot of the argument scheme selection menu of *Araucaria* in Figure 2.1. How the scheme fits the example is shown on the right.

At the bottom of the screenshot of the menu in Figure 2.1 some of the critical questions matching the scheme for argument from correlation to cause are shown.

Now we can see how to analyze the argumentation in this case. The two explicit premises "In Soviet Georgia they eat a lot of yogurt" and "In Soviet Georgia a lot of people live past 100" go together to support the implicit conclusion that the eating yogurt is causing the people in Soviet Georgia to live past 100. The argumentation scheme that binds these two premises together in support of the conclusion is argument from correlation to cause. But we can analyze the argument still further by showing how this argument

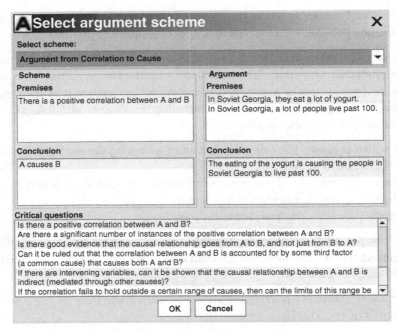

Figure 2.1: Screenshot of the Argument Scheme Selection Menu of *Araucaria*

leads to the conclusion that if you want to live longer you should eat yogurt. This conclusion, in turn, taken together with the implicit premise that you want to live longer, which can be seen as a goal premise, leads to the ultimate conclusion that you should eat yogurt.

These two premises work together, based on the argumentation scheme for practical reasoning, to support the ultimate conclusion. The structure of the argumentation as a whole is displayed in Figure 2.2.

The analysis of this case is interesting because it shows not only an ad with an implicit conclusion, but one with an implicit sub-conclusion used to link one part of the argument with another. Also, two argumentation schemes can be applied to the structure of the chain of argumentation. We essentially have to chain two arguments connected to each other because an implicit conclusion of the one argument functions as a premise supporting the premise in the other argument.

An interesting discussion point in the analysis of this particular example is whether the argument commits the *post hoc* fallacy – the error of leaping from a correlation to a premature causal conclusion. There are good grounds for concluding, on the analysis above, that the argumentation in this case does

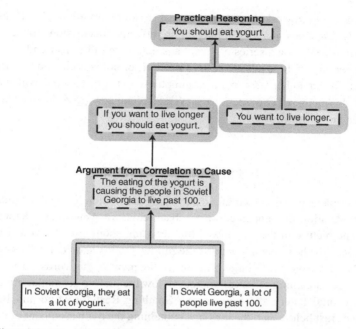

Figure 2.2: *Araucaria* Visualization of the Argument in the Yogurt Example

commit the *post hoc* fallacy. The analysis of it shown in the diagram in Figure 2.2, along with the argumentation scheme and list of critical questions given in Figure 2.1, provide the right kind of evidence needed to support such a criticism. So, here we have a widely successful ad that, arguably, is an instance of the *post hoc* fallacy. But to go into the matter a little more deeply, we have to look at the context of dialogue.

This ad was successful during an earlier time, when people were aware of the longevity of the farmers in Georgia and it was widely thought to be a remarkable phenomenon because there appeared to be no explanation for why they would live so long. The ad exploited this common knowledge very successfully by allowing the reader to jump (precariously) to an explanation that serves the marketers of yogurt products. The same ad would very likely be laughable today, or at any rate would not be effective, as commonly held opinions about aging and nutrition have changed. As times have changed, so has the context in which ads are used for mass persuasion. Now there is an aging population that spends a lot on health-related products but also tends to be more sophisticated about health issues. For these readers, ads that are targeted to real health problems that they have, and that address the problem by offering solutions that seem likely to work, based on practical reasoning of a kind that is not so obviously fallacious, may seem like a more effective persuasion strategy. We now turn to analyzing a series of recent ads that seem to fit this trend.

Whether any of these ads are really fallacious or not is tricky, however, and depends on a number of general assumptions discussed in the concluding section. In the next two sections, several recent ads from *Newsweek* are analyzed and discussed.

2.3 The Lunesta Example

This example is part of a lengthier chain of argumentation in an ad for Lunesta sleep medication that appeared on the back cover of *Newsweek*, October 8, 2007. The picture in the ad showed the head and shoulders of a young man, asleep with his head resting against the pillow. On his shoulder a fluorescent butterfly was depicted. In large print above the picture, the words, "The sleep you've been dreaming of" were printed. Below the picture in smaller print, but also in capital letters, the expression, "Soothing Rest for Mind and Body" appeared. Just below that, the message containing the main argument of the ad appears. This text comprises most of the argument, but two sentences just after the part quoted have been deleted: "It's what you've been craving. Peaceful sleep without a struggle. That's what Lunesta is all about: helping most people fall asleep quickly, and stay asleep all through the night." It is easy to see that this text presents an argument directed toward getting the readers of the ad to buy Lunesta. However, at first it may be a little harder to see what the premises are that are put forward to support this conclusion, and what the form of the argument is. The argument evidently has some sort of structure, but it may not be apparent what that structure is. We begin by making a so-called key list of the statements that make up the explicit premises and conclusion of the argument:

> Premise: Your goal is to have peaceful sleep without a struggle.
> Premise: Taking Lunesta is the best means to have peaceful sleep without a struggle.
> Premise: Lunesta helps most people fall asleep quickly.
> Premise: They stay asleep all through the night.

When stated in this way, the argument can be analyzed as having the form of the argumentation scheme called practical reasoning. This scheme represents goal-directed reasoning of the following sort: I have a goal; this action is a means to help fulfill the goal; therefore I should carry out this action. There are

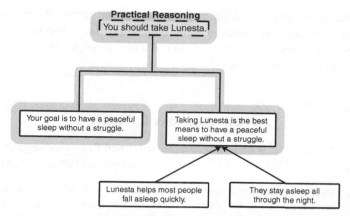

Figure 2.3: *Araucaria* Visualization of the Argument in the Lunesta Example

three basic components of this scheme. One premise describes an agent's goal. A second premise describes an action that the agent could carry out and that would be a means to accomplish the goal. The third component is the conclusion of the inference telling us that the agent should carry out this action.

We can analyze the argument in the Lunesta example by applying the scheme for practical reasoning to the statements in the key list. The main problem is that the conclusion does not appear to be stated explicitly in the given text. However, since the argument is part of an ad, we can reasonably take it that the purpose of the ad is to persuade the readership that taking Lunesta would be a good thing (from a prudential viewpoint) for them to do – the purpose of the ad is to sell the product, and it looks like the argument is directed to this sort of conclusion. Hence, in the analysis shown in Figure 2.3, we have inserted the conclusion as the implicit statement 'You should take Lunesta.' In Figure 2.3, we can see how the two explicit premises are linked together, based on the scheme for practical reasoning, and work together to support the conclusion. The conclusion is displayed in a text box with a dashed border, indicating that the statement in the box is implicit.

The remaining two statements, at the bottom of Figure 2.3, are depicted as providing two individual reasons, each of which stands on its own to support the statement above it ("Taking Lunesta is the best means to have peaceful sleep without a struggle"). It is interesting to note that the implicit statement in this case is the conclusion, as contrasted with the more usual sort of case in which the implicit statement is one of the premises.

The Lunesta example is relatively simple, and represents a common kind of argument structure found in commercial ads for drugs, herbal products, or foods that claim to have health benefits, except that it may be one of the premises in the argument, rather than the conclusion, that is implicit. We now turn to a brief mention of some other examples that are slightly more complex, and that raise interesting issues.

2.4 The Mucinex Example

An ad for Mucinex shows a large character fashioned from what appears to be mucus (*Newsweek*, February 18, 2008, 5). The text under the visual reads:

> When mucus gives you major congestion, you need a major mucus fighter, new maximum strength Mucinex. Just one pill has the most mucus fighting medicine available, to break up and loosen congestion for a full 12 hours. In fact, it's the longest lasting nonprescription chest congestion medication you can buy. So when maximum mucus happens to you, overpower it with maximum strength Mucinex.

The basic argument in this ad can be put in the form of practical reasoning as follows: Your goal is to reduce congestion by reducing the amount of mucus in your chest; taking maximum strength Mucinex is a means to realize this goal; therefore you should take maximum strength Mucinex. Another interesting aspect of the argumentation in the ad is that it mentions the claim that the product breaks up and loosens congestion for a full twelve hours. Then it states that the product is the longest lasting non-prescription chest congestion medication you can buy. This claim answers one of the critical questions matching the scheme for practical reasoning – namely, the question of what alternative actions to the one being consid-ered would also bring about the goal. It would very likely be known to both the reader of the ad and those who crafted it that there are competing products available that claim to achieve the same goal. So, the consumer who reads the ad has a choice between different means of carrying out the goal: buying this product, or buying some competing product. This ad displays the interesting strategy of proleptic argumentation – the technique of putting forward an argument containing a reply to an objection even before the objection is made by the respondent in the argument. Proleptic argument amounts to making two moves at one turn in a sequence of dialogue. In this instance, the argument based on practical reasoning is put forward in such a way that it contains a reply to one of the critical questions matching the scheme.

One problem with standard argument diagramming is that critical question-ing cannot be represented on the diagram, but there is a qualification to be made

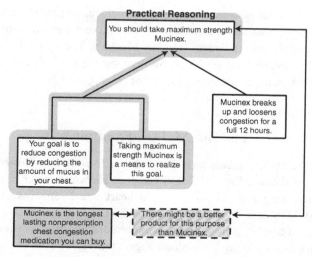

Figure 2.4: Using Refutation to Represent Answering a Critical Question

on this claim. It can be represented to some extent through the device of refutation. Let's examine the example shown in Figure 2.4.

The basic Mucinex argument is shown on the left as an instance of practical reasoning. The statement in the darkened box with the dotted border is shown joined to the practical reasoning argument by a double arrow. The double arrow stands for what is called refutation in *Araucaria*, which is supposed to be like negation. The statement in this text box, stating that there might be a better product for this purpose than Mucinex, operates like asking a critical question matching the practical reasoning argumentation scheme – namely, the critical question of what alternative actions to the one being considered would also bring about the goal.

Hence, the device of refutation does allow us to express the notion of a critical question being asked in response to an argument matching a parti-cular scheme. However, *Araucaria* treats the refutation as being a statement, and no distinction is drawn between making a statement and asking the question. Then, the statement which appears in the left-hand darkened box, stating that Mucinex is the longest lasting non-prescription chest congestion medication you can buy, is drawn as a refutation of the refutation that appears to its right. In other words, this example illustrates the refutation of a refutation.

This ad has an interesting visual aspect. The mucus man is a burly and threatening looking figure who also looks mildly disgusting. He is portrayed as somebody or something bad, who is about to do harm to you (the reader of the ad).

This visual part of the ad uses value-based practical reasoning. The argument is telling the viewer that he needs to take steps to protect himself from this bad individual, and the way to do that is to buy Mucinex. The visual part of the ad highlights the written text in the ad by drawing the reader's attention to a problem he might have, and then to a way of solving it.

2.5 The ACTOS Example

An ad for ACTOS, a medication for diabetes (*Newsweek*, November 26, 2007, 25) has the headline: "ACTOS has been shown to lower blood sugar without increasing the risk of having a heart attack or stroke." The ad presents ACTOS as a way for the reader who has type 2 diabetes to solve the problem of lowering blood sugar. It expresses this sort of argument: You have the goal of lowering your blood sugar; taking ACTOS is a means to realize this goal; therefore you should take ACTOS. The ad also responds to critical questions proleptically (in advance of their being put forward), by including a response to CQ_5 to the effect that the negative consequences of increasing the risk of heart attack or stroke will not occur.

Critical questioning cannot (straightforwardly) be represented on the diagram, but the potential rebuttal could be diagrammed as a pair of arguments fitting the scheme for argument from negative consequences mentioned in Chapter 1. An argument diagram showing how the proleptic argumentation in the ACTOS example works is presented in Figure 2.5.

The basic practical reasoning structure of the argument is shown on the bottom, displaying the argumentation scheme for practical reasoning as applied to the argument. The statement "Therefore you should not take ACTOS" is displayed at the top in a darkened box, indicating refutation in *Araucaria*. Refutation is something like negation, indicated in *Araucaria* by a double-headed arrow. The refutation is supported by argument from consequences, as shown in the middle. What is also shown is that the premise 'If ACTOS is taken there will be a risk of heart attack or stroke' is itself refuted by another claim. This is shown by the statement in the darkened box at the middle-left of Figure 2.5.

2.6 The Caduet and Plavix Examples

Argumentation from negative consequences is extremely common in the *Newsweek* ads, where it is used to cite possible side effects of a medication or, as in the ACTOS example, to argue proleptically. Some of the ads deal at

Figure 2.5: Argument Diagram for the ACTOS Example

great length with possible side effects of taking the medication advertised. For example, an ad for Caduet (*Newsweek*, December 29, 2008, 29), a drug promoted as one pill that reduces both high blood pressure and high cholesterol, offers many details concerning side effects. In a section entitled Possible Side Effects of Caduet, it lists headache, constipation, swelling of the legs or ankles, gas, feeling dizzy, upset stomach, and stomach pain. It also mentions unexplained muscle weakness, nausea, vomiting, brown or dark-colored urine, feeling more tired than usual, and the skin and whites of your eyes turning yellow.

The next ad shows a picture of a woman, and beneath that it says, "I have poor leg circulation. And I have a good reason to try to reduce the risk of heart attack or stroke that comes with it." Further below, more argumentation is presented:

> Peripheral artery disease (PAD) is often described as poor leg circulation, which puts you at the double risk of heart attack or stroke. That's because, if you have poor blood circulation in your legs, you may also have it in your heart and brain. You may feel nothing, but the most common symptom of PAD is pain or heaviness in the legs. Take the next step. So if you're diagnosed with PAD, ask your doctor about a treatment clinically proven to

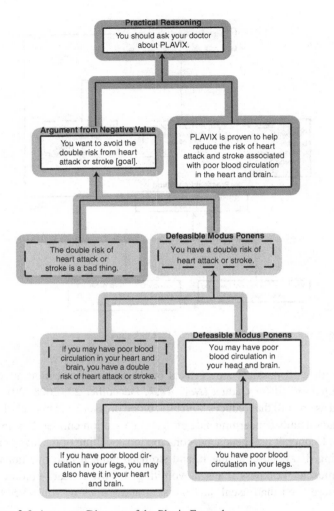

Figure 2.6: Argument Diagram of the Plavix Example

help reduce your risk of heart attack and stroke associated with PAD. PLAVIX helps keep blood platelets from sticking together and forming dangerous clots, the cause of most heart attacks and strokes. Ask your doctor about PLAVIX.

This chain of argumentation is fairly complex, and there could be many ways to diagram it, but one way that captures the practical reasoning structure is shown in Figure 2.6.

The three statements in the darkened boxes with the dashed lines around them are implicit premises that have been inserted. The explicit premises are listed as follows:

You want to avoid the double risk of heart attack or stroke [goal].
If you have poor blood circulation in your legs, you may also have it in your heart and brain.
You have poor blood circulation in your legs.
You may have poor blood circulation in your heart and brain.
PLAVIX is proven to help reduce the risk of heart attack and stroke associated with poor blood circulation in the heart and brain.
You should ask your doctor about PLAVIX.

In one instance, an implicit premise also plays the role of an implicit conclusion by forming a chain of reasoning. This form of argument is illustrated by the goal premise in the practical inference at the top of Figure 2.6, supported by argument from values.

2.7 The Lap-Band Example

The argument in the next ad is an interesting contrast to the one in the yogurt example. This ad is a more recent one (*Newsweek*, September 28, 2009, 61), and has several interesting features that are also different from any of the other ads studied above. It shows a large picture of an attractive young woman who appears to be visibly overweight. The text of the ad is printed against a backdrop of a picture of this young woman. Two sentences are displayed in large text in the middle of the page. One says: "If I lost the weight, I could stop taking so many medications." The other says: "So I talked to my doctor about the Lap-Band system." The next part of the text reads as follows:

If you're ready to finally lose weight and keep it off, then you may be ready for the Lap-Band System. The Lap-Band System is a device that's placed around the upper part of the stomach – often as an outpatient procedure – to help you feel fuller faster and longer. It's a healthy way to lose a significant amount of weight, and enjoy long-term results! Unlike gastric bypass surgery, there's no stomach cutting or stapling, plus it's adjustable for your needs, and can even be removed if necessary.

The remainder of the ad is concerned with contraindications and possible side effects. For example, it is stated that the system is not for those who are pregnant or suffer from certain disorders, and that band slippage, stomach injury, vomiting, and heartburn may occur. On an adjoining page (60) a detailed list of contraindications, warnings, and possible adverse effects is presented.

One of the interesting aspects of this ad is that it presents the young woman whose picture is displayed in the ad as an example of someone who has taken this medical treatment and is now offering advice to the reader of the ad, supposedly based on her personal experience. It is interesting because the woman pictured in the ad has certain goals that are either stated or may be attributed to her, and the assumption is that certain target readers of the ad to whom its argumentation is directed are presumed to share these goals. The woman pictured in the ad has supposedly carried out an action, namely taking this treatment, and it has enabled her to successfully achieve these goals. One of her goals, prominently stated in the large print at the beginning of the ad, was for her to stop taking so many medications. It is presumed that a significant number of potential readers of the ad would be in the same position as this young woman – namely, taking a lot of medications that they would like to stop taking.

Thus, the ad has a dialogue structure with two levels of practical reasoning in it. One is the young woman's description of her own process of practical reasoning, whereby she took steps to go ahead with this treatment based on her goal to stop taking so many medications. The assumptions are that she is in a position to know about the treatment because she has actually taken it, and that the target readers of the ad who are in the same position can benefit from her experience. There are also some implicit goals that can be seen as enthymematic premises. Although it is not stated explicitly in the wording of the ad, it is clear that her goal was to lose weight. There is also an implicit assumption that taking many medications is undesirable. It is well known that taking a lot of medication has side effects that can be made more complicated, and even dangerous, if the side effects conflict with each other in ways that may be impossible to predict. This can be presumed to be common knowledge among the readers to whom the ad was directed.

In the main argument, quoted above, several sub-arguments may be distinguished. One is that the device is installed as an outpatient procedure, as opposed to gastric surgery that has to take place in a hospital – a procedure that presumably most people would be less comfortable with. Another is the statement that it helps the person feel full faster and for longer, a premise that shows how the technique works, and makes the claim that it does work. Finally, other advantages over gastric bypass surgery are cited: no stomach cutting or stapling, it's adjustable for your needs, and it can be removed if necessary. The conclusion of the ad directed to the reader is that if he or she is in the same position as the young woman pictured in the ad, and has the same goals, he or

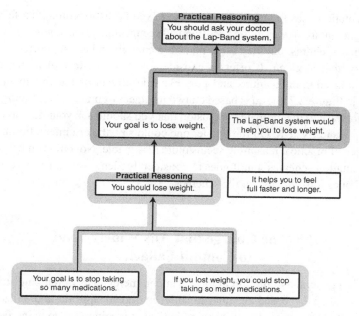

Figure 2.7: Visualization of the Practical Reasoning in the Lap-Band Example

she should consider this treatment. More specifically, the reader of the ad is advised to take the first step of talking to his or her doctor about trying this treatment. The practical reasoning part of the argument can be diagrammed as shown in Figure 2.7. This part of the argumentation is interesting because it is an example of chaining of practical inferences into a sequence of practical reasoning.

Some other parts of the argumentation are also interesting to comment on. The critical question of whether there are better alternatives to the proposed course of action is addressed by several arguments. One alternative that is mentioned is gastric bypass surgery. The ad states that unlike gastric bypass surgery, there's no stomach cutting or stapling. The implicit value premise is that stomach cutting or stapling is a negative value for the reader of the ad. These would be taken to be negative consequences of any weight loss treatment; hence, they are reasons *for* the Lap-Band System and *against* the alternative of gastric bypass surgery. Two other reasons are given to support the Lap-Band System against other possible alternatives: it is adjustable for your needs, and it can even be removed if necessary.

The general contrast between this example and the yogurt example is interesting to observe. The latter example could be used to illustrate deceptive argumentation uses in an ad. The argument even arguably commits a fallacy. The argumentation used in the Lap-Band ad seems highly reasonable. It makes a number of claims, but they seem plausible enough and are supported by the evidence that is given. It offers a considerable body of factual information concerning contraindications and possible side effects of the treatment. As shown in Figure 2.7, the ad is based on two instances of practical reasoning that chain forward to the ultimate conclusion that you should ask your doctor about the Lap-Band System. On the whole, one could say, the argumentation in the sequence of practical reasoning seems quite reasonable. Not only is it based on argumentation schemes, but it goes to considerable lengths to answer relevant critical questions that match the schemes.

2.8 The Charge that Ads Widely Tend to Commit Fallacies

There is a general assumption in logic that commercial ads of the kind studied above tend to be based on questionable emotional appeals and fallacious arguments, as contrasted with genuine logical reasoning that contains factual information of the kind useful to a consumer considering taking steps to solve a practical problem (Slade, 2003). Many commercial ads are commonly cited in logic textbooks in the sections on informal fallacies as examples of fallacious arguments. As shown in Section 2, it has been argued that these ads commit fallacies.

Groarke (2009, section 10) analyzed an example of a vodka ad in which a giant bottle of vodka is shown being poured onto a sleepy village, transforming it into a glittering city with skyscrapers. He analyzed the message conveyed in the picture (p. 2) as expressing the following argument:

> Explicit Premise: If you add vodka to your life, your sleepy life will be transformed into a life of cosmopolitan excitement.
> Implicit Premise: A life of cosmopolitan excitement is desirable.
> Conclusion: You should add vodka to your life (i.e., purchase vodka).

Groarke (p. 2) concluded that this argument is fallacious, on the basis that it is an instance of a "normative variant" of the fallacy of affirming the consequent. The fallacy of affirming the consequent has a deductively invalid argument form of argument: if A then B; B; therefore A. An example would be: if I have graduated, I have paid my tuition fee; I have paid my tuition fee; therefore I have graduated. This form of reasoning is invalid from the viewpoint of deductive logic.

Birdsell and Groarke (1996) and Slade (2003) were quite right to draw attention to the significance of the visual aspect of argumentation in ads. Images were used in all of the ads studied in Sections 4 and 5, although in some instances they were highly significant and in other cases minimal. Some were highly evocative emotionally and were directed toward the values of the targeted readers. The Lunesta butterfly hovering over the sleeper's pillow evokes drug safety. The Mucinex man evokes mild disgust toward mucus. The Mucinex ads varied over the period studied, with different depictions of the mucus man as a hooligan attacking the cold sufferer but being repelled by Mucinex. In one such ad (*Newsweek*, December 7, 2009, 35), the mucus man is depicted as a muscular, threatening biker being blown off his motorcycle by Mucinex. Here some mild emotions of fear are appealed to, but in the Plavix ad the fear of clogged arteries is graphically exploited by a picture of a blood vessel being plugged up by cholesterol. The reader can easily imagine the consequences of this situation. These pictures in the ad can be analyzed as putting arguments forward (Slade, 2003; Groarke, 2009), but they also perform a function of drawing the reader's attention to a problem that may affect him and that needs to be solved. Presumably, most readers of *Newsweek* ignore the ads, or pay little attention to them, but a graphic that relates to their specific problem(s) will grab their attention.

The visual aspect of argumentation in the ads is one focus of the allegation that the ads commit logical fallacies. Groarke's example of the giant vodka bottle being poured onto the sleepy village was taken to express the following argument: [Explicit Premise] If you add vodka to your life, your sleepy life will be transformed into a life of cosmopolitan excitement; [Implicit Premise] A life of cosmopolitan excitement is desirable; [Conclusion] You should add vodka to your life (i.e., purchase vodka). Groarke evaluated this argument as fallacious by classifying it as an instance of the fallacy of affirming the consequent. It is questionable, however, whether this is the best way of representing the form of this argument, for the implicit premise is about whether a life of cosmopolitan excitement is desirable. A better way of representing the form of the argument is as an instance of practical reasoning. The goal is a life of cosmopolitan excitement, the means is to employ vodka, and the conclusion is to buy vodka. Instead of measuring the argument against the standard of deductive validity, we can view it as fitting the argumentation scheme for practical reasoning.

Seen as an instance of defeasible practical reasoning, the argument is not fallacious – or, at any rate, the basic structure of the argumentation in the ad is reasonable. As an instance of practical reasoning, it can be seen as reasonable depending on two assumptions:

1. Whether the premises are true, and
2. Whether it takes the appropriate critical questions for practical reasoning into account.

It can be argued that it fails on both counts, and, indeed, Groarke's criticisms of some of the weak points in the argument can be fitted nicely into this format. For example, it can be pointed out that there are negative consequences of drinking vodka, it can be argued that the excitement it provides is temporary, and so forth. Perhaps there are also grounds for alleging that the example is an instance of fallacious use of practical reasoning, but by categorizing the argument as a deductive one that needs to meet standards for deductive reasoning, Groarke's analysis fails to recognize that the underlying structure of the argument is that of practical reasoning – a defeasible form of argument that is most fully evaluated by seeing how well it stands up to critical questioning based on its argumentation scheme.

As shown at the end of Section 2, pharmaceutical health product ads have come under even more detailed criticism for committing fallacies. Using methods of argumentation theory to analyze examples of ads for pharmaceutical products Rubinelli (2005) concluded that some of the arguments in the ads can be said to have committed informal fallacies. Rubinelli cited an ad for Allegra that failed to include information about side effects of taking the product, possibly leading someone to ask his/her doctor for a medication that is not appropriate for them: "We are here dealing with a clear fallacy of omission, based on a failure to present information" that is relevant for consumers (Rubinelli, 2005, 89). Rubinelli, Nakamoto, and Schulz (2007, 1213) cited an ad that claimed that the product advertised is better than the comparable products on the market, but provided no support for this claim. They also cited ads (1213) that either failed to mention side effects, or printed them in a small font using technical language that would not be familiar to all readers. The fallacy is taken to be a failure to provide relevant information. One general failure of the DTCA (direct to consumer) ads they cited is that they commit the fallacy of omission, based on their failure to present information to consumers (Rubinelli, Nakamoto, and Schulz, 2007, 1214). A further series of DTCA ads analyzed by Rubinelli, Nakamoto, and Schulz (2008, 53) were said to show that the ads commit a fallacy of relevance by emphasizing certain aspects in a more inviting way – for example, by using larger print in a more prominent place, "inviting the reader to ignore crucial information."

The underlying issue is whether a failure to present information in an argument in an ad is fallacious. The answer depends on whether the purpose of the ad, or part of it, is to present information to the reader. Supporters of DTCA see it as a way of providing people with information about the benefits and risks of medication, arguing that pharmaceutical companies have more scientifically based information than any other sources (Rubinelli, Nakamoto, and Schulz, 2008, 49). However, detractors emphasize the financial interests of the pharmaceutical companies, arguing that their aim is to sell product by creating brand recognition (Rubinelli, 2005, 76–77). Hence, a good part of the dispute seems to be about the supposed purposes of this type of advertising. As a result, in order to properly judge whether arguments used in such health product ads are fallacious or not, we have to look at the context of use of the ad in a type of dialogue.

Omitting to present information in an argument is not always fallacious. It depends on whether the unstated information is relevant, and this in turn depends on what type of dialogue the argument is supposed to be part of. Proof standards are different in different types of dialogue (Gordon and Walton, 2009). The proof standard in a scientific investigation, or in evidence-based medicine, should properly be higher than the proof standard required for an argument placed in an ad in a magazine. Given this difference, it was remarkable that the *Newsweek* ads presented so much information on side effects. Even if such an ad fails to tell the reader about all of the possible side effects of taking the medication in question, inferring that the argument used in the ad therefore commits a fallacy of omission is a logical leap. Sometimes omitting information can be reasonable in argumentation, depending on what the goal of the dialogue is supposed to be.

2.9 Issues of Argument Evaluation Raised by the Ads

According to Kukafka (2005, 29), applying argumentation theories to consumer healthcare informatics for behavioral change has turned out to be a complex undertaking because of the limitations of some of the tools used. The natural language generation systems used to provide explanation and advice to consumers proved to exhibit limitations and shortcomings. One problem is that they do not explore planning mechanisms that account for the generation of text consisting of multiple arguments. Another is that although they have attempted to improve the construction of persuasive argument through rhetorical structure theory, these attempts lack a theory of how persuasive arguments in health communication are put together in a coherent sequence. At the same time, although proving to be a successful method, the tailored approach to health communication – where the behavioral change strategy is intended to reach a specific person – clearly needs better argumentation tools that allow the health informatics communicator and the person to whom the message is directed to interact in a dialogue format where arguments can be put forward by both parties in a way that responds to the previous arguments and questions of the other party. The ads studied in this chapter show that the argumentation scheme for practical reasoning, along with its matching set of critical questions and the accompanying application of the argument diagramming technique, are the tools that are needed.

Many health product ads contain pictures or other graphics as well as text. Birdsell and Groarke (1996) have studied visual ads that express arguments with premises and conclusions in very much the same way that arguments are put forward in written discourse. They admit that visual ads can be vague and ambiguous, and admit to all sorts of difficulties about justifying an interpretation of what the argument is supposed to be. However, they point out that written messages in ads, or any natural language texts of discourse, are confronted with these problems too. They stress (Birdsell and Groarke, 1996, 6) that context – including not only sequences of images, but also verbal context and implicit assumptions about what the readers of the ad can be expected to know or accept – is very important in interpreting visual ads. Their findings suggest that the visual components of health product ads need to be taken into account.

Another dialectical aspect of a health product ad that needs to be taken into account is whether information-seeking dialogue needs to be embedded into the persuasion dialogue in order for the argumentation in the ad to be reasonable enough to meet standards for an acceptable argument of this sort. As an additional part of the practical reasoning strategy used in the ad, the advertiser must also provide information that can be used to answer the reader's critical questions. For example, in the case of some health products, the reader will be concerned about potential side effects of taking a medication. The advertiser needs to adopt the strategy of crafting the ad in such a way that critical questions, like those concerning negative consequences of carrying out the designated action, are responded to. Thus, the advertiser's task is an empathic one of not only targeting a particular readership by formulating a goal, but also of being aware of reservations that the reader would have about carrying out the action proposed in the conclusion.

In evaluating the argumentation in the ads studied above, there are controversies about whether a failure to present information in an argument in an ad is improper, or even represents fallacious argumentation. An underlying issue with health product ads is whether the purpose of the ad is (or should be) (a) to persuade the reader to buy the product depicted in the ad, or (b) to give the reader information about the product in the ad. There is also the possibility that these aims are combined, and so we have to recognize the phenomenon referred to in the argumentation literature as the "dialectical shift" (Walton and Krabbe, 1995, 100–116). In a common kind of example, there is a shift from deliberation dialogue to an information-seeking type of dialogue. For example, suppose there is a debate in a legislative assembly on whether to pass a bill to install a new dam, but before those in the assembly can vote on the issue, they need to find out many facts about the proposed dam and its projected costs. They will call in experts, such as engineers and accountants. When this occurs there is a shift from the original deliberation dialogue to an information-seeking dialogue. This shift would be classified as an embedding in the system of Walton and Krabbe (1995, 102), meaning that the goal of the deliberation is supported by the information-seeking dialogue. But some dialectical shifts are illicit, meaning that the advent of the second dialogue interferes with the progress of the first (Walton and Krabbe, 1995, p. 107). Illicit shifts of this sort can be associated with fallacies, according to Walton and Krabbe (1995).

It is a commonplace of discussion of advertisements in visual media to claim that they use irrational appeals and faulty logic to sell products (Slade, 2003). Logic textbooks have propounded this view for years by telling us that such ads tend to use emotional appeals that shortcut logical reasoning, and even commit logical fallacies. One of the most widely used logic textbooks (Copi and Cohen, 2005, 128) tells us that commercial ads are designed by "ballyhoo artists" who persistently use relentless illogical appeals to emotions of every kind. Recent studies of argumentation in pharmaceutical ads (Rubinelli, Nakamoto, and Schulz, 2007, 2008) appear to confirm that these ads commit logical fallacies. Direct-to-consumer advertising (DTCA) of pharmaceutical products is illegal in all countries of the Western world except for the United States and New Zealand (Calfee, 2002, 176). However, it reaches all over the world via the Internet (Rubinelli, Nakamoto, and Schulz, 2008, 49). Thus, the question of whether they commit fallacies is significant and controversial.

Using methods of argumentation theory to analyze examples of ads for pharmaceutical products, Rubinelli (2005) concluded that some of the arguments in the ads can be said to have committed informal fallacies. She criticized an ad that failed to include information about side effects as having committed a fallacy of omission (Rubinelli, 2005, 89). Rubinelli, Nakamoto, and Schulz (2007, 1213) also alleged fallacies of failing to present relevant information about side effects. Supporters of DTCA ads defend them, however, as a way of providing people with information about the benefits and risks of medication (Calfee, 2002). Detractors (Lexchin and Mintzes, 2002, 197) cite evidence that many ads surveyed did not contain the basic information a person would need to make an informed decision about the usefulness of a treatment.

These allegations of committing fallacies stem from the perception that there is a failure to provide relevant information in DTCA ads. The assumption that the ads should provide information leaves them open to allegations of having committed fallacies of omission by not providing enough information (Rubinelli, 2005, 76–77). But how much is enough? Should the purpose of these ads be to present information, when we all know that a pharmaceutical company is not an unbiased source of information on the benefits or risks of the product it sells? Questions are raised here about the context of use of the ad for some communicative purpose in a dialogue setting.

It is true that pictures (graphics) can appeal to emotion more directly and more powerfully than words, especially if combined with words, and that pictures contain arguments in many instances (Birdsell and Groarke, 1996). But should appeals to emotion of these kinds be treated as fallacious arguments just because they appeal to emotion? Should emotional thinking always be treated as the opposite of logical reasoning? Is an appeal to emotion always logically defective as a good reason for accepting a conclusion? For a long time, the answer to these questions was affirmative, but more recently it has come to be recognized that the traditional blanket condemnation of appeals to emotion in argumentation is not warranted (Walton, Reed, and Macagno, 2008). Appeals to emotion should be generally recognized as having legitimate standing as being, under the right conditions, reasonable arguments carrying some weight in shifting a burden of proof in a balance of considerations case where exact calculation of the outcome is not a practical possibility. It is necessary to judge the argument in each ad by evaluating the purpose of its use in a dialogue context.

Consumers in a free market economy are not so naïve that they don't know that the ads are using all kinds of clever strategies to try to get them to pay attention to the message in the ad, to remember it, and to view the product favorably. Both sides in the persuasion dialogue know the game. Practical reasoning is a reasonable form of argumentation if used properly. The examples suggest that the underlying argumentation for practical reasoning used in the problem/solution ads is inherently reasonable, even though the standard of rationality appropriate for its use is not the same as the standards used in traditional deductive and inductive reasoning. Certainly it is the dominant argumentation scheme used in the ads, and by far the most common scheme that was identified.

2.10 Conclusions

It was interesting to find such a number of ads appearing during this period that exhibited the use of practical reasoning. Each ad in the series of examples is meant to be a persuasive argument to get consumers to buy a product. The intent was not empirical, however, but to study how each argument used particular schemes for this purpose, to evaluate strengths and weaknesses in the arguments by using the set of critical questions matching each scheme. The aims were to identify the argumentation strategies used in the ads so we can get a better idea of how they work as sequences of logical reasoning that can be broken down into parts and combined in argumentation structures. Each argument was visualized using an argument map that shows its parts, including its unstated premises or conclusions. This process helps us to see how the argumentation in the examples is not only based on practical reasoning, but is situated in a framework of supporting and attacking arguments.

Chapter 2 proved to be an instructive starting point for moving toward a deeper analysis of the logic of practical reasoning, in two ways. The first is that it was based on real examples of the use of practical reasoning of the kind that are very common in natural language argumentation. The second concerns the tool of argument diagramming used to represent the reasoning found in these examples. The use of this tool in Chapter 2 revealed five characteristic features essential to any analysis of practical reasoning:

- The diagram method forced the argument analyst to identify the premises and conclusion of the argument that is taken to be an instance of practical reasoning.
- The diagram method visibly showed how chains of arguments built up of practical reasoning combined with other kinds of arguments moved from the specification of means to the specification of a goal.

- The application of the diagram method can be used to represent the structure of how these other arguments not only support practical reasoning, but are also used to attack practical reasoning, by attacking its premises, its conclusion, or the inferential link that joins the premises to the conclusion.
- What makes *Araucaria* particularly valuable as an argument diagramming tool is that the argumentation scheme for practical reasoning, as well as other argumentation schemes, can be applied in bringing out the reasoning used in a particular example.
- The critical questions matching this scheme are presented to the argument analyst, and this feature is a particularly valuable one for studying how practical reasoning can be attacked or even refuted in particular cases.

These five features yield valuable information about practical reasoning, providing us with a set of desiderata that can work as focal points for a deeper analysis of the logical structure of practical reasoning. Hence, the diagram method provided a way of bringing out and summarizing the essential features of how practical reasoning is used in a given case.

The examples studied also showed how the scheme for practical reasoning is used in these health ads in interesting ways by combining it with the use of enthymemes. The examples show how schemes can help reveal implicit premises and conclusions in the arguments. For instance, the yogurt example shows how an analysis can help to uncover implicit assumptions in a chain of reasoning that should be open to critical questioning. The fourth critical question, which asks if the correction could be accounted for by some factor other than the one cited as cause, is especially important in this case. In this instance it would be fallacious to jump to the conclusion that the eating of the yogurt is the cause of the longevity. Drawing this conclusion is questionable, given that many other factors – such as environment and life style, not to mention other foods – need to be taken into account. Hence, the argument in this example can justifiably be judged to be fallacious.

The arguments in the other examples studied are basically reasonable, by virtue of their using practical reasoning to offer the reader of the ad a solution to a problem that he or she might have. What is shown is that there is a current trend to base the argumentation on practical reasoning, and that this kind of reasoning is not fallacious in the way claimed, even though it may be based on premises that are not always explicit or are not very well substantiated. What has been shown is a way to help overcome deficiencies in techniques of tailored health communication in consumer health informatics by using argumentation schemes, argument visualization tools, and dialogue models to frame these persuasive communication messages. The evidence collected

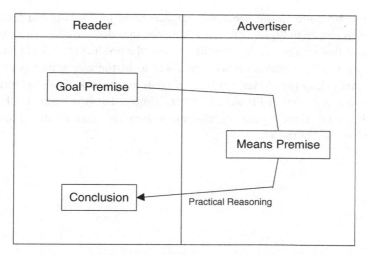

Figure 2.8: Persuasion Dialogue in Which Two Parties Use Practical Reasoning

has been shown to be useful in exploring the planning mechanisms that account for the generation of text consisting of multiple arguments in health product communications.

The provisional hypothesis proposed on the basis of the study of these examples of argumentation structure of health product ads takes the basic form of a persuasion dialogue between the advertiser who designs the ad and publishes it, and the reader to whom the ad is directed. Each contributes to a part of the inference leading to the conclusion based on the argumentation scheme for practical reasoning. The advertiser targets a particular group of readers who are presumed to have some problem they need to solve, and hence are presumed to have a goal that can be determined. It is the reader who contributes this goal. The advertiser provides a means that the reader can use to fulfill this goal, and presents this means to the reader. The reader is supposed to draw the conclusion that he or she can fulfill the goal, or at least take some steps toward its fulfillment, by drawing the conclusion that he or she should carry out the action recommended in the means premise.

The structure of the argument as a whole is that of practical reasoning, as shown in Figure 2.8, which displays the two parties and indicates the role each has in the reasoning used to derive the conclusion. In this way, the two parties both take part in the reasoning process, even though they do not have a dialogue in the literal sense that they take turns speaking and replying. Still, their argumentation interaction does have what might be called a dialogue structure in the sense of that described by Walton and Krabbe (1995), as shown in Figure 2.8. The advertiser, in order to make a successful argument that will persuade the reader to buy the product (or ask his doctor about it), needs to base it on what he takes to be the commitments of the reader, including the reader's presumed goals and values. The structure of the argument shown in Figure 2.8 is very simple, but it represents a basic hypothesis for representing the communication structure of the practical reasoning used in the ads.

3

Formal and Computational Systems
of Practical Reasoning

In Chapter 2 we examined some relatively simple (but real) cases in which argument diagramming tools, along with argumentation schemes and critical questions, were used to identify and analyze practical reasoning. Now we need to go more deeply into the subject to address the question of how the kind of practical reasoning we have identified can be formally modeled. There are some existing formal models in artificial intelligence that can model this kind of practical reasoning, in addition to the value-based system introduced in Chapter 1. Some of these formal models have been implemented in computational systems that contain argument diagramming tools. In Chapter 3, the reader will be introduced to these formal models and computational tools, in order to show how they can be used to model practical reasoning.

The way *Araucaria* is applied to the various examples of arguments in health ads in Chapter 2 was very instructive because it showed how the scheme for practical reasoning, along with other arguments – some of them also based on known schemes – can be structured in a way that makes the sequence of reasoning in a case easy to interpret and analyze. A nice feature of *Araucaria* was that once the scheme is identified as fitting a particular segment of the chain of argumentation represented in the argument diagram, the menu can be displayed showing the critical questions matching the scheme. This particular device turned out to be extremely helpful because, as indicated in Chapter 1, the main tool needed for evaluating instances of argumentation containing practical reasoning is the list of critical questions matching a scheme.

Argument diagramming, even along with argumentation schemes, is not sufficient to yield a model of the structure of practical reasoning as a species of rational argumentation. For that purpose, we need a precise formal model that goes more deeply into the structure of practical reasoning. In this chapter, it will be shown how some existing formal argumentation systems can be applied to practical reasoning. It will also prove helpful if the formal model is implemented in a working computational system that has additional features useful for analyzing practical reasoning, including an argument diagramming interface.

The system of value-based practical reasoning introduced in Chapter 1 is itself a formal model, based on an underlying structure called an abstract argumentation framework (Dung, 1995). The first job of this chapter, carried out in Section 1, is to introduce the reader to abstract argumentation frameworks. The first formal computational system that is introduced (ASPIC+) is also based on such a framework. Section 2 introduces the reader to an argument diagramming tool called ArguMed, which is based on a formal logical system called DefLog. The third formal computational system described in the chapter, the Carneades Argumentation System (CAS), also has an argument diagramming tool. CAS is computational, because it consists of a mathematical structure whose operations are all computable. In the beginning of its development, CAS used graphs in its argument diagrams that were acyclic, meaning that they could not contain circles. However, the more recent versions of the model overcame this limitation by mapping CAS argument frameworks onto abstract argument frameworks, and now it has been shown that CAS can be translated into ASPIC+ (van Gijzel and Prakken, 2012).

This chapter will explain how these formal systems can model practical reasoning. In particular it will be shown how CAS has incorporated the critical questions matching practical reasoning, and other schemes as well, into the argument diagram that is used as the basic tool for analyzing an argument. CAS will be applied to some of the examples studied in Chapter 2 to bring out some points of discussion on how formal systems model key features of practical reasoning, especially those relating to the employment of critical questions.

3.1 Abstract Argumentation Frameworks

Prakken (2011, 65) built a formal model of argumentation called ASPIC+, built around the idea that defeasible forms of argument such as practical reasoning do not guarantee the truth of a conclusion, but merely make a conclusion more plausible if its premises are true. He cites the following example of value-based practical reasoning. Suppose that we have the goal of increasing productivity because we think that increasing productivity is good. And suppose we think that reducing taxes is the way to increase productivity. Then we should conclude that taxes should be reduced. However, we also accept the premises that reducing taxes increases inequality, that increasing inequality is bad, and that equality is more important than productivity. Hence, we should conclude that we should not reduce taxes. The second argument defeats the first one, even though the conclusion of the first argument was acceptable before the second argument was considered. Given these observations, Prakken's solution (66) is to work toward developing a logical system that is inherently dialectical. This means that an argumentation system of the kind that can be used to model practical reasoning has to be such that an argument is successful in proving its conclusion if – and only if – it meets three requirements: first, the argument has to be properly constructed; second, it has to be capable of being defended against counter-arguments; and third, it needs to be actually defended against counter-arguments that have been brought forward. Prakken has shown that ASPIC+ has these three characteristics.

ASPIC+ is built on the basis of abstract argumentation frameworks (Dung, 1995). An argumentation framework is a structure used to determine which arguments can be accepted among a set of arguments in which some arguments defeat others. The proponent starts with the argument he wants to prove, and when the opponent has his turn he must provide a defeating counter-argument. An abstract argumentation framework (*AF*) is defined as a pair (*Args, Def*), where *Args* is a set of arguments and *Def* ⊆ *Args* × *Args* is a binary relation of defeat. Since the notion of an argument is primitive in an argumentation framework, the model does not analyze the internal parts of an argument, its premises, conclusion, or the nature of the inferential link joining them. Both the notion of an argument and the notion of argument defeat are taken as given. The idea is that each argument can be defeated by other arguments, which can themselves be defeated by other arguments. In any given set of arguments we can have a sequence of the following general sort: for arguments a_1-a_n, a_2 defeats a_1, a_3 defeats a_2,..., a_n defeats a_{n-1}.

We can have cycles of arguments, and any given case of an argument framework can be represented as a directed graph in which the arguments are represented by the nodes of the graph and the arrows joining the nodes represent defeat relations. Let's start with the simple linear example shown in Figure 3.1.

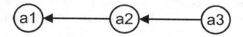

Figure 3.1: Example of an Argumentation Framework Graph

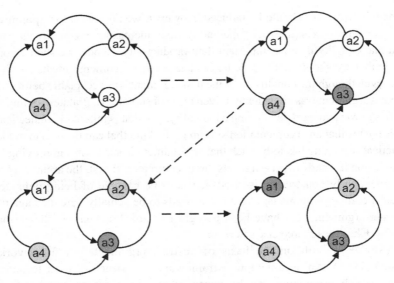

Figure 3.2: Four Evaluation Steps in the Argumentation Framework Example

First we note that a1 is defeated by a2, and so it seems that a1 should not be accepted. But then we observe that a2 is defeated by a3. Moreover, a3 is not defeated by any other argument, so whatever the outcome, a3 should be accepted. But if a3 is accepted then it defeats a2. And if a2 is defeated, it no longer defeats a1. So ultimately a1 should be accepted. The application of this model provides a kind of semantic procedure that can be used to tell which arguments are acceptable and which are not in a given case where arguments defeat other arguments.

The easiest way of understanding how such a semantic procedure works is to introduce what are called labelings, which determine whether an argument is *in*, *out*, or *undecided*. An argument is said to be *in* if all its defeaters are out. An argument is *out*, however, if it has a defeater that is in. An argument that is neither out nor in is undecided.

A simple example of how the semantic procedure works is shown in Figure 3.2. In this example there are four arguments: a1, a2, a3, and a4. The arrows represent defeat relations. If an argument is in, its node is shown with a light gray background. If an argument is out, its node is shown with a dark gray background. If an argument is undecided, its node is shown with a white background. The dashed lines indicate the order of steps from one argument to the next.

At the start of the procedure, in the top left diagram, let's say that the given situation is that a4 is in and a1 is undecided. So, a4 is shown with a light gray background and a1 is shown with a white background. What happens next? First, because a4 is in, a3 is out. Hence, in the right top diagram, a3 is shown with a dark gray background. But since a2 is not defeated by any other argument that is accepted, it is in. This situation is shown in the bottom left diagram. But since now both a4 and a2 are in, a1 is defeated by both these accepted arguments (even though one would be enough). Therefore a1 is out. Hence, in the bottom right diagram, a1 is shown as dark.

In addition to using the definition of an abstract argumentation framework as a set of arguments and a binary relation of defeat, ASPIC+ also offers a positive notion of argument defense to supplement the notion of argument defeat defined in standard abstract argumentation frameworks. The definition of this notion of argument defense runs as follows: a set B *defends* an argument A_i iff for each argument $A_j \in A$, if A_j defeats A_i, then there exists A_k in B such that A_k defeats A_j (Prakken, 2011, 67). In English, this means that an argument is defended if – and only if – for every argument that defeats it there is a set of arguments that defeat the defeating argument. In other words, an argument is defended, and therefore acceptable, only if it defeats all attacking arguments. The analogy of the gunfighter is often used to illustrate this condition. The gunfighter is successful in staying alive only if he defeats every other gunfighter that is trying to attack him.

In addition to incorporating abstract argumentation frameworks, ASPIC+ is built on a logical language containing a contrariness function, a set of strict and defeasible inference rules, and an ordering of this set of inference rules (Prakken, 2010). The system works by determining the success of rebutting and undercutting attacks that compare conflicts in arguments at the points where they conflict. ASPIC+ is based on the system of Pollock (1995), where an important distinction was drawn between two kinds of refutations called rebutting defeaters and undercutting defeaters (often referred to as rebutters versus undercutters). A rebutter gives a reason for denying a claim by arguing that the claim is false whereas an undercutter defeater attacks the inferential link between the claim and the reason supporting it (Pollock, 1995, 40). Pollock used a famous example (1995, 41) to illustrate his distinction. According to the example, if I see an object that looks red to me, that is a reason for thinking it is red, but if I know that the object is illuminated by a red light, that is an undercutter because red objects look red in red light too. This is not a reason for thinking the object is not red, but it is a reason for undercutting the argument that it is red. Despite the attacking argument, the object may be red, for all we know. As an undercutter it acts like a critical question that casts an argument into doubt rather than strongly refuting it. The use of three kinds of counter-arguments that can be used to attack any given argument is highly characteristic of ASPIC+. The three kinds of counter-arguments are undercutters, rebutters, and premise attacks.

Another important characteristic of ASPIC+ is that not only can it represent deductive reasoning, such as predicate logic, but it can also represent defeasible argumentation schemes, such as practical reasoning. The system uses a modified form of the Walton et al. (2008) schemes for arguments from positive consequences and arguments from negative consequences, combined into one scheme (Prakken, 2011, 72): Action A results in consequence C; C is good (bad); therefore A should (not) be done. This scheme is employed by Prakken in the way that is normal in argumentation systems: it has a matching set of critical questions that can be used to undercut or rebut a given argument fitting the scheme. Comparable to the CAS Argumentation System explained in the next section, the premises of an argument can be of three types: assumptions, presumptions, and exceptions. Assumptions are similar to what are called the ordinary premises of a scheme in CAS. Presumptions appear to be additional premises that are taken to hold unless questioned. Exceptions, said to be similar to contradictories (Prakken 2010, 117), are additional premises that only fail to hold when the questioning of them is backed up by an argument. How these three kinds of premises are treated in CAS will be an important topic in the next section.

3.2 ArguMed Based on DefLog

In 1999, Bart Verheij began to build an automated argument assistant called ArguMed, which helps a user to construct an argument diagram in order to analyze and evaluate a given argument (Verheij, 2003a, 320). The development of this system was guided by his parallel research on the logical system called DefLog (Verjeij, 2003a), which represents the underlying structure of the reasoning displayed by ArguMed. ArguMed is available at no cost on the Internet (http://www.ai.rug.nl/~verheij/aaa/argumed3.htm). The argument diagrams that can be produced using this system look somewhat similar to those produced with *Araucaria*. The ultimate conclusion, called the issue in ArguMed, appears in a text box at the top of the diagram, and the premises supporting it form arguments that can be linked together, and that lead by arrows to the conclusion. The user can input statements directly into the boxes shown on the screen and then, in a way comparable to *Araucaria*, can draw

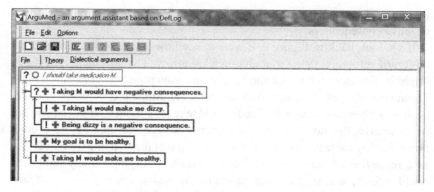

Figure 3.3: An Example of Practical Reasoning Drawn with ArguMed

arrows representing argument support and argument refutation. An example illustrating the use of practical reasoning is shown on the screenshot of the user interface pictured in Figure 3.3.

The box containing the statement shown at the top in Figure 3.3 – the statement that I should take medication M – has a question mark in it, indicating that this statement is at issue (is the ultimate conclusion). An exclamation mark indicates that the statement is of the assumption type. The + indicates a statement that has been evaluated as justified.

The two statements at the bottom are premises of a practical reasoning argument. This argument is shown as linked, called "conjoint" in ArguMed, and indicated by the line from each of them going into the long vertical line pointing by an arrow to the ultimate conclusion. The text box just under the ultimate conclusion is an undercutter, indicated by a line drawn from it to the long vertical line going from the premises of the practical inference to the ultimate conclusion. This text box, which states that taking M would have negative consequences, is supported by the pair of conjoint premises just under it. One can see from looking at these premises that the two premises and its conclusion, all taken together, represent an instance of argument from negative consequences. Since the undercutter (the statement that taking M would have negative consequences) is supported by these two premises, and both premises are justified, the main argument supporting the ultimate conclusion is defeated by this undercutting argument. For this reason, ArguMed automatically changes the vertical line at the left into a squiggly line, whereas before being defeated the argument was represented as a solid black line. The argument from negative consequences is an undercutter represented by the X at the end of the top arrow where it meets the squiggly line. In short, the example represents a case where the ultimate conclusion was initially supported by practical reasoning, but then the support for it was defeated by an argument from negative consequences.

If we look back to Figure 2.4, we can see how *Araucaria* visualizes the notion of refutation using a double-headed arrow. The statement that there might be a better product for the purpose of reducing chest congestion than Mucinex was used as an argument to attack the ultimate conclusion that the person to whom the ad was directed should take maximum strength Mucinex. In *Araucaria*, this notion of argument attack was represented by the double arrow joining these two propositions, meaning that the first one was meant to be a refutation of the other one. But refutation could mean many things. It could refer to a strong kind of refutation in which one argument defeats another, or it could refer to a weaker kind of refutation whereby one argument undermines support for the other one. Looking again at Figure 2.4, we see that there is another instance of refutation represented in the diagram as well. The argument that was doing the refuting is now refuted by another argument stating that Mucinex has the longest lasting non-prescription chest congestion medication you can buy. In other words, in this case we had a refutation of a refutation.

An advantage of ArguMed over *Araucaria* and other comparable systems of argument diagramming is that it can model and visually represent the distinction between these two kinds of argument attack and defeat. One way of representing the Mucinex example shown earlier in Figure 2.4 in the style of DefLog is shown in Figure 3.4. The circled X represents negation, indicating an argument being attacked (refuted, defeated).

In Figure 3.4, we see the practical reasoning argument represented by the two conjoint premises near the bottom. The second of these premises is backed up by the statement that Mucinex breaks up and loosens congestion for a full

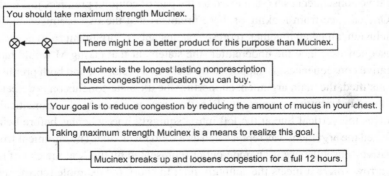

Figure 3.4: Refutation in the Mucinex Example Shown as an Undercutter

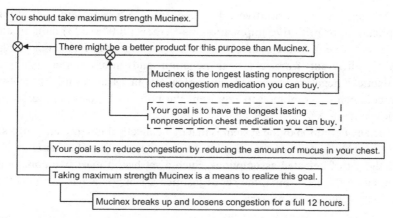

Figure 3.5: Refutation in the Mucinex Example Shown as a Rebutter

12 hours, shown at the bottom. But then we notice that just under the ultimate conclusion shown at the top, there is an attack on this practical reasoning argument, posed by the claim that there might be a better product for this purpose than Mucinex. The problem posed is whether this attack should be represented as undercutter or a rebutter. In Figure 3.4 it is shown as an undercutter because it is displayed on the diagram as attacking the practical reasoning argument itself.

But the possibility remains that the argument could be interpreted in a different way. Instead of attacking the previous argument, the statement that Mucinex is the longest lasting non-prescription chest congestion medication you can buy could be represented as a rebuttal of the statement that there might be a better product for this purpose than Mucinex. In order to show better why this interpretation is also plausible, the argument could be penalized more deeply by adding an implicit premise. This is shown in Figure 3.5.

The statement in the text box with the dashed border is shown in Figure 3.5 as an implicit premise that forms part of the linked argument taken together with the other premise to attack the statement that there might be a better product than Mucinex. If Mucinex is the longest lasting non-prescription chest congestion medication you can buy and your goal is to have the longest lasting non-prescription chest medication you can buy, these two premises together form a very strong argument against the claim that there might be a better product for this purpose than Mucinex. Hence, when the argument is interpreted this way it can be represented as a rebutter rather than merely being an undercutter.

DefLog uses two primitives. The connective $\sim>$ represents defeasible implication, or primitive implication, as Verheij (2003a, 323) calls it, and the connective X is the symbol for dialectical negation. Dialectical negation is different from classical negation and intuitionistic negation. Dialectical negation represents the defeat of an assumption. These two symbols can be combined to represent the notion of attack, expressed as follows: $A \sim> XB$.

The key definition of the system is that of a dialectical interpretation of a set of sentences divided into two disjoint subsets: the set of justified assumptions and the set of defeated assumptions. Such a set has to meet two conditions (Verheij, 2007, 197). First, the set of justified assumptions has to be conflict free. This requirement means:

1. that there must be no sentence A in the set such that the defeat sentence XA follows from using defeasible *modus ponens*, and
2. the defeat of sentence XA of each sentence in the set is in the justified subset or follows from it using defeasible *modus ponens*.

Given these requirements, it follows in a dialectical interpretation of a set of assumptions that each consequence of the justified subset is justified. However, this does not mean that all the assumptions are actually justified, for some of them can be defeated by the justified assumptions. According to Verheij (2007, 187), the abstract argumentation systems of Dung (1995) are extensions of DefLog, essentially because the notion of an argument a_1 attacking an argument a_2 can be expressed in DefLog as an undercutting defeater in Pollock's sense as: $a_1 \sim> Xa_2$.

The only rule of inference supported by primitive implication is that of defeasible *modus ponens*:

$$A \sim> B$$
$$A$$
$$\text{Therefore } B$$

Instead of taking on the values true and false characteristic of standard deductive logics, the propositions in DefLog are assumptions that can either be positively evaluated as justified, or negatively evaluated as defeated.

As an example of primitive implication Verheij (2003a, 324) uses the conditional 'If an object looks red, it is red,' which is of course the famous example that Pollock used to illustrate defeasible reasoning. Consider the following inference, which contains two premises and a conclusion that Verheij describes as *prima facie* assumptions:

looks_red
looks_red ~> is_red
Therefore is_red

The two premises represent the assumptions that a particular object looks red and the conditional assumption that if it looks red, it is red. The conclusion represents the assumption that the object in question is red. The conclusion follows in virtue of a form of argument called defeasible *modus ponens*.

Next, consider another instance of a Pollock-style argument that illustrates how dialectical negation is used:

looks_red
illuminated by a red light
looks_red ~> X(looks_red ~> is_red)
Therefore X(is_red)

The first premise is the same as that in the above inference. It states that the particular object in question looks red. The second premise, however, states a particular fact about the case, namely that in this instance the object in question is illuminated by a red light. The third premise states that in these particular circumstances, it is defeated that the object is red if it looks red. The conclusion is the assumption that the object is red, and it is defeated.

3.3 The Carneades Argumentation System

CAS is a formal mathematical model of argumentation, and is at the same time a working computational system that can be used to construct arguments, to visualize them as argument diagrams and to evaluate them (Gordon, 2010). The visualization tool for CAS, and a manual explaining how to use it, can be accessed at http://carneades.github.io/. CAS was originally developed to support deliberation on legal and policy issues for applications to electronic democracy, and therefore it is highly applicable to modeling practical reasoning concluding in a recommended policy or course of action. The model represents arguments by using different types of premises called ordinary premises, assumptions, and exceptions to represent critical questions in an argument diagram format (Gordon and Walton, 2006).

CAS formally represents a sequence of argumentation as a graph, a structure made up of nodes that represent premises or conclusions of an argument, and arrows joining points to other points. Each arrow represents an argument from a premise or a set of premises to a conclusion. The chain of arguments

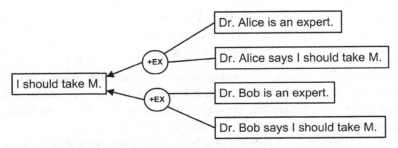

Figure 3.6: A Linked and Convergent Argument Structure

having this graph-type structure can be visualized as an argument diagram, or so-called argument map. Technically speaking, an argument graph is defined as a bipartite directed graph, consisting of statement nodes and argument nodes connected by edges, or arrows representing inferences from statements to other statements. More precisely, an *argument graph* is a bipartite, directed, labeled graph, consisting of statement nodes and argument nodes connected by premise and conclusion edges. Formally, an argument graph may be defined in the CAS framework as a 4-tuple $\langle S, A, P, C \rangle$, where S is a set of statement nodes, A is a set of argument nodes, P is a set of premises, and C is a set of conclusions. If we look at Figure 3.6, for example, the proposition in the text box at the left stating that I should take medication M is the conclusion of the argument.

There are two argument nodes, represented as circles. The name of the argumentation scheme appears in the circle representing the argument. In this instance the notation EX represents the scheme for argument from expert opinion, and the plus sign indicates that it is a pro argument supporting the conclusion. In Figure 3.6 there are two argument nodes, and each of the two arguments is shown as fitting the argumentation scheme for argument from expert opinion. The four propositions in the text boxes at the right are premises. The top two propositions – the proposition that Dr. Alice is an expert, and the proposition that Dr. Alice says I should take medication M – are premises in the argument represented by the top node. Similarly, there are two premises in the bottom argument. Each of the two arguments is a linked argument, follow-ing the terminology of Chapter 2, while the two arguments together make up a convergent argument configuration. Essentially CAS models a convergent argument as two separate arguments. The one argument supports the other, strengthening support for the conclusion.

CAS is capable of representing deductive and inductive arguments, but is most useful to represent defeasible arguments of the kinds represented by argumentation schemes, like argument from expert opinion, abductive argument, argument from cause and effect, and so forth. The characteristic feature of such arguments is that they are best seen in the most typical uses as defeasible, meaning that they lead only to a presumptively acceptable conclusion that may later need to be retracted as more arguments in a case are brought forward. CAS was developed in the field of artificial intelligence and law, and therefore has mainly been tested on examples of legal argumentation. But it is open domain software, meaning that it can be used in any context of argumentation, including everyday conversational argumentation.

The first step in understanding an argument diagramming system is to see how it represents linked and convergent arguments. A linked argument is one where two (or more) premises go together to support the conclusion. A convergent argument is one where each premise (or group of premises) functions together to support the conclusion. In the example in Figure 3.6, there are two arguments, and each one is an argument from expert opinion, as indicated by the EX in each argument node. As stated in Chapter 1, the + symbol denotes a pro argument. Each argument is a linked argument because the two premises function together to support the conclusion. But if you look at the diagram as a whole, we have a convergent argument because there are two separate arguments supporting the conclusion. CAS treats a convergent argument as two separate arguments, each of which individually supports the conclusion.

Next, let's change the example to illustrate how two opposed arguments from opinion could be represented. In Figure 3.7, the argument at the bottom is a con argument.

Figure 3.7 represents the classic battle of the experts. Expert Alice is pro taking M, while expert Bob is contra. This example represents what is sometimes called argument attack or argument rebuttal. We will study different kinds of argument rebuttal below (see Section 4).

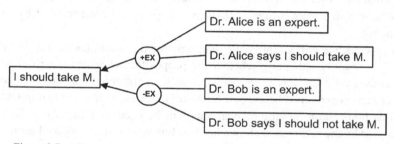

Figure 3.7: A Pro and a Con Argument

Figure 3.8: Simple Example of Practical Reasoning

In this case we have a stalemate. The one argument from expert opinion is pitted against the other, but both arguments are legitimate instances of the scheme for argument from expert opinion. Which argument should win out over the other? To approach this question let's get a better idea of how CAS can be used to evaluate arguments.

3.4 Evaluating Practical Reasoning with Carneades

Let's look at an instance of practical reasoning, a typical case of deliberation about medical treatment. As shown in Figure 3.8, the conclusion of the argument is that I should take medication M. The top premise expresses the circumstances representing the present state of the world. The middle premise is the goal premise. The bottom premise is the means premise.

So, this argument is a linked argument that has three premises. We can see that the three premises function together to support the conclusion if we recall from Chapter 1 that the scheme for practical reasoning can be expressed in a form that has these three premises.

On a Carneades argument diagram, as it appears on the computer screen, each proposition that is a premise or conclusion in some argument appears in a text box. When applying CAS to a real argument found in a text, the user begins by constructing an argument diagram representing the premises and conclusion(s) of the argument and the inferential links joining them together. The user also inputs a judgment on which premises are accepted by the audience.

However, we will simplify the diagrams for the examples treated in this book by merely indicating whether the proposition is accepted (in) or not accepted (out). The way CAS evaluates such an argument depends on some other factors explained below (see Section 5), but, for purposes of simplicity, in this book the following conventions will be used. A proposition that is accepted by the audience is shown in a text box with a light gray background. A proposition that is rejected by the audience is shown in a text box with a

Figure 3.9: Proving the Conclusion by an Argument with All Premises Accepted

dark gray background. A proposition that is neither accepted nor rejected by the audience is shown in a text box with a white background. This simple way of visualizing argument evaluation will be sufficient for our purpose of showing how CAS can be used to model practical reasoning. CAS also contains a knowledge base of argumentation schemes. If the audience accepts all the premises of the given argument, and if the argument fits one of these argumentation schemes, CAS automatically calculates the conclusion of the argument as accepted. See section 10 for further remarks.

A simple example of how the evaluation procedure will work is shown in Figure 3.9. In this example, all the premises have been accepted, as indicated by their appearing in the four light gray boxes on the right. The argument node containing the scheme for practical reasoning is also shown in a light gray circular node, indicating that the scheme applies correctly to the argument. CAS therefore automatically puts the conclusion in a light gray box, showing that the audience also needs to accept this proposition.

For purposes of easy exposition in this book, some other features of CAS are not used, or not used extensively. One of these is the variability of standards of proof. Whether a proposition in a text box is accepted or not according to CAS depends on the standard of proof that the user puts into the system when he or she makes the argument diagram. CAS is built around the idea of modeling sufficiency of an argument by using standards of proof that specify how strong the argument needs to be in order to prove its conclusion. The conclusion of an argument is said to be acceptable if it meets its burden of proof, according to the applicable proof standard for the type of dialogue. The default in CAS is set to the preponderance of the evidence standard, meaning that a given argument is accepted if it is stronger than the arguments against it. But the user can input higher or lower standards, such as clear and convincing evidence, beyond reasonable doubt, and so forth.

Another feature not used in this book is the capability to input numerical weighting of arguments representing how strongly the audience accepts a given argument. In CAS the strength of acceptance of the conclusion of an

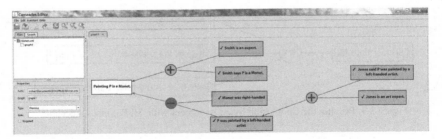

Figure 3.10: Screenshot of an Example in CAS

argument depends both on the acceptance of the premises by the audience and also the strength of acceptance of the argumentation scheme by the audience. In this book, evaluation will be simplified by determining the acceptance of the conclusion based only on two factors: whether the audience accepts the premises, and the evidential link (argumentation scheme) joining the premises to the conclusion. In cases where no known argumentation scheme fits an argument node, the scheme for defeasible *modus ponens* (DMP) can be used. This scheme sets a number of requirements representing the premises of the scheme as the antecedent of a conditional premise, and states that if all these antecedents are met by the argument in the case, the consequent of the conditional follows defeasibly as the conclusion of the argument (Walton, 1996). It is similar to deductive *modus ponens* except that the conditional is defeasible instead of the standard material conditional of deductive logic.

How a user inputs the information on the standard of proof and represents the argumentation in a case can be illustrated by showing a simple picture of the CAS screen displayed in Figure 3.10. The argument shown at the top is a pro argument, and the one shown at the bottom is a con argument. In the pro argument at the top, both premises are shown as accepted. Text boxes that are accepted are shown in the screen in green (lighter gray) boxes with a checkmark in front of the proposition in the box.

Text boxes containing propositions that are rejected are shown in a text box with red (darker) box with X mark in front of the proposition. In Figure 3.10, the con argument at the bottom has two premises, and one of those premises is supported by a linked pro argument. This linked pro argument, like the pro argument shown at the top, is an argument from expert opinion. Although the scheme for argument from expert opinion is not shown in the node on the screen in either instance, it is represented in the underlying data model of the argument graph.

At the left of the screenshot, the menu is shown where the user can input information about the argument – for example, the proof standard. The user can also insert the status of a given proposition: whether it is accepted, rejected, or neither accepted nor rejected. Once the user has inserted this information, CAS automatically adjusts all the arguments in the diagram accordingly. For example, if a particular argument has all of its premises accepted, as indicated by the user, and the argument fits an argumentation scheme listed in the catalogue of schemes in the CAS system, then CAS will automatically indicate that the conclusion is accepted by coloring its text box green and inserting a checkmark in front of the proposition in the text box. In the example in Figure 3.10, both main arguments have all premises accepted, and the con argument has some additional support. If neither argument can rebut the other strongly enough to defeat it decisively (according to the proof standard required), the conclusion is evaluated as neither accepted nor rejected.

Our concern in this book will be to model practical reasoning in deliberation dialogues on what course of action should be taken in a given set of circumstances based on the goals of the individual or group needing to make a decision. For this purpose we will not need to worry about applying some of these more advanced capabilities of CAS such as proof standards and argument weights. It will be enough to evaluate examples of practical reasoning using argumentation schemes, CAS argument diagrams, and the critical questions matching a given scheme.

3.5 Managing Critical Questions with Carneades

The scheme for argument from expert opinion was formulated in Walton (1997a, 210) as follows:

Major Premise: Source E is an expert in field F containing proposition A.
Minor Premise: E asserts that proposition A (in field F) is true (false).
Conclusion: A may plausibly be taken to be true (false).

An argument from expert opinion can be evaluated by asking one or more of the six basic critical questions matching the scheme (Walton, 1997a, 223):

CQ_1: *Expertise Question*: How knowledgeable is E as an expert source?
CQ_2: *Field Question*: Is E an expert in the field F that A is in?
CQ_3: *Opinion Question*: What did E assert that implies A?
CQ_4: *Trustworthiness Question*: Is E personally reliable as a source?

CQ$_5$: *Consistency Question*: Is *A* consistent with what other experts assert?
CQ$_6$: *Evidence Question*: Is *E*'s assertion based on evidence?

CQ$_1$ refers to the expert's level of mastery of the field *F* as an expert. CQ$_4$ refers to the expert's trustworthiness. For example, it could be questioned whether the expert is biased if he has something to gain financially by advocating *A*.

The problem is that questions cannot (at least easily) be represented on an argument diagram. But if these critical questions could be represented as additional implicit premises of the scheme, that would solve the problem. According to Walton (1997a), if the respondent asks any one of the six critical questions the burden of proof shifts back to the proponent's side to respond to the question appropriately or else the argument will be defeated. The asking of the critical question temporarily defeats the argument, until the critical question has been answered successfully. This might suggest rephrasing each critical question as an additional premise of the argument. Such a premise would have to be defended if questioned, just like the regular premises. But unfortunately, not all of the critical questions work this way.

Some of the critical questions appear to shift the burden merely by being asked, while others can only defeat the argument if backed up by evidence. The trustworthiness question and the consistency question fall into this latter category. If you ask the trustworthiness question, the arguer might simply reply, "Of course the expert is trustworthy. If you think not, you will have to give some evidence to back up this allegation." Similarly, if asked the consistency question, the arguer may simply shift the burden of proof by replying, "Show me some expert who disagrees."

This view of the matter is open to discussion, however, and may depend on the context, the type of dialogue, and the stage the dialogue is in. Some might argue that the respondent should have the burden of proof to back up all these critical questions with specifics. Others might argue that just asking any one of the questions should be enough to make the original argument default until the question has been answered satisfactorily. A similar view can be presented for dealing with the critical questions matching the value-based scheme. Some could be classified as assumptions, while others, such as the value premise (CQ$_2$), could be classified as exceptions. Still, burden of proof issues often have to be decided on a case by case basis. But if the critical questions can be classified as either assumptions or exceptions, we can then insert them as propositions that are premises of practical reasoning on an argument diagram. Once such a classification has been made in a given case, we can dispense with the dialogue concept of critical questioning, and represent the argument as a set of premises and a conclusion.

For these reasons it was decided in CAS to divide the critical questions into three categories. How this is done can be shown using the scheme for argument from expert opinion (shown below), as taken from the catalogue of argumentation schemes in CAS. The assumptions represent critical questions that, like the ordinary premises, are assumed to hold, but need to be supported by the arguer if questioned. The burden of proof is on the proponent. The exceptions, the third category, are assumed not to hold. The 'id' is the identifier of the scheme, and saying it is strict means that this type of argument is defeasible.

Shown here is the way the argumentation scheme for argument from expert opinion is configured in the catalogue of schemes in CAS:

id: expert opinion
strict: false
direction: pro
conclusion: A
premises:
- Source E is an expert in subject domain S.
- A is in domain S.
- E asserts that A is true.

assumptions:
- The assertion A is based on evidence.

exceptions:
- E is personally reliable as a source.
- A is inconsistent with what other experts assert.

This configuration shows by example how all the schemes are represented in CAS.

3.6 Managing Critical Questions for Practical Reasoning

How should the critical questions matching the scheme for practical reasoning be modeled in CAS? Suppose a proponent of an argument based on practical reasoning is being critically questioned by a respondent (questioner) in a deliberation dialogue in which the two are trying to decide on a prudent course of action in a given situation. When the respondent asks one of the critical questions, does that alone refute the argument until the question has been satisfactorily answered by its proponent? Or does the questioner have to give some evidence to back up the question before the argument is defeated? Let's consider the six critical questions, one at a time. It might generally be assumed to be true that I have no other goals that should be considered that would conflict with G, or, if I have, the respondent needs to say what they are. It might also generally be assumed to be true that if there are alternative actions to be considered, they have been taken into account, and that bringing about A is the best of the set. It would generally be assumed to be true that it is possible for me bring about A, if I am seriously thinking of bringing A about. Taking this view, critical questions CQ_1, CQ_2, CQ_3, and CQ_4 could be classified as presumptions. However, it can be assumed to be false that there are alternative actions that should be considered (on the basic scheme) unless the respondent can specify what they are. And it can be assumed to be false that there are consequences of the proposed action that have not been taken into account, unless the respondent can specify what they are. Taking this view, CQ_5 and CQ_6 could be classified as exceptions. In this view, issues of burden of proof concerning the critical questions for the basic scheme can be dealt with in a standard way by diagramming additional nodes that are classified as assumptions of the original argument or exceptions to it.

To see how this approach will work in practice, let's go back to the examples of practical reasoning analyzed using *Araucaria* in Chapter 2 and consider how the same arguments might be represented using CAS.

3.7 Visualizing the Health Ad Examples with Carneades

The Lunesta example was the most straightforward example for illustrating this scheme for practical reasoning using *Araucaria*. It was represented in the argument diagram in Figure 2.3. The way it is represented using CAS is shown in Figure 3.11.

The implicit conclusion of the argument is that you should take Lunesta. In CAS, the conclusion is shown on the left, as contrasted with the *Araucaria* diagram in Figure 2.3, where the conclusion is shown at the top. This difference is merely one of notational convention.

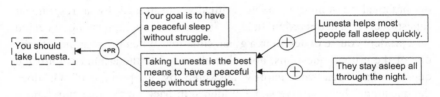

Figure 3.11: CAS Visualization of the Lunesta Example

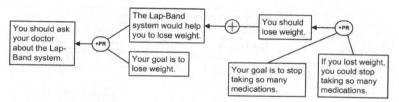

Figure 3.12: CAS Visualization of the Lap-band Example

The notation used to mark an implicit premise or conclusion is to use a dashed borderline of the text box. In this instance, the dashed border of the text box around the proposition 'You should take Lunesta' indicates that this proposition is an implicit conclusion. We can see that in Figure 3.11 the scheme for practical reasoning is represented in the argument node at the left. The part of the argument on the right is a convergent argument consisting of two independent arguments for the conclusion that taking Lunesta is the best means to have a peaceful sleep without struggle.

The next example is the version of Figure 2.7, the *Araucaria* visualization of the practical reasoning in the Lap-Band example. In CAS it is visualized as shown in Figure 3.12.

This argument illustrates chaining together two instances of practical reasoning. The way of representing the argument in CAS is very similar to the way it was represented in Figure 2.7 using *Araucaria*. It illustrates chaining together two instances of the scheme for practical reasoning. So far, there appear to be little in the way of significant differences between the way *Araucaria* represents practical reasoning and the way CAS represents it.

How CAS represents the practical reasoning that was employed by *Araucaria* in Figure 2.4 to analyze the Mucinex example begins to reveal some key differences between the two systems. In Figure 2.4, the argument basically fitted the scheme for practical reasoning based on a linked argument and a single argument. However, the interesting aspect of Figure 2.5 was how *Araucaria* used refutation to raise the critical question concerning alternative means to solve the problem of reducing congestion by reducing the amount of mucus. In *Araucaria*, the device used was to insert an implicit premise stating that there might be a better product for this purpose than Mucinex. What was shown in Figure 2.4 is an example that contains a refutation of a refutation. The additional statement that Mucinex is the longest lasting non-prescription chest congestion medication you can buy is brought forward to refute the proposition that there might be a better product on the market than Mucinex.

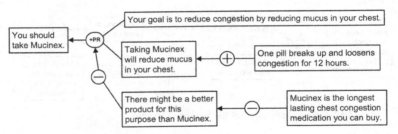

Figure 3.13: The CAS Version of the Mucinex Example

CAS has a different way of representing the practical reasoning in this example, shown in the argument diagram in Figure 3.13. According to the way the Mucinex example is represented in Figure 3.13 by CAS, the basic argument from practical reasoning shown at the top of the diagram is straight-forward. The user's goal is to reduce congestion by reducing mucus in his chest, and taking Mucinex is said to be the means to carry out this goal. Now the question is how CAS will visually represent the refutation of the refutation shown earlier in Figure 2.4. CAS represents the first refutation as an exception. In other words, the practical reasoning argument that Mucinex is the method of choice for reducing congestion in the user's chest is brought into question by posing the critical question of whether there might be an alternative means; hence, the statement that there might be a better product for reducing conges-tion than Mucinex is treated as an exception. It can defeat the argument from practical reasoning if some evidence is given to back it up. However, what happens in this instance is that this statement is attacked by a counter-argument. The claim is made that Mucinex is the longest lasting chest congestion medica-tion you can buy. In other words, this statement represents a refutation of the exception that was originally intended to refute the argument from practical reasoning.

What is especially interesting about the way the sequence of argumentation is represented in Figure 3.13 is that the bottom argument containing the sequence of the two refutations is shown by means of the arrow paths leading to the argument node containing the scheme for practical reasoning. What this shows is a feature characteristic of CAS. It contains argument diagrams where one argument node is joined by an arrow to another argument node. In *Araucaria*, in common with the majority of argument diagramming tools, there can only be arrows leading from text boxes to other text boxes. Hence, as shown in Figure 2.4, refutation has to be represented by a special kind of double arrow joining two text boxes. In CAS, just as in ASPIC+, a critical question can be represented as an exception that undercuts the argument to which it was

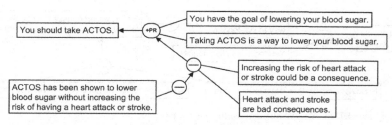

Figure 3.14: CAS Version of the Argument Diagram for the ACTOS Example

directed.To model this idea of refutation, CAS uses the device of visually showing one argument attacking another by drawing an arrow from the attacking argument node to the node of the argument that was attacked.

Another example that shows the difference between the two systems is the *Araucaria* argument diagram for the ACTOS example shown in Figure 2.5. This example also illustrates the use of the double arrow and as well as an instance of a refutation of a refutation. In this example the original argument was an instance of practical reasoning used to support the conclusion that the user should take ACTOS. But then the side effects critical question was raised on whether there might be negative consequences of taking ACTOS. The side effects argument was then countered by the claim that ACTOS has been shown to lower blood sugar without increasing the risk of having a heart attack or stroke. How the same argument is represented by CAS is shown in Figure 3.14.

In the CAS version, the sequence of argumentation is also shown as a refutation of a refutation. The structure is similar to that in the last example because the notion of a refutation of a refutation is visualized as one con argument node leading by an arrow to another con argument node. This way of drawing the argument diagram in the case makes the argumentation more graphically clear and easier to follow.

Finally, we will take a look at how the *Araucaria* visualization of the yogurt example shown in Figure 2.2 can be rendered in the CAS.

In the *Araucaria* version shown in Figure 2.2 the basic argument uses the scheme for practical reasoning to support the conclusion that you should eat yogurt. Supporting this argument is another one based on the argumentation scheme for argument from correlation to cause. In the CAS version shown in Figure 3.15, the implicit conclusion that you should eat yogurt is shown at the left. Both premises of this argument are also implicit, and so they, like the conclusion, are shown in text boxes with darkened borders. In Figure 3.15 the argument from correlation to cause is shown as supporting one premise of

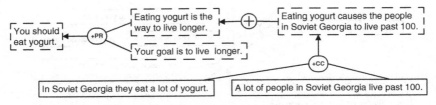

Figure 3.15: CAS Visualization of the Yogurt Example

the practical reasoning argument. How CAS could extend the analysis of this argument would be to consider the various critical questions shown in Chapter 2 to be attached to the argumentation scheme for argument from correlation to cause. It is the consideration of these critical questions that revealed the fallaciousness of the yogurt example. In CAS, these critical questions would be represented as additional assumptions or exceptions attached to the argumentation scheme for argument from correlation to cause. If one of these critical questions is treated as an assumption, merely asking it temporarily defeats the argument from correlation to cause. If it is an exception, of course, some evidence has to be given to back it up before it defeats the argument from correlation to cause.

3.8 The Smart Car Example

So far in this chapter we have been assuming that we are using the instrumental form of practical reasoning to analyze these examples, but now we need to consider how to analyze cases of value-based practical reasoning. Let's go back to the Smart Car example given in Chapter 1, Section 6. In this example, I have been having problems with my car, and as a way of solving the problem I decide to look for a new one. My goal is to buy a new car. But, of course, it is not that simple. I will not just go into the nearest dealership and buy the first car I find for sale. Cost is involved, and I have certain requirements in mind, based on my situation. Nearly all of my driving is in the city, and so I am looking for a car that will fit these circumstances and do the job at the least cost. I also have factors like style and comfort in mind. Another factor that is very important for me is concern for the environment. All these factors narrow down the search to a car that will not use too much fuel, and so I concentrate on small cars. As I discuss matters with a salesperson in the showroom, she argues, "The Smart Car uses less fuel than the other cars you are considering. Also, it has style and comfort." This example is the Smart Car case.

To identify the argumentation in the Smart Car case, we begin with a key list that identifies all the propositions that are premises or conclusions.

> Your goal is to buy a car.
> The Smart Car uses less fuel that the other cars you are considering.
> The Smart Car has style.
> The Smart Car has comfort.
> Any car that uses less fuel than others you are considering is less harmful to the environment.
> You should buy the Smart Car.

We could also add some implicit premises to the argument that show how each of the three explicit premises is based on a value of the buyer.

> Concern for the environment is a value of yours.
> Style is a value for you.
> Comfort is a value for you.

These values could also be weighted, or assigned an order of importance, but to keep the example simple, we will not consider this possibility here. Bench-Capon (2003) gives a formal account of how values can be assigned a preference ordering in practical argument. How should these values be represented as having some role in the argumentation? There are two possible ways of representing them that need to be discussed.

One way of representing the structure of the argumentation in the Smart Car case is displayed in the argument diagram in Figure 3.16. According to this

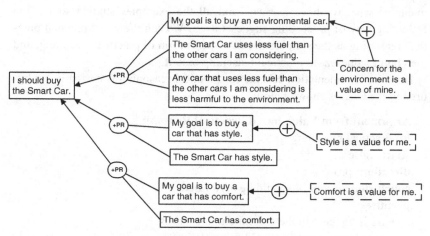

Figure 3.16: CAS Diagram of Analysis 1 of the Smart Car Argument

analysis, each value acts as further support for a premise. The structure of the two arguments on the left is not analyzed as deeply as that of the one on the right. The argument on the right is shown as an instance of practical reasoning. It is a linked argument with three premises: A, B, and E. The argumentation scheme for practical reasoning is shown binding the three premises together as linked support for the conclusion F. V1 is analyzed as a value that supports E. Alternatively, perhaps V1 could be seen as a value that supports the goal stated in A.

On this analysis, each value is an underlying basis for a goal premise that supports the practical reasoning leading to the ultimate conclusion. But there is also another way of modeling such cases. We can represent arguments from values (positive or negative) as additional arguments supporting or challenging an argument from practical reasoning. Either way is possible.

3.9 Instrumental and Value-based Practical Reasoning

In this section the problems of how to fit the two practical reasoning schemes together is addressed. The values premise can be seen as supporting the goal premise. It can also be seen as a premise in a linked argument that also contains other premises. Additionally, it can be seen as a warrant that supports the linked argument from the other two premises. Values can be treated in the manner of Atkinson, Bench-Capon, and McBurney (2005), where they function solely as support for goals. This problem remains unsolved. The last method was the one applied to the Smart Car example in the previous section. To fit the requirements of what we have learned from all the examples studied so far, the following way of proceeding suggests itself. We can view instrumental practical reasoning as the simpler and more basic form of practical reasoning, and then build value-based practical reasoning onto it.

How the argumentation scheme for practical reasoning is currently configured in the CAS is shown below.

Argument from Value-based Practical Reasoning
id: practical reasoning
strict: false
direction: pro
conclusion: Action A should be performed.
premises:
  - $S1$ is the case in the current circumstances.
  - Performing A in $S1$ would bring about $S2$.

- *G* would be realized in *S2*.
- Achieving the goal *G* would promote the value *V.*

assumptions:
- *V* is a legitimate value.
- *G* is a worthy goal.
- Action *A* is possible.

exceptions:
- There exists an action that would bring about *S2* more effectively than *A*.
- There exists an action that would realize the goal *G* more effectively than *A*.
- There exists an action that would promote the value *V* more effectively than *A*.
- Performing *A* in *S1* would have side effects which demote *V* or some other value.

The above version of the scheme follows the view of practical reasoning in Atkinson and Bench-Capon (2007), which sees value-based practical reasoning as primary. What the examples analyzed so far suggest is a different approach. In this approach, a distinction is drawn between instrumental and value-based practical reasoning so that instrumental practical reasoning is taken to be the basic argumentation scheme. Then value-based cases of practical reasoning can be treated by considering values as additional implicit or explicit premises. As suggested by the Smart Car example, considerations of values can be added on to the basic scheme as additional implicit premise or arguments.

In line with this approach, the following new version of the instrumental scheme for practical reasoning has been configured in the CAS format.

Argument from Instrumental Practical Reasoning (new version)
id: practical reasoning
strict: false
direction: pro
conclusion: Action *A* should be performed.
premises:
- *S1* is the case in the current circumstances.
- Performing *A* in *S1* would bring about *S2*.
- *G* would be realized in *S2*.

assumptions:
- *G* is possible.
- Action *A* is possible.

exceptions:
- There exists an action that would bring about *S2* more effectively than *A*.
- There exists an action that would realize the goal *G* more effectively than *A*.
- There are intervening actions required to move from the action *A* to the goal *G*.
- Performing *A* in *S1* would have side effects that need to be taken into account.
- There is another goal *G'* that is incompatible with *G*.

These are the two schemes for practical reasoning we will use in the rest of this book. But, as the examples treated in the following chapters will show, the best way to work is to use the instrumental scheme where values considerations are not in the forefront, but bring in the value-based scheme in cases where it is important to take values into account.

3.10 Evaluating Practical Reasoning

A question that has now been partly but not completely answered is how practical reasoning should be evaluated as weak or strong in a given instance. As shown in this chapter, the formal systems we examined employed sets of critical questions matching the schemes for the two types of arguments from practical reasoning. These questions function as what Pollock (1995) called undercutters of a defeasible argument, modeled as exceptions that leave the argumentation scheme in place as holding, but defeat or question its applicability to the case at issue. But there are also rebuttals, or counter-arguments, that defeat the original argument, to be considered by posing a counter-argument to the conclusion of the prior argument being attacked. Using some examples this chapter has shown how these undercutters and rebuttals should be employed in evaluating practical reasoning, and how they work in shifting a burden of proof.

As promised under figure 3.9, further remarks on how arguments are evaluated in CAS are in order. There are four major versions that CAS has evolved through (see https://github.com/carneades). Version 1 (2006–2008) was implemented in the programming language Scheme. Version 2 (2011), the desktop version with the graphical user interface illustrated in figure 3.10, is still available. Version 3 is the web-based version of Carneades, developed in 2010–2015, illustrated by the example of drafting copyright legislation described in chapter 6, section 3. Version 4 is currently under development. In version 2, an argument is evaluated as justifying its conclusion if the premises of the argument are acceptable and the argument has not been undercut by other arguments that defeat it. A third criterion available in CAS is the attaching of numerical weights to the argument representing the strength of the argument according to the audience, represented as a fraction between zero and one. Version 2 cannot evaluate cumulative arguments, whereas version 4 can. Version 4 evaluates arguments by two criteria: (1) whether the audience accepts the premises and (2) whether the argument properly instantiates an argumentation scheme.

For purposes of simplicity of treatment of examples of practical reasoning, the criterion for argument evaluation used in this book is that of version 4. This means that in a graph of an example of an argument, if the premises are colored gray, and the argument node is colored gray (showing the argument properly instantiates a scheme), the conclusion is automatically colored gray.

We have shown to some extent how formal argumentation systems can be used to evaluate practical reasoning. One point is that some standard of proof has to be set in place if an argument will lead to a decision at the end that will decide the contested issue of what to do in a given set of circumstances. But what if collecting more information about the circumstances might lead to a better decision than acting on what is currently known? It is an ideal of rational argumentation that the procedural setting in which argumentation is put forward should have rules that define the closure of the practical reasoning procedure shown in Figure 1.5.

Practical reasoning is about deciding what to do by taking some course of action in the future that appears prudent now, as a way of realizing a goal. But one problem is that, in the so-called real world, we are never really sure what is going to happen in the future, especially in complex situations relating to social and economic policies, political decisions, or business planning. In simple cases of practical reasoning, openness of the database can be closed off by an assumption. In these cases – most notably in the famous blocks world example – the closed world assumption (meaning that the agent knows all there is to know) is held to apply. In the blocks world, there is a simple task where an agent, whether it is a person or a robot, has to rearrange some small set of numbered blocks on a desk in a designated pattern in which some of the blocks have to be stacked on top of other blocks. In simple cases of this sort, the sequence of reasoning has only a few moves, and after the sequence of possible moves has been exhausted, the agent either succeeds in carrying out the task or not. So here the practical reasoning is complete because there is a definite closure point. This assumption in such a case requires that the inflow of data to the knowledge base of the agent is closed off. This principle is called the closed world assumption.

For example, the closed world assumption can be applied to a case of deciding whether there is a flight from Pasadena to Reno by looking at the listing of flights on a televised flight monitor in an air terminal (Reiter, 1980, 69). The closed world assumption implies that if a flight being searched for is not listed, it can be concluded that there is no such flight. Since the search through the database rests on the assumption that all the information required to make a decision can be found in the database listed, it can be concluded even by the negative finding that no flight is listed on the monitor. If no flight is listed from Pasadena to Reno, this non-finding means it can be concluded that there is no flight from Pasadena to Reno. The case is closed.

These observations may suggest the hypothesis that practical reasoning can be viewed as a deductive form of argumentation if the knowledge base is closed. However, there is no general consensus at present on whether practical reasoning can be viewed as a deductively valid form of argument if the knowledge base is closed. Still, Searle (2001) has offered a detailed argument to show that that there can be no deductive logic of practical reasoning. However, in the vast majority of real instances, the closed world assumption is not realistic because there is a lack of knowledge of what will happen in the future and therefore the reasoning must be carried out under conditions of uncertainty. A common problem of practical reasoning, for example, is whether it is better to act promptly to take an advantage of an opportunity that may not last, or to collect more relevant data about the circumstances and resist jumping to a hasty conclusion. Such factors suggest the wisdom of the use of defeasible reasoning of the kind used by DefLog, ASPIC+, and CAS.

The methods we have explained so far in the formal and computational argumentation system examined in this chapter include the use of argumentation schemes, standards of proof, argument diagrams, and sets of critical questions matching schemes. These methods are the primary resources for identifying and analyzing instances of practical reasoning. They also provide us with extremely useful resources for helping a decision-maker with the task of evaluating practical reasoning. The prudent rational agent can ask the appropriate critical questions needed to probe into the weak points in an argument based on practical reasoning, and even identify fallacies of practical reasoning of the kind illustrated in the yogurt example.

Even so, there is quite a bit more that needs to be said about how to solve these problems to provide useful advice on how to implement practical reasoning in automated systems of rational deliberation where the choice needs to be made on what to do under conditions where a decision needs to be made even if all the data one would like to collect is not available. It will be argued in the rest of this book that this problem of closure needs to be solved in order to get closer to the goal of achieving a fully adequate method of evaluating practical reasoning. Dealing with this problem in Chapter 5 will bring the reader to the idea of a dialectical setting of an argument as a framework that can be used to evaluate the success or failure of the argument depending on the purpose the argument is supposedly being used for. In Chapter 6 a formal model of deliberation will be presented as the contextual setting for determining closure.

The next problem, confronted in Chapter 4, is that practical reasoning is used in explanations as well as arguments. Therefore, we need to come to understand how it is used in explanations, and how we can tell in the given case of practical reasoning whether it ought to be evaluated as successful or not depending on whether the case represents an explanation or an argument.

4

Practical Reasoning in Arguments and Explanations

The previous chapters have shown how practical reasoning is used in arguments, but it will turn out to be vitally important to understand how it is used in explanations. It will even be shown at the end of this chapter how the same example of practical reasoning in a discourse can combine explanations with arguments. Hence, there arises the problem of building a model of explanation to reveal precisely how practical reasoning is used in explanations. The key to solving it, as will be shown in this chapter, is to broaden the study of practical reasoning to take into account not only its structure as a chain of reasoning, but also how that same kind of reasoning can be used in different ways in different communicative settings. An argument will be shown to be a response to a particular kind of question, while an explanation will be seen as a response to another kind of question.

Recent work in artificial intelligence has taken the approach that an explanation is best seen as a transfer of understanding from one party to another in a dialogue where one party is a questioner who asks why or how something works and the other party attempts to fulfill this request (Cawsey, 1992; Moore, 1995; Moulin et al., 2002). Recent literature in philosophy of science seems to be gradually moving toward this approach, but there is an open question of how it can be represented using a formal structure (Trout, 2002). Since explanations and arguments are sometimes hard to distinguish, the first step is to provide some way of representing the distinction between them in their formal structure. In this chapter, the Why^2 Dialogue System is presented as a formal model showing how the difference between argument and explanation resides in the pre- and post-conditions for the speech act of requesting an argument and the speech act of requesting an explanation. It is an extension of earlier dialogue systems (Walton, 2004, 2007a, 2011).

The second step is to show how a successful explanation transfers under-standing from one party to another in such a dialogue. This is done by using two connected devices. One is a script – a sequence of actions or events joined together in a pattern that represents a normal way of doing something, or a sequence of connections of a kind familiar to both speaker and listener (Schank, 1986; Schank and Abelson, 1977; Schank and Riesback, 1981; Schank, Kass, and Riesback, 1994). This device is already widely familiar and is increasingly being used in artificial intelligence (Leake, 1992; Bex, 2011; Cassens and Kofod-Petersen, 2007). The second device is that of the explanation scheme, modeled in this chapter as an abstract sequence into which a script fits by instantiation. These two devices are shown to work together as components of an explanation that can be used to transfer under-standing in a dialogue.

Section 1 outlines the elements of the traditional deductive-nomological model (DN model) of scientific explanation, and describes a traditional alter-native to it: an agent-centered view based on practical reasoning. Section 2 gives an example that shows why it is difficult in some cases to determine whether something is an argument or an explanation. Section 3 offers a brief account of the key differences between argument and explanation. Section 4 presents a dialogue model originally built to represent argumentation, but expanded in this chapter so that it can also accommodate explanation. Section 5 explains how recent work in artificial intelligence has adopted the view that an explanation is a transfer of understanding based on the notion of a script. Section 6 presents the main example used to show how the dialogue theory, using the notion of a script, can provide a model of scientific explana-tion. Sections 7, 8, and 9 model some examples of scientific and agent-based explanations. Section 10 provides some conclusions.

4.1 Traditional Approaches to Scientific Explanation

According to the deductive-nomological (DN) model (Hempel, 1965, 174), an event or fact to be explained – called the *explanandum* – is explained by deducing it from a set of general laws and a set of factual circumstances expressed by atomic propositions. This model is based on three sets of vari-ables. $L_1, L_2, \ldots, L_n$ is a set of general laws. Presumably each of these statements begins with a universal quantifier. $C_1, C_2, \ldots, C_n$ is a set of statements describing particular occurrences. E is a proposition describing an event to be explained. The structure of an explanation, in the DN model, can be expressed as a deductive inference of the following form:

$L_1, L_2, ..., L_n$
$C_1, C_2, ..., C_n$
Therefore E.

An example used to illustrate DN theory (Achinstein, 1983, 8) is the following sequence of three statements:

All metals expand when heated.
This metal was heated.
Therefore this metal expanded.

The event to be explained is represented by the third statement. The first and second statements together are taken to provide a scientific explanation in the DN model of why the metal expanded, under the given circumstances. The explanation is that the metal was heated, and all metals expand when heated.

Although in its original inception the DN model used only deductive reasoning, it was later expanded to include inductive reasoning as well. This later variant was called the inductive-statistical (I-S) type of explanation. Hempel (1965, 301) offered an example of a child who had the mumps, explained by pointing out that he had recently been playing with a friend who had mumps. The antecedent factors (Hempel, 1965, 301) are the child's exposure to mumps and the fact that he did not have mumps before.

It is an interesting observation that because the DN model was based on logical reasoning, it makes it seem that argument and explanation are closely connected, or even possibly that explanation is a species of argument. Perhaps it could be conjectured that, in the DN model, an explanation could be treated as a sequence of abductive reasoning that goes backward from the conclusion that the metal expanded to the premises that (1) all metals expand when heated and (2) this metal was heated. At any rate, what is interesting to note is that 'all' is taken, in deductive logic, to admit of no exceptions, as represented by the universal quantifier in logic. Since inductive reasoning was allowed in later versions of the DN model, however, perhaps there could be some room for defeasible reasoning within the model.

The main opposition to the DN model of explanation was that it did not apply to historical explanations, because these are not based on general laws in the way scientific explanations are, but are concerned with unique occurrences. What is to be explained is not a natural event, but the actions of human agents who autonomously decide what to do based on what reason requires in their particular circumstances. According to historians such as Collingwood (1946), historical actions have an inside, as well as an outside, where the inside represents the goals and intentions of the agent who arrived at a decision on what to do in a historical situation. In his view, to understand an action, the historian must rethink the process of thought that went through the mind of the original agent when he or she arrived at a decision on what to do (Collingwood, 1946). According to Dray (1964, 11), for example to explain the action of a Roman emperor, the historian must re-enact in his own mind the experience of the emperor and how he saw the alternatives that were available in his situation at the time in ancient Rome, and the reasons for choosing one over another. This way of putting it appears to make it necessary for the historian to go into the emperor's mind in a way that requires simulation of a kind that is mysterious or even impossible. But perhaps there could be a way of reconstructing the emperor's presumed goals and intentions based on the historical evidence that is available, even if the conclusions derived are merely hypotheses. A provisional hypothesis, even one that is merely a provisional explanation of why an action was carried out, can be supported or refuted by factual historical evidence about what happened. Interestingly, Dray even links this process of historical reconstruction of a past agent's presumed states of mind to practical reasoning. In his description of it (Dray, 1964, 11), Collingwood's theory requires us to "enter the practical deliberations of an agent trying to decide what his line of action should be." Such a procedure would include the goals the agent wants to achieve, knowledge about the agent's knowledge of the facts of his given situation, and his knowledge of the means that might be used to achieve the goal. Seen this way, the historian must reconstruct the emperor's practical reasoning to reconstruct how it led from his goals and his knowledge of the situation to the action he actually carried out, as recorded by historical evidence, including testimony and documents.

This agent-centered view of historical explanation saw the opposed theory (the DN model) as based on a philosophy of logical positivism that took what the positivists presumed to be the forms of reasoning used in natural science as the basis for their model of explanation. In the positivist view, all scientific reasoning – all rational thinking, for that matter – must be based only on observable events and inferences drawn from them using deductive logic, or in some instances inductive logic based on probability. It is evident from the description of their position outlined above that the opponents of the DN model based their approach to explanation on practical reasoning. The problem they had in maintaining a viable alternative that could compete with the DN model was that they had no clear and precisely formulated logical model of practical reasoning to offer. It wasn't until the advent of interest in building models of practical reasoning in artificial intelligence that there appeared to be much hope of building an agent-centered view of practical reasoning of a scientific kind that could be applied to computational fields such as planning, multi-agent reasoning, robotics, legal argumentation, and other important applications of agent-centered computational models.

Before we can proceed further, some important questions need to be answered. What is the basis of the distinction between an explanation and an argument? How can each of these concepts be defined? How can we tell by means of evidence when trying to analyze a text of discourse in a given case whether it is an argument or an explanation?

4.2 Criteria to Determine Whether Something Is an Argument or an Explanation

The first problem in attempting to analyze the concept of an explanation is to attempt to provide criteria for determining when some piece of discourse that looks like it could be either an explanation or an argument should be taken to fit into one category or the other. This distinction is vitally important from a logical point of view, as it would be a fundamental error to criticize an argument as falling short of standards for acceptability or validity of a rational argument, when in fact the text that was put forward was meant as an explanation, and not an argument. It is an error to criticize something as a bad argument if it is not really an argument at all. For this reason, introductory logic textbooks attempt to give students advice on how to classify pieces of text that might look superficially like an argument in order to determine whether they should properly be treated under the category of argument or explanation.

For example, Copi and Cohen, in the textbook *Introduction to Logic* (1990, 31), posed the question of whether the following piece of discourse should be classified as an explanation or an argument:

> a decaying satellite can look like an incoming warhead to a sensor. That is the reason we have a man in the loop. (General James Hartinger, Chief, Air Force Space Command, 'Nuclear War by Accident – Is It Impossible?' interview in *U.S. News & World Report*, December 19, 1983, 27)

The answer given in the textbook is that the text in this case should best be treated as an explanation rather than an argument: "Here we have an explanation for our having a man in the loop, not an argument intended to prove that we do" (Copi and Cohen, 1990, 506). They add, however, "the fact that a decaying satellite can look like an incoming warhead may also serve as the premiss of an argument of which the conclusion is that a human being *ought* to be involved in the system used for detecting approaching warheads" (506). The interpretation of this passage as an argument can be seen as based on argument from negative consequences and practical reasoning, if we interpret the passage as justifying the prudential rationality of having a man in the loop for reasons of safety. Presumably the reason for having a man in the loop is the possibility of the accidental triggering of a nuclear response by the automated system because there is no human decision-maker who would be there to override this wrong response. The conclusion of the argument, in this interpretation, is that the decision of having a man in the loop is prudentially reasonable because of the highly negative consequences that might come about if there is no man in the loop.

However, what seems to be a more plausible interpretation is that the passage represents an explanation of why "we have a man in the loop." Hence, even though the passage uses the term "reason," perhaps suggesting an argument, it also presupposes the factual assumption that there is a man in the loop in the existing system that is being discussed. In this interpretation, the passage can be interpreted as an explanation for why the group designing the system put a man in the loop. The explanation is that because a decaying satellite can look like an incoming warhead, there is the possibility that the system could be triggered accidentally by an event such as a decaying satellite. This explanation helps the person to whom it was directed to understand why a man was put in the loop. We should also note that the explanation can be reconstructed as based on practical reasoning. Safety is presumably an important goal for any automated system that could trigger a nuclear explosion. Having a man in the loop as a check against accidental triggering is a means to prevent such a negative consequence. So interpreted, the explanation is an instance of abductive practical reasoning, which traces backward from the known fact that a man is in the loop to a goal that explains the reason for this feature of the system. It helps to fulfill the goal of safety by preventing the accidental possibility of a nuclear accident.

This case is an interesting one because it could possibly be interpreted either way. If the statement that there is a man in the loop is taken as factual, and not subject to doubt, the passage can be interpreted as an explanation for why there is a man in the loop. On the other hand, if the passage is taken as justifying a man being in the loop by means of practical reasoning, it could possibly be interpreted as expressing an argument. The distinction between an explanation and an argument appears to be contextual – that is, based on the supposed purpose of the text of discourse in a given case. The purpose of an argument is to remove doubt about some proposition that is in question. The purpose of an explanation is to convey understanding to the questioner concerning some proposition, event, or action taken to be factual. For example, when the various explanations for the Challenger space vehicle disaster were offered, it was presumed by all parties that the event really happened. There was no doubt about this, and it was widely known because for many years it was an iconic televised image.

4.3 Defining Argument and Explanation

How, then, given the text of discourse, are we to determine based on some testing procedure whether the text is better taken to represent an argument or an explanation? One test that has been widely adopted in logic textbooks proceeds on the basis of the following distinction. In an argument there is a proposition that is in doubt, and that has to be proved and supported before it can be accepted. This statement is the claim made which expresses the conclusion of the argument. By definition, an argument is a sequence of reasoning used to remove doubt about some unsettled proposition, namely the conclusion that is claimed to be true but is not known to be true by both parties to the discussion. By definition (Walton, 2004a), an explanation is a speech act put forward by one party in a discussion to try to help the other party to understand something that he/she presently does not appear to understand. We could put this in a different way by saying that there are two different kinds of why questions. In one type of why question, the speaker asks the hearer to prove some claim made by giving evidence to support it. This type of why question asks for an argument. In another type of why question, the speaker asks the hearer to help him understand something that he presently does not understand.

   This distinction can be drawn as one of a difference in the purpose of the discourse. The purpose of offering an argument is to resolve doubt about some proposition by offering evidence to show that it is true (or false). The purpose of offering an explanation is to help a questioner understand something that he does not understand very well, or at least has claimed that he does not understand, as indicated by his having asked a question. Since the distinction is drawn this way, in terms of the supposed purpose of discourse in which the argument or explanation is embedded, it can be seen to be based on a dialogue model of communication in which a speaker and a hearer take turns in putting forward speech acts such as arguments and explanations

   Dialogue models of explanation computing have been put forward, based on numerous examples of dialogical sequences of questions and answers in which one party tries to explain to another party how some machinery works (Cawsey, 1992; Moore, 1995). The nice feature of such dialogue models is that they can incorporate user feedback, thereby enabling an explanation sequence to recover from misunderstandings from a previous attempt at an explanation. An abstract dialogue model of explanation CE of this sort can be found in Walton (2007a). In this model, both the speech acts of asking for and providing an explanation are represented types of moves (speech acts) definable by pre- and post-condition rules in dialogues. Bex and Budzynska (2010) have shown how the same sequence of reasoning can be used as an explanation in one context and as an argument in a different context. In their account, the illocutionary force of the speech act in a dialogue determines whether the reasoning is argumentation or explanation.

This push toward building a different model of explanation from the traditional positivistic one, so long taken as the received wisdom in philosophy, can be assisted by building on formal dialectical systems of argumentation. Once we come to understand the characteristics of the formal models representing argumentation, we can better come to understand how argument is inherently different from explanation. From there we can have a basis for devising better criteria for distinguishing between an argument and an explanation in a given case based on a solid theoretical grounding.

4.4 A Dialogue Model for Argument and Explanation

Hamblin (1970) built the fundamentals of a methodology called formal dialectic that can be traced back to its roots in Aristotle, and perhaps back even further to the Greek philosopher Zeno (Krabbe, 2013). The simplest form of a formal dialectical system represents argumentation as a framework in which two agents take turns asking questions and putting forward arguments. Krabbe surveys the field of formal dialectics by showing that there are different formal dialectical systems that have different purposes and that represent different kinds of argumentation. In the systems surveyed by Krabbe, one party, the proponent, has the goal of using concessions from the other party, the respondent to prove some designated proposition to the respondent based on premises that are concessions (commitments) of the respondent. The two parties take turns, and there have to be rules governing when each party can speak and what form his move needs to take. There also have to be rules to determine whether the one party or the other can be declared the winner of the dialogue. The general types of systems modeled by Krabbe represent the type of dialogue called persuasion dialogue in the classification of different types of dialogue put forward in Chapter 2, Section 1. The critical discussion (van Eemeren and Grootendorst, 1984, 2004) is a type of persuasion dialogue that is well known in the field of argumentation studies. Krabbe (2013) has even shown how the critical discussion type of dialogue can be modeled as a formal dialectical structure that has roots in the ancient Aristotelian procedures for academic debates. As indicated in Chapter 2, however, there can be other types of dialogue that have different goals from rational persuasion. One of these is the deliberation type of dialogue, where the goal is for the participants to make a decision on what to do in a situation that requires a choice to be made. This type of dialogue will be studied in detail in Chapter 6. What is of interest here is that it is possible to apply such formal dialectical models to explanation as well as argumentation. Let's begin with the Hamblin systems designed to model argumentation and then see how their basic structure can also be used to model explanation.

In Hamblin's (1970, 265–276) formal dialectical Why-Because System with Questions, there are two participants called White and Black, who take turns making moves in a sequence that has a start point and an end point. At each move, each party contributes a locution of a kind that would now be called a speech act. Dialogue protocols determine that the two parties must take turns contributing a speech act, and the response of each party must be appropriate to the previous move made by the other party. Hamblin (1971, 130) specifies a set of participants P and a set of locutions L, and then defines a locution act (speech act) as a set of participant–locution pairs (1971, 130). For example, $\langle P_0, L_4 \rangle$ is a locution act where P_0 is the first participant and L_4 is the fourth type of locution allowed in the dialogue; L_4 may be the speech act of asking a why question. A dialogue of length n is defined as a member of a set of sequences of locution acts. Hamblin illustrates this definition by giving an example of a small dialogue of length 3: $\{\langle 0, P_0, L_4 \rangle, \langle 1, P_1, L_3 \rangle, \langle 2, P_0, L_2 \rangle\}$. In this example, participant P_0 starts the dialogue at move 0 by uttering a locution of type 4. At move 1, participant P_1 replies by putting forward a locution of type 3. At move 2, participant P_0 replies using a locution of type 2. Generally a dialogue is an ordered sequence of moves of this sort. How any particular type of dialogue is defined depends on what locutions are allowed and how these locutions or speech acts are defined.

A record of each party's commitments is kept throughout the dialogue and updated at each move. In Hamblin's definition, "a speaker is committed to a statement when he makes it himself, or agrees to it as made by someone else, or if he makes or agrees to other statements from which it clearly follows" (Hamblin, 1971, 136). In this view, a commitment is not necessarily a belief, although a speaker's commitment to a proposition can often be an important indicator that the speaker believes that this proposition is true. At each move, as the speech act is put forward by one party or the other, commitments will be either inserted into or withdrawn from the commitment store of the one party or the other.

Assertion, or making a claim, is one type of speech act that can be put forward in a move in such a dialogue. For example, if Black asserts that snow is white then the proposition that snow is white will be inserted into Black's commitment store. Another kind of speech act is the asking of a question. One particularly important kind of question is the so-called why question, which is essentially a request for an argument to support a claim. So, for example, after Black has asserted that snow is white, White can challenge Black's claim by asking the question, 'Why is snow white?' This sort of move on White's part looks like it could be a request for an explanation, but Hamblin is not concerned at all with explanations. The only appropriate responses that can be given to a why question in the Hamblin system are (1) to retract the assertion, or (2) to provide an argument to support it (Hamblin, 1970, 166).

Next, we need to recognize that a why question can be ambiguous. Hamblin was primarily concerned with argumentation, and therefore he treated a why question as being a request for an argument needed to support a claim made by the other party. But a why question could also be a request for an explanation. Walton (2011b) constructed a dialogue system for explanation that was loosely based on Hamblin's dialectical framework, but has speech acts and protocols that are appropriate for a dialogue in which one party requests an explanation by asking a why question, and the other party responds with a speech act that attempts to help the first party to come to understand what is being asked about something that he/she purports not to understand. In this system, the function of an explanation is seen as the transferring of understanding from one party to another in a dialogue. In a way comparable to Hamblin's dialogue system, a speech act (locution) is a type of move made by one or the other party at some appropriate point as a dialogue proceeds. One speech act is the asking of a why question, now seen as the request by one party to the other party to offer an explanation of something the first party claims not to understand (Walton, 2004). For each type of move, there are pre-condition rules that set the conditions under which a party is allowed to make that type of move, and post-condition rules that set the allowable replies to each type of move by the other party.

Generally, the participants take turns as follows. The explainee makes the first move by asking for an explanation, and then the explainer gets a chance to respond by offering one. If the explainer offers one, the explainee can simply accept it by saying 'I understand.' If she replies by saying she does not understand, she can then proceed to ask further questions about it. The dialogue is closed when this sequence of questioning has been exhausted. Here we combine these two systems to create a new system we call the Why^2 System.

The leading characteristic of this new system is that it has two kinds of why questions. One is a request to provide an argument, while the other is a request to provide an explanation.

Below are six kinds of especially significant speech acts in this new dialogue system:

Assertion: Putting forward a statement, p, q, r, ..., is a permissible locution, and truth-functional compounds of statement-letters are also permissible locutions.

Factual Question: The question 'p?' asks 'Is it the case that p is true?'

Argument Request: The speech act 'Why[1] p?' makes a request to the explainer to provide an argument that supports p.

Explanation Request: The speech act 'Why[2] p?' makes a request to the explainer to provide understanding concerning p.

Ambiguous Request: The speech act 'Why p?' either makes an argument request or an explanation request.

Explanation Attempt: A response to a previous explanation request made by the explainee that purports to convey understanding of p to the explainee.

A rule of Hamblin's system (1970, 271) that is significant for our purposes here is that the question 'Why[1] p?' may not be asked unless p is a commitment of the hearer and not of the speaker. Yet another rule (Hamblin, 1970, 271) requires that the answer to a why question, if it is not 'Assertion p' or 'No commitment p,' must be in terms of statements that are already commitments of both speaker and hearer. This rule is not suitable for the new system, however, and has to be appropriately modified. In general, we can see that both the asking and the answering of a why question are governed by protocols that Hamblin formulated and that involve the commitments of both parties at any particular move in a dialogue where the speech act is put forward and responded to. Here a lengthy discussion of these protocols would be interesting, but we have no space for this. We need to focus on what happens if White makes an ambiguous request. Such a request is a problem for the continuation of the dialogue, unless Black can find some way to disambiguate White's move.

Here is the solution to the problem of how to distinguish between an argument and an explanation using the dialogue model. If both Black and White are committed to p, this evidence gives Black the right to assume that White is asking for an explanation. Our grounds for this, in light of our previous discussions of the function of an explanation, is that it can be assumed that White is already committed to p, and so White is not in doubt about p. However, if White is not committed to p, evidence of this lack of commitment gives Black the right to assume that White is asking for an argument. According to this solution, explanation and argument can be used in conjunction. Indeed, it is to be expected that an explanation can be supported by evidence taking the form of an argument supporting one or more of its parts. However, this solution also allows for explanation and argument to be different. This difference becomes clear in a dialogue where the speech act, or rather its illocutionary force, is made clear by evidence that can be found in the context of the dialogue – that is, in the commitments indicated by the previous moves of the two parties. In this theory, the difference between argument and explanation is contextual.

The features of an explanation generally are that it occurs in a dialogue in which one party is taken by the other to understand something while the other party (the questioner) is presumed to lack this understanding. The dialogue begins when one party asks a why question (or in some instances, a how-question or other type of question requesting an explanation). When the explainer offers the explanation, the questioner may accept it, or ask further questions in a continuing dialogue. To be successful, the explanation must remove the questioner's lack of understanding. Success can be indicated in various ways. The explainee may say "OK, now I understand it," or there may be some testing procedure to judge how well the explainee really understands it. For example, there may be an examination dialogue (Dunne et al., 2005).

4.5 Transfer of Understanding in Dialogues

The capability for defining explanation using a dialogue model of explanation as a speech act put forward by a speaker with the aim of transferring understanding from a speaker to a hearer raises further questions. What is understanding? How can it be transferred from one party to another? These seem like very hard questions, but there is a way toward getting some good answers to them. There have been attempts to define a notion of understanding suitable for use in artificial intelligence and cognitive science by bringing in the notion of a script. In these theories, understanding is making sense of something by using common knowledge to fill gaps in a script that is puzzling for some reason. A script is a sequence of actions and events that are connected together in a way we understand based on common knowledge of the way things can be generally expected to go from the evidence of our past experiences. For example, the following sequence is a script: my swinging a golf club, hitting the golf ball, the golf ball flying through the air, the golf ball landing on the grass, the golf ball rolling toward the putting green and ceasing its motion at the edge of the green.

The dialogue model of explanation can base the notion of transfer of understanding on the mutual comprehensibility by two or more parties of a script, a connected sequence of events or actions that both parties understand by virtue of their common knowledge about the ways things can be generally expected to happen in situations both are familiar with (Schank, 1986; Schank and Abelson, 1977; Schank and Riesback, 1981; Schank, Kass, and Riesback, 1994). The sequence of speech acts characteristic of the offering and accepting of an explanation in a dialogue (Walton, 2011a) can be summarized as follows. The dialogue has an opening stage, an intervening sequence of exchanges where arguments and explanations are put forth, and a closing stage:

- The speaker and hearer taking part in a dialogue share common knowledge about some domain that represents the subject of the dialogue.
- The hearer finds an anomaly in the domain, something that she does not understand.
- She assumes that the speaker understands it and can explain it.
- She request that the speaker offers an explanation, and he replies by attempting to give an explanation using a script they both understand.
- The explanation is successful if it gives an account of the anomaly that enables the hearer to understand and fix the part of the script where the anomaly was noted.
- Either the explanation is successful in transferring understanding to the hearer or not.
- If it is successful, the dialogue stops.
- If it is not successful, the dialogue can continue until closure is reached.

ACCEPTER (Leake, 1992) is a computational system for explanatory understanding, anomaly detection, and explanation evaluation that fits this sequential pattern. In this system, explanations are meant to fill knowledge gaps revealed by anomalies. There are numerous detailed examples of explanations processed by ACCEPTER along the lines of the dialogue sequence given above. These include explanations of the explosion of the space shuttle Challenger, the recall of Audi 5000 cars for transmission problems, and an account of an airliner that leaves from the wrong departure gate (Leake, 1992, 38).

Cawsey's work (1992) on computational generation of explanatory dialogue and Moore's dialogue-based analysis of explanation for advice-giving in expert systems (1995) are based on a dialogue approach. Moore (1995, 1) defines explanation as "an inherently incremental and interactive process" that requires a dialogue between an explainer and an explainee who has asked a question requesting an explanation. An analysis of understanding has been presented and refined by Schank and his colleagues in cognitive science using many detailed examples (Schank, 1986; Schank and Abelson, 1977; Schank, Kass, and Riesbeck, 1994). Schank (1982) recognized a spectrum of degrees of understanding, ranging from complete empathy to a minimal kind of understanding he called "making sense." It is fragmentary, conjectural, and incomplete.

Understanding is modeled using the well-known device of the script originated by Schank and Abelson (1977). Schank, Kass, and Riesbeck (1994, 77) memorably describe scripts as "frozen inference chains stored in memory." They represent knowledge about familiar situations and routine ways of doing things taken from plan libraries representing the ways things can normally be expected to go based on situations familiar from past experience. Their examples are taken from everyday life in a social science setting, however, and it is open to question how well they might apply to explanations of natural events of the kind that require knowledge of principles from science or engineering. The rest of this chapter is taken up with an exploration of two simple examples of explanations of this sort.

4.6 The Radiators Example

In the following example (Walton, 2006, 77), somebody asks why the radiators are usually located under windows in a room, when windows are the greatest source of heat loss. This seems to be an anomaly, because we generally try to avoid any heat loss in building construction where possible, in order to avoid wasting energy. Here is the example of the explanation that is offered as the answer to this why question:

> The windows are the coldest part of a room and when air in the room comes in contact with them, it falls to the floor. The cold air from the window is heated when it passes the radiator, then it rises and a moving current of air continuously circulates around the room. If the radiator were placed against an inside wall, that inside area of the room would stay warmer than the coldest part of the room, the area where the windows are. We would have a noticeable temperature difference in the two areas that would not be comfortable for those in the room.

To see how the explanation works, we have to begin by realizing that it is based on common knowledge of the way things can be normally expected to work in a heated room. The speaker appears to be operating on the assumption that the questioner knows that when warm and cold air are both present in different areas in a room under otherwise normal conditions, the warm air rises and the cold air falls. The speaker outlines a sequence of events showing how placement of the radiator under the window in a room leads to a convection current that circulates the warm and cold air around the room. The convection current mixes the cold and warm air, resulting in the production of a moderate

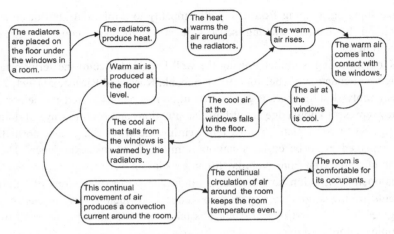

Figure 4.1: The Positive Radiators Script

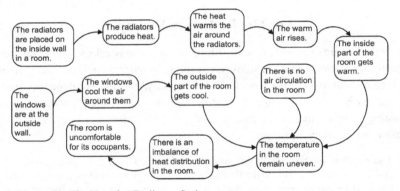

Figure 4.2: The Negative Radiators Script

temperature throughout the room. The moderate temperature that is the outcome of the process is a state that is comfortable for the people in such a room.
The explanation resolves the anomaly and thereby conveys understanding to
the questioner by giving an account of heat circulation in a room.

If we look at the explanation in the example more carefully, we can see that
there are two contrasting accounts that can be extracted from it, each of which
can be represented as a script. The first script explains to the questioner why
the heat loss is not as great as the questioner initially appeared to assume. The
second script shows to the questioner why putting the radiators elsewhere in the
room would have negative consequences. The structure of each of these
contrasting scripts is displayed in Figures 4.1 and 4.2.

The text boxes in Figure 4.1 contain propositions that describe parts of a situation we are familiar with from everyday experience.

We know, for example, that the radiators are normally placed on the floor under the windows in a room. We know that radiators produce heat. The arrows joining the text boxes are sometimes causal, but not always. They represent transitions from one state to another that we are familiar with based on common knowledge. We know, for example, that when radiators produce heat, the heat they produce warms the air around the radiators. Then, following through the other propositions in the sequence, we understand how the rising and falling of the air, which results in a convection current that makes a continual movement of air around the room, keeps the room temperature even for the occupants. As the last step in the sequence, we have included the statement that the room is comfortable for its occupants. This outcome indicates that the sequence of events represented in Figure 4.1 explains why the radiators are placed on the floor under the windows in a room. Essentially, the explanation is that this placement of the radiators results in a situation where the room is comfortable for its occupants.

Note that the graph structure in Figure 4.1 contains a cycle. If you start from the first text box on the left containing the proposition that the radiators are placed on the floor under the windows in a room, and then follow each step to the right after the seventh step, the inference arrow goes back to the third step, producing a cycle. This cycle represents a feedback relationship. As the warm air rises from the radiator it comes into contact with the windows where the air is cool. The cool air falls to the floor, where it is warmed by the radiators, producing warm air at the floor level, which then rises and comes into contact with the windows. As shown in Figure 4.1, it is this circular process that leads to the three-step sequence at the bottom. The continual movement of air produces a convection current which tends to keep the room temperature even. It is the production of this convection current around the room and its tendency to keep the room temperature even, and therefore comfortable for the inhabitants of the room, that explains why the radiators are placed on the floor under the windows.

What provokes the need for an explanation in the radiators example is the apparent anomaly that placing the radiators under the windows would be a waste of heat because the warm air would simply escape out of the window. It might appear initially that this placement of the radiators would waste heat, because it would conserve the heat in the room much better to place the radiators against the wall away from the windows.

This additional dimension to the explanation can be seen by examining the contrasting script presented in Figure 4.2. This script explains what would

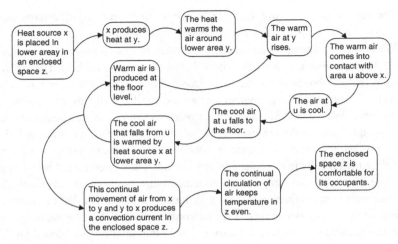

Figure 4.3: Explanation Scheme for the Radiators Example

happen if the radiators were placed on the inside wall of the room, as opposed to the situation represented in Figure 4.1. As shown in Figure 4.2, the outcome is unsatisfactory, because the placement of the radiators would make the inside part of the room warmer, separating the room into two parts – a warm part and a cool part. Air circulation would be poor between these two parts because the convection current represented in the sequence in Figure 4.1 would not occur. The ultimate outcome of the sequence of events represented in Figure 4.2 is the proposition (shown at the bottom left) stating that the room would be uncomfortable for its occupants.

We now proceed to a higher level of abstraction by using an explanation scheme to bring out the generality implicit in the positive radiators script.

When we look at Figure 4.3, we can see that each propositional function is connected to the next propositional function in the sequence by a defeasible generalization. For example, let's look at the arrows joining the first text box to the second one. We know that if heat source x is placed in an area y in an enclosed space z, x will produce heat at y. Next let's look at the transition between the second text box and the third one. We know that if x produces heat at area y, the heat will tend to warm the air around area y. And we know that if the heat warms the air around area y, that warm air will rise.

Perhaps we could also say that there is an even broader generalization supporting this inference, namely the generalization that warm air rises. This observation could support the DN model, but it is not true that heat always rises, only that heat generally tends to rise under the appropriate conditions – for example, in an enclosed space, or if there is no wind or a fan blowing on the source of the heat.

4.7 The Heated Metal Example

The DN model could sometimes usefully provide an explanation of why a piece of metal expanded by saying that this piece of metal was heated and that all metals expand when heated. One problem with this explanation is that the deductive model doesn't work because the generalization is defeasible. Metals generally expand when heated, but only while the pressure is held constant. However, in the special case of solid materials such as metals, the pressure does not appreciably affect the size of the object. So, with these qualifications, at best we can say that generally metals expand when heated, except for small changes that may occur under conditions of varying pressure. Perhaps the DN model could be rescued in this instance by bringing in its inductive variant. However, it is a better explanation to say that thermal expansion of the metal when heated can be explained by the particles in the middle moving more, and thereby increasing the distances between them, which accounts for the expansion.

Such an explanation can be given as follows. The excited metal molecules rapidly accelerate when the metal is heated, and this excitement causes them to collide more frequently than usual and in more drastic and random motions. This increase in kinetic energy promotes expansion as the molecules separate from each other. It is this sequential procedure that explains both why a particular piece of metal expanded when heated and also why metals expand when heated in general. This sort of explanation can be modeled by a script sequence as shown in Figure 4.4.

Just as in the radiators example, there is a sequence of events that tie together, and, when put in order, provide a script – an account that presents an explanation of the proposition to be explained. In this particular instance the sequence is the series of inferential steps from one event to another. In the

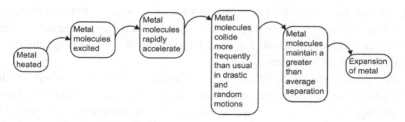

Figure 4.4: The Heated Metal Script

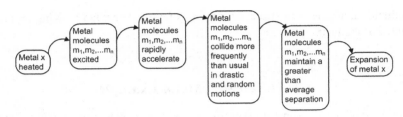

Figure 4.5: Explanation Scheme for the Heated Metal Example

radiators example the explanation was prompted by an anomaly, something about the heating arrangements in the room that the explainee did not understand.

The sequence of events represented in Figure 4.4 is comparable to the radiators script shown in Figure 4.1. There is a sequence of events described by propositions placed in an order that represents a sequence of events we can all understand with a little background knowledge of atomic theory in science. In the heated metal example, the explainee is asking for a theoretical scientific explanation. The latter example is simpler because there is no anomaly of the same kind as before, and no need for a contrastive explanation of the kind shown in Figure 4.2 of the radiators example. But in a comparable way to the radiators example, we can get a more general explanation by representing the sequence at a higher level of abstraction by fitting the script into an explanation scheme as an instance of it. This procedure of matching the script with the scheme requires that each variable in the explanation scheme be replaced by the individual fitting the variable in the explanation script in a uniform substitution. The explanation scheme for the heated metal example is shown in Figure 4.5.

Comparing this scheme-based explanation to the explanation for why metal expands when heated provided by the DN model (in Section 1), we see that there are two aspects that they have in common. Both include the particular circumstances of the metal being heated, and both include the expansion of metal as the thing to be explained. The new script-based explanation has more information in it, as it includes four intervening steps in the causal sequence. We would say, therefore, that this explanation is more informative than the DN one, and hence is generally a better one. At least it is a deeper one, and would be more practically useful – say, for purposes of giving an explanation to students in a general science class.

That said, however, in general which explanation is better depends on the context of the dialogue. The explanation shown in Figure 4.5 could be deepened by including further details of how the molecules react to heat by becoming 'excited.' An explanation of the expansion of metal in a physics seminar might be expected to be more detailed and technical, while the one in Figure 4.5 might be suitable for a high school class in general science. Questions could be asked about it, and evidence (in the form of arguments) could be given to support the propositional nodes or the inference steps.

4.8 The Hawk Example

In this case a hawk was found in the rafters of Dillon Hall, a building containing classrooms at the University of Windsor. To deal with the situation a company called Bob's Animal Control was called in. In the news report it was explained that the hawk could possibly be a danger to students going to classes in the building, even though it was high up in the rafters. Bob's Animal Control explained that there was a danger that the hawk might become dehydrated if it stayed in the building too long, and might become weak from lack of food if it could not get outside. Accordingly, they captured the hawk in a net and released it outdoors at a time when students were not present.

In this case the problem was presented, and the first step toward the solution of the problem was for the university administration to call Bob's Animal Control. The solution proposed by Bob's Animal Control was to capture the hawk using a net. The possible consequences that could be taken into account included, on the one hand, danger to students using the building, and, on the other hand, danger to the hawk unless it could be released back into the wild in a safe manner. They solved the problem by capturing the animal in a net when no students were around and releasing it into the environment.

This case represents a typical example of everyday problem-solving where some action had to be taken to deal with an unusual situation. The setting is one of a deliberation in which some means had to be found to solve the problem posed by the hawk found in Dillon Hall. The situation urgently required a decision because there was danger to students as well as to the bird. University officials who had to deal with the problem decided that the means to solve it was to call experts to get advice. They chose this as the first step to take. From there they decided to call an animal control service, which resulted in the hiring of such an organization. This step led to the arrival of the worker who took charge and removed the bird by using the net to capture it and then released it outside. So, if you look at the sequence of goals and actions, it does represent practical reasoning, as shown in Figure 4.6. The practical reasoning moves forward from the initial problem situation through a series of steps involving the chaining of goals and actions to an ultimate sequence of actions that solve the problem. Note also that the example

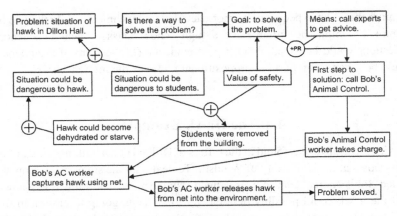

Figure 4.6: Problem-Solving in the Hawk Example

involves not just a single agent, but a group of agents acting together with other agents in a collaborative manner.

4.9 Practical Reasoning and Explanations

An interesting observation about the hawk example is that we can also see it as representing an explanation that might be put forward after the event to explain to someone else – for example, a reporter from the local newspaper – what transpired and how the problem was solved by the administration officials. In this instance, the same structure of practical reasoning as is shown in Figure 4.6 could also function as a sequence of practical reasoning representing an explanation. The reporter might ask the university officials how the problem was solved, and they might essentially reply by tracking backward from the last point where the animal control worker took charge and released the hawk into the environment. From there it could track backward to explain how the officials solved the problem by calling an animal control agency, and explaining how their goal was to solve the problem in accord with the value of safety, given that the situation could be dangerous to students as well as to the animal. The tracking sequence and its components are shown in Figure 4.7.

Figure 4.7 represents the problem-solving reasoning in the example by breaking it down into three components: the circumstances that created the problem, the practical reasoning that led to the solution of the problem, and an argument that was important to see how the solution to the problem was worked out. The argument, shown in the middle of Figure 4.7, is an instance of

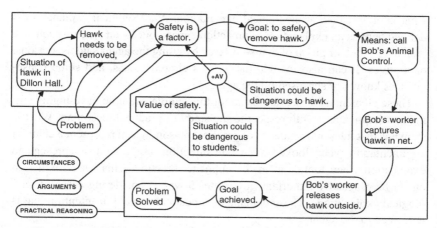

Figure 4.7: Tracking Backward in the Hawk Example

argument from positive values that has three premises. This argument supports one of the event descriptions that is part of the script in the formulation of the problem, namely the statement that safety is a factor. In other words, what we see represented in Figure 4.7 is an instance of explanation combined with argumentation. This aspect will prove to be very important, and will be further investigated, in the next chapter.

The practical reasoning part of the explanation is shown in the diagram at the top right of Figure 4.7, going down the right side of the diagram and then moving along the bottom. During this sequence of practical reasoning

1. the goal is stated,
2. the means to carrying out the goal is stated,
3. a consequence of the action taken as the means is stated,
4. a second action related to the prior one is stated, and
5. it is shown that the goal is achieved.

The end of the sequence of practical reasoning is that the problem is solved. This sequence illustrates a typical chaining of practical reasoning of the kind illustrated in Chapter 1.

There are several interesting observations to be made about this way of representing the reasoning in the hawk example. One is that it combines argument with explanation. The argument supports one part of the explanation. Another is that the explanation is not about natural events, as was the case in the radiators example. It is about a human action that was taken. In other words, to the extent that the sequence shown in Figure 4.7 represents an explanation, it is what is often called a teleological explanation. A teleological explanation is defined here as an explanation of an action carried out by an agent – such as a human or robot, or group of them – offered by citing the agent's goals, reasons, or motives. It can also include the agent's circumstances, and some consequences known or surmised by the agent.

These elementary observations about this simple example have highly significant implications with respect to the study of practical reasoning. What is shown is that the same sequence of practical reasoning can represent a chain of argumentation when looked at in one direction, but can also represent an explanation when looked at in the opposite direction. This lesson will turn out to be especially important in Chapter 5 when considering cases of teleological explanations. These explanations postulate a goal or intention that is attributed to the agent.

4.10 Conclusions

The Why^2 Dialogue System is a formal model showing how the difference between argument and explanation resides in the pre- and post-conditions for the speech act of requesting an argument and the speech act of requesting an explanation. Consider an example of a text of discourse where there is a problem about deciding whether to take it as an explanation or an argument, based on the evidence that is possessed. The solution is provided by examining the evidence. In many instances, the text may not contain the why question, but only the proposition given in the explanation or argument that was presumably a response to a prior why question by the other party. The evaluator has to look at this proposition and ask whether it is a commitment of both participants in the dialogue or not, by examining their commitment sets and perhaps by drawing inferences from the propositions in these commitment sets using the dialogue protocols called commitment rules (Walton and Krabbe, 1995). If it is in both commitment sets, the speech act is an explanation. If it is not in both commitment sets, the speech act is an argument. In other words, the determination depends on what is taken to be the function of the why question in the dialogue, and this has to be inferred from the textual evidence in the case at hand.

In the dialogue theory, the function of an explanation put forward by an explainer is to transfer understanding to the explainee. Understanding is defined in terms of scripts – sequences of events or actions joined together in a way that is familiar to both parties in the dialogue based on their common knowledge of how things can be normally expected to go in situations both have encountered previously. Understanding is conveyed by presenting a script that fits together, that is supported by evidence, and that is coherent with normal patterns of this kind familiar to both parties. Scripts are represented as sequences of nodes and arrows in a graph structure that is most often linear, or a tree structure, though in some instances they can also contain cycles, as shown in the radiators example. A cycle can represent a feedback relationship in a sequence of nodes, as shown by the example in Figure 4.1. At a higher level of generality, a script is an instance of an explanation scheme, which has variables in place of the constants in the explanation script. The explanation is provided by the structural matching of the script and the scheme.

The issue of judging whether examples of scientific explanation are best modeled by the DN theory or by the dialogue theory is complicated by the fact that in explanation schemes the nodes are joined by inferences that can be represented by or supported by generalizations. This appears to leave some room for exponents of the DN theory or its probabilistic variant to apply their model of explanation. However, the two examples studied in this chapter suggest that the dialogue model goes deeper because it brings out more than just how a general law fits with a single instance. It also brings out:

1. How the connected inferential steps in a script-based explanation fit together into an organized sequence familiar to both parties.
2. How the script can be matched with an explanation scheme.
3. How these two sequences can fit with each other.
4. How this matching can transfer understanding in a dialogue.

5

Explanations, Motives, and Intentions

Ascription of an intention to an agent is especially important in law. In criminal law the intent to commit a criminal act, called *mens rea*, refers to the guilty mind, the key element needed to prosecute a defendant for a crime. For example, in order to prove that a defendant has committed the crime of theft of an object, it needs to be established that the defendant had the intention never to return the object to its owner. Studying examples of how intention is proved in law is an important resource for giving us clues on how reasoning to an intention should be carried out. Intention is also fundamentally important in ethical reasoning where there are problems about how the end can justify the means.

This chapter introduces the notion of inference to the best explanation, often called abductive reasoning, and presents recent research on evidential reasoning that uses the concept of a so-called script or story as a central component. The introduction of these two argumentation tools show how they are helpful in moving forward toward a solution to the longstanding problem of analyzing how practical reasoning from circumstantial evidence can be used to support or undermine a hypothesis that an agent has a particular intention. Legal examples are used to show that even though ascribing an intention to an agent is an evaluation procedure that combines argumentation and explanation, it can be rationally carried out by using a practical reasoning model that accounts for the weighing of factual evidence on both sides of a disputed case.

The examples studied in this chapter will involve cases where practical reasoning is used as the glue that combines argumentation with explanation. Section 1 considers a simple example of a message on the Internet advising how to mount a flagpole bracket to a house. The example tells the reader how to take the required steps to attach a bracket to the house in order to mount a flagpole so that the reader can show his patriotism by displaying a flag on his house. The example text is clearly an instance of practical reasoning.

The author of the ad presumes that the reader has a goal, and he tells the reader how to fulfill that goal by carrying out a sequence of actions. In other words, the author is explaining to the reader how to carry out this task. Simply put, the text contains an explanation that uses practical reasoning. Another interesting aspect of the example is that the text partly involves an argument as well as an explanation. These aspects pose a number of highly significant problems for practical reasoning, already partly addressed in Chapter 4, and that will be solved in Chapter 5.

Chapter 5 uses CAS to model the explanation in the flagpole example using argument diagrams that represent that structure as a sequence of practical reasoning. It turns out to be possible, at least up to a point, to model the sequence of practical reasoning in the flagpole example using argument diagrams and argumentation schemes. Section 3 goes on to consider an example of practical reasoning used in problem-solving. This example shows that the same sequence of practical reasoning can represent both argumentation and explanation. Section 6 analyzes the logical structure of practical reasoning used in this way to reason from an action to a motive. Section 7 introduces inference to the best explanation. Sections 8 and 9 consider the more difficult kind of case in which practical reasoning is used to reason from a motive to an intention. CAS is applied to some legal examples to illustrate how this kind of backward reasoning works. Section 10 provides some conclusions.

5.1 The Flagpole Example

The following example is a short text found on the Internet (see: http://www.homeconstructionimprovement.com/2008/07/install-flag-pole-bracket-on-vinyl.html). The text, as quoted below, tells you how to mount a flagpole bracket to the vinyl siding on your house so you can show your patriotism by displaying a flag on your home. It seems like a simple example that is easy to understand, and it looks very much like it uses practical reasoning:

> Attaching a flagpole bracket to vinyl siding is an easy home improvement project that will allow you to show your patriotism on your home. It's important to install the bracket properly so you don't damage your vinyl siding. The easiest way to install a flagpole bracket (or hanging flower pot bracket or similar) is to screw the bracket to a vinyl surface mount block. The surface mount block has a profile routed out of the back so that it will fit the siding profile. The trick to successfully installing the bracket and surface mount block is to pre-drill holes in the siding. You want to drill a

hole slightly larger than the screws you're going to use so that the siding can move as it expands and contracts due to temperature.

The first part of the text starts out as an argument telling the reader that installing such a flagpole bracket is easy, and that it is a good thing because it enables you to show your patriotism. The remaining part of the ad, quoted below, gives other details of how to carry out the task of mounting the bracket on your house:

> Vinyl siding moves a LOT when it heats and cools throughout the year. If you put a screw right through the vinyl siding it will prevent the siding from moving and therefore cause it to buckle. So I pre-drilled the surface mount block first. This allowed me the ability to pre-mark the siding. Then I drilled a 1/4″ diameter hole in the siding where each of the three screws would go. Then it's as simple as installing three long screws to attach the bracket and surface mount block at the same time. Make sure you use screws that won't be so long that they hit some wires.

The latter part of the text quoted just above gives a description of how the author of the ad installed such a bracket himself and gives warnings to the reader about some potential negative consequences of installing the bracket in a different way.

The practical reasoning in the text is sufficiently clear that the reader can get a useful message about the project of installing a flagpole bracket on his house. But there is an aspect of it that is puzzling from a point of view of understanding practical reasoning. The text seems to start out by putting forward an argument, but then it slips over into a different kind of practical reasoning that conveys an explanation of how to do something. To try to grasp this transition, it is helpful to start with the argument part.

The very first sentence of the quoted text appears to express an argument suggesting to the reader that attaching a flagpole bracket to the vinyl siding of his house would be a good idea. That is the conclusion of the argument. One premise is that such a project will allow you to show your patriotism on your home. The other premise is that it is an easy home improvement project. This argument can be visually represented using the argument diagram in Figure 5.1. A dashed border around a proposition indicates that the proposition is an implicit premise in the argument.

The argumentation scheme in both instances is the one for argument from positive value, represented in the two nodes by the notation +AV. The next two sentences in the text of the example can also reasonably be interpreted as expressing an argument. This argument is shown in Figure 5.2.

As shown in the diagram in Figure 5.2, the way this argument is configured is based on two argumentation schemes: one for instrumental practical reasoning,

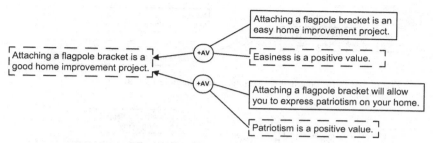

Figure 5.1: First Argument in the Flagpole Example

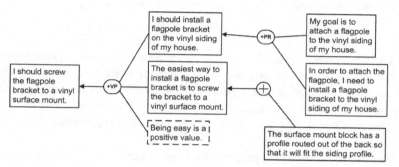

Figure 5.2: Second Argument in the Flagpole Example

and the other for value-based practical reasoning. The value-based practical reasoning scheme is represented by the notation +VP. Up to this point, then, the text can be fairly straightforwardly represented as an argument, and its structure can be modeled using CAS in the way shown in Chapter 3.

5.2 Practical Reasoning in the Flagpole Example

The rest of the text is clearly based on practical reasoning, but takes us in a different direction because it appears to be an explanation. It is not difficult to see that practical reasoning is essentially involved in this latter part of the sequence of reasoning in the flagpole example. Even so, let's move ahead and see if we can use argument diagrams in the CAS style to represent a sequence of practical reasoning in this part of the text.

Figure 5.3 uses a CAS argument diagram to show the structure of another part of the practical reasoning in the example.

Figure 5.3: Basic Practical Reasoning in the Flagpole Example

Figure 5.4: Evaluation of the Practical Reasoning Using CAS

The person who conveyed the advice given in the explanation in the example presumes that the reader may also have a goal of attaching a flagpole to his house, or be considering such a project. The explanation given in the text tells the reader that in order to achieve this goal, first you must install the flagpole bracket to which the flagpole can be attached once it is eventually mounted on the house.

The two premises of the practical reasoning structure shown in Figure 5.3 are merely stated but not proved. However, suppose that the reader accepts both of these propositions. Suppose that the reader has a goal to attach a flagpole to his house, and suppose that the reader accepts the statement that in order to do this, a flagpole bracket needs to be installed to the vinyl siding of his house. If these two premises are accepted, CAS shows both of them as in, and the text boxes containing these two statements are darkened, as shown in Figure 5.4.

Once the premises have been accepted, CAS will automatically show the conclusion as accepted, given that the structure of the argument fits the argumentation scheme for practical reasoning. Once both these conditions are met, CAS will display the conclusion as accepted, as shown in Figure 5.4.

In the second block of text quoted above, the author is warning the reader that unless the bracket is installed in a certain way, it could damage the vinyl siding on his house. This part of the practical reasoning contained in the message conveyed to the reader is shown in Figure 5.5.

The argument shown at the bottom fits the scheme for argument from negative consequences. What happens when both premises of this argument are accepted, and the argument properly fits the form of the scheme for

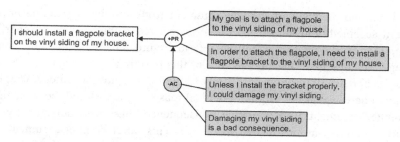

Figure 5.5: Possible Negative Consequences Taken into Account

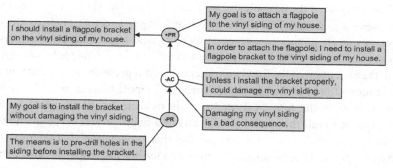

Figure 5.6: Counter-argument to the Previous Counter-argument

argument from consequences? The answer is that this argument undercuts the previous practical reasoning argument. In Figure 5.5, it is shown that once the premises and the argument node of the argument at the bottom have been accepted, the argument from practical reasoning is defeated. There has been an exception. Hence, the ultimate conclusion – the statement that I should install a flagpole bracket on the vinyl siding of my house – is now shown in the text box with white fill, meaning the conclusion is no longer accepted. Essentially what has happened is that the argument from negative consequences has defeated the practical reasoning, and therefore the conclusion of the practical reasoning no longer holds.

Tracing the sequence of practical reasoning in the example, the next step is to recognize that the person offering the advice is conveying the message that there is a way to deal with the potential negative consequences shown in Figure 5.5 by drilling holes in the siding before installing the bracket. Using CAS, this next part of the reasoning can be represented as a counter-argument against the previous argument from negative consequences. This way of exhibiting the sequence of practical reasoning in the example is shown in Figure 5.6.

Once the premises of the con argument from practical reasoning have been accepted, and the scheme for practical reasoning has been properly applied, as shown at the bottom left in Figure 5.6, the argument from negative consequences is defeated. For this reason, the pro argument from practical reasoning shown at the top of Figure 5.6 is now accepted. What is shown here is that the original practical reasoning is restored, because the counter-argument from negative consequences has been defeated by a further counter-argument that attacks it. This latter counter-argument is also shown to be an instance of practical reasoning, like the original argument.

The analysis of the flagpole example to this point has shown how it can be represented as a sequence of practical reasoning connecting goals to means to carry out the goals while responding to critical questions about negative consequences. But there is a problem. The text in the flagpole example, with the exception of the first two sentences, is not presenting an argument to the reader telling him that he should install a flagpole bracket to his house. If you look over the text as a whole, it is evident that it is meant as an explanation to tell the reader how to attach a flagpole bracket to his house without causing damage to the house. But this explanation also seems to be based on practical reasoning. The author is telling the reader how to carry out the task of installation if the reader wishes to adopt the goal of attempting to do so. The author explains to the reader that the trick is to pre-drill holes in the siding, slightly larger than the screws, so that when you attach the bracket, there is room for expansion, preventing the vinyl from buckling. As the author goes on to explain in more detail how to do this, one can see that the sequence of actions fits the structure of practical reasoning explained in Chapter 1. In such a sequence there is a chaining of actions, so that each action leads to the next one in a whole sequence of actions leading toward the goal.

In this case we have a big problem – the problem of telling us whether the sequence of practical reasoning of this sort represents an argument or an explanation. We can represent it as a sequence of reasoning that is very much like an argument, as shown by the reconstruction above using CAS. But really it is an explanation rather than an argument. Although this observation poses a problem, it also reveals some insights that are very interesting:

1. it suggests that practical reasoning is used in explanations as well as arguments;
2. it suggests that arguments and explanations can be intertwined together in an interesting way;

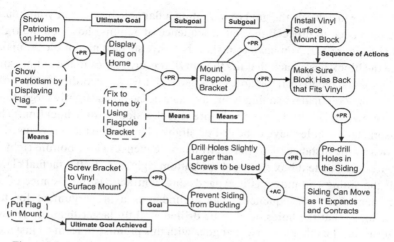

Figure 5.7: Practical Reasoning in a Teleological Explanation

3. it calls out for a clarification that is of broad import for logic and the study of argumentation, a clarification between reasoning and argument;
4. it suggests that reasoning is involved in both explanations and arguments.

It is vitally important to clarify all of these issues if we are to get a better grasp of practical reasoning. Another example might be useful to clarify these matters a bit further.

5.3 The Flagpole Example as an Explanation

The forward and backward reasoning is displayed in Figure 5.7. First, the sequence of practical reasoning can be seen as a sequence of steps starting from the ultimate goal shown at the upper left of Figure 5.7. The ultimate goal is for the person to whom the explanation was directed to show patriotism on his or her home. As shown just below the ultimate goal, there is an implicit premise, indicated by the broken boundary surrounding the proposition, that the means to show patriotism is by displaying the flag. These two premises lead together by practical reasoning to the conclusion to display the flag on your home. This conclusion is then reused as a premise in a second step of practical reasoning that employs as its other implicit premise the action of fixing the flag to your home by using a flagpole bracket. The conclusion of this instance of practical reasoning is the proposition that you should mount a flagpole bracket on your house.

In order to achieve the goal of mounting a flagpole bracket on your house you then need to proceed through a sequence of actions shown on the right side of Figure 5.7. You have to install the vinyl surface mount block, make sure the block has a back that fits the vinyl, pre-drill holes in the siding, and finally you have to drill the holes in a particular way. According to the next step in the practical reasoning, you have to drill the holes slightly larger than the screws to be used in order to prevent the siding from buckling. The reason that the holes have to be drilled slightly larger than the screws used is shown by the instance of argument from consequences at the bottom right of Figure 5.7. The text box shown at the bottom right, stating the factual claim that the siding can move as it expands and contracts, is the premise of an argument from consequences. The argument is a pro argument for the conclusion that the holes need to be drilled slightly larger than the screws to be used. The other premise that goes with this premise to form an instance of practical reasoning is the proposition that the goal of this procedure is to prevent the siding from buckling. Once all the steps in this sequence of practical reasoning have been carried out, they lead to the penultimate action of screwing the bracket to the vinyl surface mount. This action in turn leads to the final goal being achieved by the action of putting the flag in the mount block on the house.

So, as you look over the whole figure what you see is a sequence of practical reasoning leading from an alternate goal through a series of subgoals and actions that represent means to a final action in the sequence that represents the achievement of the ultimate goal. The sequence of practical reasoning could represent a chaining of means-end inferences of a kind that could be used in a deliberation on how to do something. It shows how to achieve the ultimate goal by carrying out a sequence of actions or events that are all linked together as a chain of practical reasoning that tells you how to proceed through the steps required. It presents an explanation of how the ultimate goal of showing patriotism on your home can be achieved. Going by the criteria used in Chapter 4 that distinguish between arguments and explanations, there is evidence indicating that this particular example represents a how-to explanation. The writer of the article posted on the Internet is trying to explain to readers of the article how to attach a flagpole bracket to his or her home in order to show patriotism.

The message is particularly directed to the reader who might have a home with vinyl siding, so special instructions are given on how to properly mount the bracket in order to prevent buckling of the siding. Buckling of the siding could be seen as a negative consequence, but in the diagram the practical reasoning has been conveyed by postulating prevention of the siding from buckling as a goal that is one premise of an instance of practical reasoning. The second part of the quoted text offers the reader a more detailed account of how to carry out the task of mounting the bracket. This part of the text represents a supplementary explanation that goes into the finer details of exactly how to carry out each step.

The description of what the text in the flagpole example is meant to do, given just before the example was presented above, states that the text tells you how to mount a flagpole bracket to the vinyl siding of your house so that you can show your patriotism on your home by displaying the flag. So interpreted, the text is telling you how to do something. In other words, it is giving you an explanation of how to carry out a task – the task of mounting a flagpole bracket to the vinyl siding of your house – so that you can carry out a goal that has value to you. The value is patriotism, and the explanation is telling you how you can show your patriotism on your home by displaying the flag on it. Practical reasoning is fairly explicit in this way of describing what the text is doing. The text is saying that if your goal is to show your patriotism, you can carry out this goal through the means of displaying the flag on your house.

In a more detailed way, an observer can see how practical reasoning is woven into the explanation by tracking the sequence of reasoning in Figure 5.7. How you can carry out the task of mounting the flagpole bracket to the vinyl siding of your house is shown in the sequence of actions at the right of Figure 5.7. However, even before that the explanation tells you how you can get from your ultimate goal of showing patriotism on your home to link up with a sequence of actions by putting two subgoals between the ultimate goal and the sequence of actions. The way to show patriotism on your home is to display a flag on it. So now displaying a flag on your home becomes a subgoal. Then, by practical reasoning, the reader is led to another subgoal – that of mounting a flagpole bracket on his or her house. From there, the sequence of practical reasoning leads from the installation of a vinyl surface mount block to other actions that fit into the sequence as a means of carrying out the installation procedure.

What can be seen is how the entire sequence of practical reasoning woven throughout Figure 5.7 hangs together and makes sense as a script that provides an explanation of how the task should be carried out and what goals will be achieved by these means. This is because the whole sequence fits together by fitting subgoals into an ultimate general goal and fitting this network of goals into specific actions that function as the means to carry out the goals. What makes the whole sequence fit together as a coherent script is the practical reasoning steps being chained together so that the sequence of reasoning as a whole makes sense by fitting the goals and the means together. Put succinctly, the whole sequence makes sense because it explains to the reader how he or she can show his or her patriotism by displaying a flag on his or her house.

The second part of the text, quoted separately at the beginning of Section 1, is an even more specific description of how the person who wrote the text carried out the task himself in his own case. This is a description of what the writer did, but it also functions as an explanation to the reader to show how the task can be carried out using the right types of screws and so forth.

5.4 Defining Key Terms

In this section some definitions are put forward that will help to guide the following discussions. The key terms to be defined are 'goal,' 'motive,' and 'intention.'

According to the BDI model, the major premise of the basic practical inference is a statement that the agent has an intention. The problem confronted by this model is that intention is a state of mind that is internal to an agent. More specifically, when it comes to analyzing practical reasoning, the problem is an evidential one. How can someone other than that agent prove – or, for that matter, disprove – that the agent has a specific intention? We might recall from Chapter 1 that whether an agent has a particular commitment or not can be inferred from the evidence of what the agent said or did in the past. But the problem of whether an agent might properly be said to have a particular intention or not is an even deeper psychological question about the agent's internal state of mind. For these reasons, it might seem prudent for one agent to avoid drawing any conclusions at all about the presumed intentions of another agent.

However, in reality we often have to draw such inferences in everyday life in order to carry out intelligent decision-making about what to do. To communicate, in the face of ambiguity and vagueness, we constantly have to make assumptions about what a speech partner intends to say. Moreover, legal and ethical reasoning is often based on imputations of intent. The notion of judging whether an action has been carried out with some particular intention in mind – for example, malice aforethought – is especially important in criminal law. Let's begin with the notion of a goal.

One of the characteristics of an intelligent rational agent set down in Chapter 1 was the capability of formulating and acting on goals. Such a rational agent is constantly acting in circumstances that are constantly changing. It may be programmed to act on certain goals, but it may also make efforts to formulate its own goals, and to change them once formulated. An agent can have an abstract goal, such as health. As indicated in Chapter 1, goals are based on values. An agent can also have a concrete goal that it wants to reach within a certain time by setting a deadline. A group of agents engaged in a deliberation can agree on shared goals and can argue about what their goals should be as a group. In this book, a goal is associated with an aim or an end that an agent persists in moving toward as it becomes aware of information about its circumstances and guides its actions forward to some aiming point that it has designated as an objective.

As pointed out by Wigmore (1935, 76), the term 'motive' is ambiguous. In one sense it refers to an internal emotion or feeling that urges or pushes a person to do or refrain from doing something. In another sense, it can be described as an evidential circumstance of the internal emotion. For example, if a person had expressed an emotion by saying that he hates a particular individual or that he wished he owned some object, this expression could be combined with circumstances known in the case to derive the conclusion that he had a particular motive. Thus, if he said that he wished that he owned some object, and the circumstances were that the object was stolen and that he had an opportunity to take it, then it could be inferred that he had a motive for the theft. A motive is an internal feeling, and therefore not directly accessible to other parties, but evidence of it can be constructed from circumstances and from statements an agent has gone on record as making. On such an evidential basis, a reasonable conclusion can be drawn that the agent has, or does not have, a particular motive based on this evidence.

The term 'intention' is a highly contested notion in moral philosophy and philosophy of mind, but its use in law, although it appears to be more specific and clear, is complex. *Black's Law Dictionary* (Garner, 2009, 881–883) distinguishes between intention and intent. Intention (883) is described as the purpose or design with which an action is done, combining knowledge with desire. Intent (881) is defined as a state of mind accompanying an act, characterized by "mental resolution or determination." This definition is psychological in nature. On the other hand, the verb "to intend" is defined (881) as follows: "to have in mind a fixed purpose to reach a desired objective." Although it uses the words "mind" and "desired," to intend, by this definition, is to have a fixed purpose to reach a goal or objective. This makes it very close to the notion of having a goal. On the other hand, Wigmore (1935, 74) uses the term "intention" as equivalent to the notion of a design, and that as being equivalent to the notion of a plan. This usage makes intention sound less psychological and more like a goal.

In the face of this lack of agreement on defining subjective notions such as intent, how can legal and everyday reasoning about intentions be justified? The way to do it is to realize that such a form of reasoning is conjectural, and best seen as defeasible, but can be based on external factual evidence that can be verified or falsified by witness testimony or scientific observations and theories.

5.5 Practical Reasoning in Multi-agent Systems

Current research into multi-agent systems is built around what is called "agent reasoning" of a kind that is basically the same as what is called practical reasoning in philosophy. An agent in such a system, as described in Chapter 1, is an entity that carries out actions, based on its goals, that has information about its external situation, that communicates with other agents, that can exchange information with these other agents, and that can even engage in collaborative deliberations with them. Thus, such agents need to have the capability of engaging in dialogue with other agents by asking each other questions, answering these questions, informing each other about states of the world, making requests or commands to perform actions, and even sharing feelings with each other (Russell and Norvig, 1995, p. 652). An agent assumes that the other agent it communicates with has goals, and it will need to base its actions on what it takes to be these goals. There is a kind of rationality assumption that needs to be involved in agent communication systems of this type. An agent will often need to operate on the provisional assumption that its speech partner will act according to the standard requirements of practical reasoning.

How do agents in multi-agent systems communicate with each other in this fashion, given that one agent cannot look directly into the inner mental states of the other? They do so in the same way that human agents perform the same communicative tasks in everyday language: they use conversational implicature to derive conclusions by plausible reasoning as hypotheses based on the circumstances of the case and common knowledge of the way things can normally be expected to work in familiar situations. In a case well known in philosophy and linguistics (Grice, 1975, p. 54), a professor reads a letter of reference written by a second professor to support a student who is applying for a teaching job. The letter states that the student has an excellent command of English and has an outstanding class attendance record, but no additional information is given. Normally in such a case the reader would expect information about the student's academic abilities, capabilities for hard work, qualities for interacting with students and colleagues, and so forth. Because nothing has been said about these important factors, the professor to whom the letter was sent would certainly draw the conclusion that the professor who wrote the letter is saying that this student would not be a good candidate to fill the position. These same kinds of methods of drawing a presumptive inference have to be used in communicative multi-agent systems.

Dragoni, Giorgini, and Serafini (2002) proposed a set of criteria to be applied when agents communicate with each other using an agent communication language that enables one agent to recognize the mental state of another that led to a specific utterance. Their system (2002, 130) uses rules governing speech acts in the multi-agent system, combined with rules for logical reasoning, as the basis for inferring the speakers presumed beliefs or intentions. Each speech act is governed by a set of preconditions and postconditions that defines the conditions for its use in the communicative structure. Each agent has a mental state that needs to be updated as it puts forward or receives a new message. In this regard, their multi-agent system is typical of the models of dialogue used in argumentation theory. The dimension their approach brings out is the multi-agent aspect of intention recognition in systems in which groups of agents interact with each other and communicate with each other using speech acts. In such a system, one agent can ask another for clarification regarding its previous utterance in a dialogue, and one agent can even ask another for an explanation regarding the previous utterance in a dialogue.

The problem Dragoni, Giorgini, and Serafini (2002) addressed was that an agent in a multi-agent communication system must not only exchange information in order to carry out their cooperative activities, but must also make assumptions about the beliefs and intentions of the other agents they are communicating with. Their solution to the problem was based on applying inference to the best explanation as the method one agent uses to derive a hypothesis about the beliefs or intentions of another agent, and applying it from the evidence supplied to an agent by its observation about the actions of the other agents and their communicative utterances. One operation of particular interest in their system is that of abductive revision (130), an operation applied when an agent explains something that is inconsistent with an observation known to another agent. Their rules for updating mental states from communication allow for an agent to perform revisions by changing its beliefs or intentions.

The BDI framework they adopt treats sets of beliefs and intentions as the basic units of their formal structure. Although they state that reasoning capabilities for communicative agents are supposed to be general-purpose reasoning machines, they use a set of rules for propositional logic. The absence of defeasible reasoning capabilities means that their system would have to be extended in this direction to model practical reasoning.

Bex, Bench-Capon, and Atkinson (2009) use the argumentation scheme for practical reasoning to construct and compare theories about how people reason with evidence in criminal cases, based on abductive reasoning. According to their approach (80), a story in a criminal case – for example, witness testimony about what happened at the crime scene – depends for its plausibility on how it conforms to our beliefs about the way things normally happen according to common knowledge. In their theory, the plausibility of such a story depends on the plausibility of the causal links between the events in the story. Their work builds on the earlier use of schemes for inference to the best explanation of practical reasoning to infer mental states of an agent by Walton and Schafer (2006), but cites (81) the lack, in this work, of providing a formal framework. To make up for this deficiency, they ground their analysis of abductive reasoning in what is called an action-based alternating transition system.

For our purposes, a problem with applying their system is the set of critical questions matching the argumentation scheme for inference to the best explanation (84). The critical questions they use for problem formulation (85), and their formal representation of the sets of critical questions, are highly complex. The result is a formal action-based alternating transition system for reasoning from the evidential circumstances of the case to the presumed agent's intentions by the structure of abductive practical reasoning that is not easy to apply to simple examples. Although their representation of reasoning from an agent's actions and utterances to its presumed intentions can be visually modeled using a value-based argumentation diagram (92), the arrows in the diagrams represent attack relations of the kind used in the abstract argumentation frameworks. Also, the arrows in their argument diagrams represent causal links between alternating action states in a way that is different from the approach suggested by the analysis of examples in this chapter.

We now turn to a further series of examples that will suggest a different approach, an extension of Walton and Schafer (2006) that also combines practical reasoning with inference to the best explanation.

5.6 Reasoning from Action to Motive

The examination of the ways in which conclusions about how motives are drawn in law can be applied as a preliminary step to confronting the more complex problem of reasoning about intentions. It has been recognized by scholars of evidence law that motive can only be proved indirectly, by inference using circumstantial evidence (Wigmore, 1940, §385, 327). This evidence comes from the circumstantial evidence in a case showing it supports a hypothesis that the agent acted from a particular motive.

Consider the following case (Leonard, 2001, 449), where defendant D was charged with the murder of victim V. However, there was circumstantial evidence showing that D had a motive. D had taken part in a car theft, and V knew about D's involvement in the theft. Moreover, V had threatened to reveal D's involvement in the theft to the police. Leonard (448) structured the evidential reasoning in this case using the following form of inference:

> EVIDENCE: D stole a car, V was aware of the fact, and threatened to inform the police.
> INFERENCE: D had a motive to prevent V from revealing the theft to the police.
> CONCLUSION: D murdered V to prevent V from revealing the theft to the police.

The way Leonard configured the evidential reasoning in this case is as follows. The first premise represents the circumstantial evidence, and the conclusion represents the ultimate claim to be proved in the trial (the allegation that D murdered V). The inferential link that joins the circumstantial evidence to this ultimate conclusion is the imputation of a motive to the defendant D.

In this case, the evidence of the threat to reveal the defendant's auto theft gives rise to an inference to the conclusion that the defendant's motive was to prevent the victim from revealing the theft to the police. This inference has the following structure:

> Premise: the victim was aware that the defendant had stolen a car, and that the victim had threatened to inform the police.
> Premise: the defendant believed that if the victim informed the police about the theft, there would likely be unwanted consequences for the defendant, i.e., imprisonment.

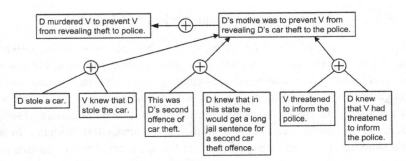

Figure 5.8: Circumstantial Evidence Used to Infer a Motive

Premise: the defendant strongly wanted to prevent these unwanted consequences.

Conclusion: the defendant had a motive for killing the victim (the motive of preventing likely unwanted consequences that he believed would otherwise happen).

This inference takes the form of the argumentation scheme for practical reasoning from evidence to motive.

The inference can be visually modeled using the CAS to show how the circumstantial evidence supports the hypothesis that D murdered V.

This evidential structure is shown in Figure 5.8. In Figure 5.8, the ultimate conclusion that D murdered V is shown at the top left, and the imputation of motive to D, upon which this ultimate conclusion is founded, is shown at the top right. The mass of circumstantial evidence supporting the hypothesis is shown in the premises of the three arguments along the bottom part of Figure 5.8.

The problem is to figure out how one gets from the mass of evidence shown at the bottom of Figure 5.8, via the imputation of motive, to the ultimate conclusion that D murdered V. The same kind of problem is posed by finding out how one gets from a mass of evidence in a case to an imputation of intent. Intent is generally an element required to prove the crime of murder in legal systems (with exceptions and variations on how this requirement is formulated and implemented in differing jurisdictions). There is also the problem of seeing how motive and intent are related. Even if motive for an action can be proved by the circumstantial evidence in a case, there is a separate step of inference to draw the conclusion that the agent intended to carry out the action. Next it will be argued that the best tool for solving such problems is provided by combining argument and explanation using the device of inference to the best explanation.

5.7 Inference to the Best Explanation

It was shown in Chapter 4 how recent research on evidential reasoning in criminal law (Bex, 2011) is based on scripts – that is, stories presenting a coherent overview of what supposedly happened in a case. The prosecution has one story, while the defense has a different story that is used to reach an opposite conclusion about what happened. A story does not have to be internally consistent, but if an inconsistency is found, probing questions will be asked during cross-examination. Examination is a complex process that typically begins with questions asking for explanations, but in cross-examination it has a tendency to shift to a critiquing phase in which the story is torn apart by findings of questionable logical gaps and even inconsistencies.

According to Bex and Walton (2012), there are seven factors that can be used to judge how acceptable or unacceptable a story is:

1. How well it helps to make sense of what happened.
2. Whether it is consistent.
3. Whether an apparent inconsistency can be resolved.
4. How well it is supported or not by the factual evidence.
5. How plausible the story is according to common knowledge about how things normally work.
6. How comprehensive it is with respect to accounting for the facts.
7. How well it stands up to critical examination.

Figure 5.7, outlining the explanation of how to mount a flagpole on your house, makes sense as a story because of the practical reasoning that connects the script together in a coherent way that the audience can understand. The structure of reasoning in a criminal case is somewhat different, however, because the primary objective is not to explain something, but to resolve a conflict of opinions by examining the evidence on both sides.

Pennington and Hastie (1993) used many case studies of criminal cases to show how the evidence in a given case can be structured into a framework of two opposed stories that each purport to explain the facts of the case. Which one is more plausible depends on evaluating the pair comparatively using the seven factors cited above; factor number 4 is especially important. One problem, however, is that a more plausible story may not be so strongly supported by the body of evidence, whereas a less plausible story may be supported by more evidence. Despite this potential imbalance, the legal reasoning used in a trial is supposed to be evidence-based. As a methodological device to deal with this problem, Wagenaar, van Koppen, and Crombag (1993) devised a special type of story structure they call an anchored narrative. The distinctive feature of an anchored narrative is that it contains arguments (in the form of evidential findings) as well as explanations, and weaves the two together.

Abductive reasoning is an unclear notion. Sometimes it refers to a kind of backward reasoning from a conclusion to the premise of an argument that the conclusion was presumably based on. But it is equated by many with inference to the best explanation (IBE). According to the influential analysis of Josephson and Josephson (1994, 14), abductive inference takes the following form, where H is a hypothesis.

- D is a collection of data.
- H explains D.
- No other hypothesis can explain D as well as H does.
- Therefore H is probably true.

In inference to the best explanation, multiple explanations of a given fact or observation can be generated, and the best explanation is selected according to criteria that express the degree to which the explanations conform to the evidence and their plausibility. This best explanation is then drawn as the conclusion of the inference.

A very simple legal example (Wigmore, 1940, 420) can be used to illustrate IBE:

> The fact that a before a robbery had no money, but after had a large sum, is offered to indicate that he by robbery became possessed of the large sum of money. There are several other possible explanations – the receipt of a legacy, the payment of a debt, the winning of a gambling game, and the like. Nevertheless, the desired explanation rises, among other explanations, to a fair degree of plausibility, and the evidence is received.

This example shows how the conclusion is arrived at as the best choice among several competing explanations of the circumstances. It also shows how IBE is a defeasible form of reasoning, meaning that its conclusion may need to be retracted as new information comes in concerning the circumstances of a case.

Josephson and Josephson (1994, 14) presented a list of six critical questions that can be used to probe into an instance of IBE that leads to a hypothesis H.

1. How decisively does H surpass the alternatives?
2. How good is H by itself as an explanation, independently of the alternatives?
3. How much confidence is there that all plausible explanations have been considered?
4. How good are the original data?

5. How can the cost of being wrong be weighed against the benefit of being right?
6. How strong is the need to come to a conclusion at all, considered against the option of collecting more information?

Wigmore's example shows how IBE can be applied to evidential reasoning in criminal cases. For example, the chain of reasoning of an agent's actions, along with his words and knowledge of circumstances, could go backward using both practical reasoning and IBE to the presumed conclusion that the agent had a particular motive or intention in acting the way he did. This can be done as shown in Leonard's example (analyzed in Section 6). Walton and Schafer (2006) showed how the reasoning used in this example is a combination of practical reasoning and abductive reasoning, or inference to the best explanation (IBE). IBE infers a conclusion from a set of given facts (data) by selecting the best one among several explanations that could account for the facts of a case. Typically, in such a case, the two sides have presented two opposed accounts, or stories, at trial, and IBE is used to point to one as the better explanation (Bex, 2011).

It can be shown how inference to the best explanation based on practical reasoning was used to lead to the hypothesis that D's motive was to prevent V from revealing D's car theft to the police, as shown in the circumstantial evidence marshaled in Figure 5.8. To see this, we need to reconstruct the practical reasoning that D presumably went through, or at any rate that we can attribute to him by virtue of what is known about the circumstances of the case. D was aware that V knew that D had stolen the car, and he also knew that V had threatened to inform the police. D also knew that this was his second offense of car theft, and in the state he would get a long sentence if he were found guilty for having committed another car theft. Getting a long sentence would be a negative consequence that he would want to avoid if possible. By reconstructing his practical reasoning, we can see that he would have a motive to prevent V from revealing the car theft to the police. The circumstantial evidence was about what D knew or didn't know and how this was related to a motive he might have had for taking action to prevent some negative consequences if he were not to take action.

By exploiting common knowledge about practical reasoning, it is possible for us to draw a hypothesis about D's motives, and to use this hypothesis to draw an inference about who killed V. By using inference to the best explanation, we can draw the plausible conclusion that D's motive was to prevent V from revealing the car theft to the police in order to prevent a long jail sentence. The IBE is a plausible argument in this case because of the explanation it is based on, provided there is no better competing explanation.

5.8 Reasoning from Motive to Intention

As Leonard (2001, 449) pointed out, there is another inference, taking the form of an argument from motive to intention, that piggybacks on the above argument from evidence to motive. In the case as outlined by Leonard, D admitted killing V, but claimed that the killing was an accident. In such a case, according to Leonard (2001, 449), the theft evidence could be admissible to prove that D intended to kill V. As Leonard put it, "The evidence of V's threat to reveal D's auto theft would give rise to an inference of a motive to prevent the revelation, and the existence of a motive would suggest that in killing V, D acted intentionally rather than by accident." The central inference in the reasoning Leonard describes can be summed up by following structure:

> Premise: D had a motive to prevent V from revealing the theft to the police.
> Conclusion: D intentionally killed V to prevent V from revealing the theft to the police.

In this inference, the first premise is based on the circumstantial evidence of what both parties knew about the defendant's previous car theft and the victim's threats to report it. The premise is itself a conclusion based on the circumstantial evidence that D stole a car, V was aware of this fact, and V threatened to inform the police. The ultimate conclusion is a claim about the defendant's intention.

The argumentation structure representing how the second argument piggybacks on the first is shown in the CAS argument diagram in Figure 5.9. The notation CO+ in the one argument node represents the scheme for argument from commitment. Basically, this scheme tells us that if an agent has gone on record as asserting proposition *P*, then that agent may be taken to be committed to *P*, assuming that the agent did not later retract commitment to *P*.

The pattern of argumentation illustrated in Figure 5.9 is one of using practical reasoning to infer the conclusion that an agent had a particular motive in carrying out an action, and then chaining the argument forward to derive an ultimate conclusion about the agent's intention.

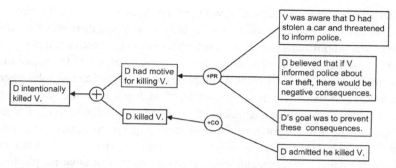

Figure 5.9: Structure of Argumentation from Motive to Intent

5.9 Reasoning from Circumstances to Intention

The concept of intention has long been a troubling one in ethics, where the so-called principle of double effect states that an agent can be responsible for harmful consequences of an intentional action, even though he did not intend the consequences to occur. This principle has been controversial and problematic in writings on ethics. Part of the problem is the issue of whether consequences that might reasonably be expected to flow from an intentional action should be themselves classified as intentional. We can note here as well that this general sort of problem involves practical reasoning and argumentation from consequences. Our concern with the problem here is how one should try to prove or disprove the claim that an agent has a particular intention, given that intention is a mental state internal to an agent. Because the notion of intentional action has proved to be so problematic in ethics and philosophy of mind, it might be better to approach it indirectly. One way to approach the problem is to begin with examining briefly how law approaches the comparable problem of proving or disproving that an agent has a particular motive.

Law has long grappled with the problem of how to reason from circumstantial evidence to an imputation of intention, and it is useful to begin with a hypothetical case that would illustrate generally how this kind of reasoning works in law. When Andrea finds out that her husband is having an affair with Barbara, a woman who lives in the neighborhood, she goes to Barbara's house one night, pours gasoline on the front porch and sets fire to it. Tragically, Barbara died in the fire. Andrea was horrified when she learned of Barbara's death, and she stated that her aim in lighting the fire was only to drive Barbara away from the neighborhood, not to kill her.

To make a judgment in a particular case of a kind that would fit the outlines of this hypothetical case above, there would be a mass of evidence collected by interviewing witnesses, consulting with experts, and collecting all the circumstantial facts of the case. In addition to the factual evidence, there will also have to be some propositions used in the evidential reasoning in the case that rest on common sense about the way things can be normally expected to happen in a case of this kind. These are often assumptions about what the reasonable agent can foresee in the situation. For example, if Andrea's intention was only to make Barbara's house uninhabitable, it would be reasonable to think that she would realize that a substantial fire would be required to achieve this goal. There are also some other assumptions relating to what the law calls the reasonable person. A reasonable person would foresee that other people apart from Barbara could be harmed by the fire, including not only the neighbors but the firefighters as well.

In this case, much depends on what Andrea's intention was, or may be inferred to be. She stated that her goal was only to drive Barbara away from the neighborhood. In the commitment model, that would be her goal, because her stating it is the kind of evidence required to show that it was a commitment of hers. But the suspicion is that she intended to harm Barbara, perhaps even to kill her. So the evidence for and against this proposition needs to be carefully weighed. If she intended to harm or kill Barbara, such a finding would be an important element in arriving at a legal conclusion in a particular jurisdiction on whether she could be found guilty of the crime of murder.

Here we begin to see that ascribing an intention to an agent is a tricky business, even though it is often done in law and history. The process of ascribing an intention to an agent, if the ascription is subject to doubt or disputation, as it often is, requires a marshaling and weighing of the factual evidence in a case. In a word, it requires argumentation that weighs the pro arguments against the con arguments. But if such a weighing of evidence requires IBE, explanations as well as arguments are involved.

Bex and Walton (2012, 121–125) used the case of Jackson v. Virginia (443 U.S. 307) to illustrate how IBE can be used to model evidential reasoning in a criminal case. When C was a member of the staff at a county jail where J was incarcerated, she had befriended him. After J's release the Sheriff and another police officer saw C and J in a diner and also observed that they were drinking. As they left the diner, the Sheriff offered to keep J's revolver until he sobered up, but he declined the offer. The next day, C's body was found in a secluded parking lot. She had been shot twice. On the day of the crime, J had been seen by witnesses shooting at targets with his revolver while drinking. The same day that he had seen the Sheriff at the diner, J had driven from Virginia to North Carolina. He was convicted of the first-degree murder of C by a Virginia court, but appealed the decision on the grounds that

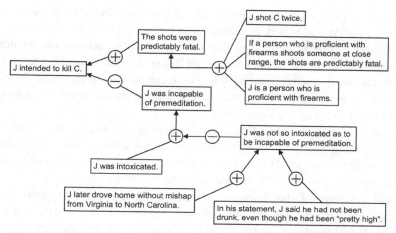

Figure 5.10: Pro and Con Arguments for a Claim about an Agent's Intention

the evidence was insufficient to support a finding that he had intended to kill her. The issue was one of intent. J claimed that there was not sufficient evidence of intent, whereas the prosecution claimed that the evidence was sufficient to prove intent.

This case is a good example of how there are pro arguments and con arguments in a case where a claim about an agent's intention has been disputed. In Figure 5.10, there is a pro argument at the top supporting the ultimate conclusion, the accusation that J intended to kill C. But there was also a con argument: J was said to be incapable of premeditation because he was too intoxicated. But at the bottom right there is an undercutter of the con argument. The undercutter argument is itself supported by two pro arguments.

This case shows how there is a network of connected pro and con arguments both supporting and attacking the claim that an agent intended to carry out an action. It shows that the method of determining whether an action is intentional or not in a given case depends on weighing the pro arguments against the con arguments. It also shows how such a weighing of evidence can be carried out using CAS.

5.10 Conclusions

How an explanation hangs together and makes sense as a sequence of plausible reasoning is shown in the analysis of the flagpole example displayed visually in Figure 5.7. Also shown by this diagram is how a chain of argumentation from an ultimate goal to an action that fulfills the goal maps into an explanation of how the goal was achieved. In contrast with the use of causal arrows by Bex et al. (2009), this model directly applies the argumentation scheme for practical reasoning. In common with the method of Bex et al. (2009), however, this way of representing practical reasoning in a case can display an argument. In this instance, it is argument from consequences supporting one of the elements of the script making up the explanation.

This new method was applied to the example of motive evidence displayed visually in Figure 5.9, showing that it is an extension using abductive reasoning to argue from the factual circumstances of the case to an agent's motive for intention first worked out in Walton and Schafer (2006).

The analysis of the flagpole example using argument diagrams and argumentation schemes in CAS has now shown how the same sequence of practical reasoning can represent both an argument and an explanation. Typically an agent in deliberation uses practical reasoning to reason forward from its goals and the known circumstances of the case to a decision to take action based on these considerations. This typical use of practical reasoning was illustrated in Chapter 1, to show that practical reasoning can be used in different ways. It was shown in Chapter 2 how practical reasoning was used in health product messages to try to persuade readers of the ad to buy a particular medication. In this kind of case, practical reasoning is used in a persuasion attempt in which the advertising agency has the goal of persuading the audience to buy the health product. In this use, one agent puts forward an argument to try to persuade another to carry out a recommended action. This use has been called persuasion over action (Atkinson et al., 2013).

Practical reasoning can also be used in a different way. One agent explains to a second agent how a third agent arrived at a decision to take action, based on the goals of the third agent and its knowledge of its circumstances when making the decision. Alternatively, it can be used by one agent in a similar way, to reason backward from observations about the actions and words of another agent to a hypothesis about the motive or intention of the second agent. As suggested in this chapter, this retrospective kind of reasoning can be modeled as an instance of IBE. It is this kind of retrospective practical reasoning that a historian uses to explain human actions based on historical data recorded in witness testimony and other sources of evidence. As the examples studied in this chapter show, this same kind of retrospective use of practical reasoning is highly characteristic of legal reasoning used in the most common examples of reasoning about evidence in criminal cases.

The problem with the BDI model has always been the lack of systematic evidential procedure that can be used to prove or disprove the ascription of an intention to an agent. The traditional problem of other minds in philosophy raises the question of how one agent can prove or disprove that another agent has a specific intention. How can a systematic procedure based on logical reasoning and external circumstantial evidence be empirically verified or falsified and used to support or undermine a hypothesis that an agent has a particular intention? As we have seen in this chapter, there have been some encouraging attempts to solve this problem. The use of argumentation schemes and argument diagramming tools employed by CAS as illustrated by the examples analyzed in this chapter have suggested an approach that runs along the same lines as some previous studies. But in this new approach the problem can be solved by seeing how practical reasoning is the glue that holds a script together so that it provides an explanation to an audience or speech partner in a multi-agent communication system. For an explanation to make sense, and thereby to convey understanding to another party or parties, all participants in the communication event must be able to grasp and apply practical reasoning, based on their common knowledge about the ways things generally work in familiar kinds of circumstances. It is these capabilities that enable agents to communicate by inferring each other's intentions.

The last example (analysis displayed in Figure 5.10) showed how ascribing an intention to an agent is typically based on a complex form of practical reasoning that has the graph structure defined in CAS to represent an argument map showing the marshaling of evidence in a given case. Using such an argumentation system has enabled us to overcome the state space explosion described in Chapter 1. What has been shown is that the procedure for verifying or falsifying a claim about whether an agent has a particular intention in a given case can be carried out using this argumentation model of weighing factual evidence on both sides of a disputed case.

6

Practical Argumentation in Deliberation Dialogue

In Chapter 2 it was shown how there are different frameworks of communication in which arguments can be put forward and critically questioned, including persuasion dialogue, information-seeking dialogue, and deliberation dialogue. This chapter will focus almost exclusively on deliberation dialogue, but will also deal with related issues where there is a shift to or from one of these other types of dialogue to deliberation dialogue. It will be shown how practical reasoning is woven through every aspect of deliberation dialogue, and how deliberation dialogue represents the necessary framework for analyzing and evaluating typical instances of practical reasoning in natural language cases of argumentation that we are all familiar with. This chapter will also show how formal models of deliberation dialogue built as artificial intelligence tools for multi-agent systems turn out to be extremely useful for solving the closure problem of practical reasoning in multi-agent settings.

The chapter begins by using four examples to show how practical reasoning is embedded in everyday deliberations of a kind all of us are familiar with. The first one, in Section 1, is a case of a man trying to solve the problem with his printer by looking on Google to get advice and then using a trial and error procedure to try to fix the problem. The second one, in Section 2, is an example of a couple trying to arrive at a decision on which home to buy, having narrowed the choices down to three candidates: a condominium, a two-story house, and a bungalow. The third one, in Section 3, is a case of a policy debate, showing how CAS employs practical reasoning in this setting. The fourth (Section 4), is a town hall meeting on a decision of whether or not to bring in no-fault insurance. Section 5 explains the essentials of the leading model of deliberation dialogue used in artificial intelligence at this point – the McBurney, Hitchcock, and Parsons (MHP) model.

Section 6 summarizes and explains an extension of the MHP model of deliberation dialogue recently developed by the author along with two colleagues in computer science (Walton, Norman, and Toniolo, 2015). In Section 7 it is shown how this system enables a practical reasoning agent to exploit an open knowledge base that makes it able to be aware of and to take advantage of knowledge about dynamic changes of its circumstances during all three stages of a deliberation dialogue. In Section 8 it is shown how the new model configures the speech act of putting forward a proposal in the context of group deliberations as a hypothesis that is put forward and advocated as the conclusion of an argument based on practical reasoning.

In computing, a protocol or communication protocol is a set of rules in which computers communicate with each other. The protocol says what part of the conversation comes at which time. It also says how to end the communication. Protocols governing the moves in a rational deliberation, including such moves as putting forward a proposal and responding to it, are formulated in Section 8. In Section 9 a set of ten criteria for determining when to properly close off the sequence of practical reasoning in a delibera-tion dialogue is presented. It is argued that a natural deliberation dialogue suitable for realistic applications in computing may be successful even if the decision on what to do, or how to solve the problem set at the opening the stage of dialogue, has not been made. Section 10 summarizes the features of the new model of deliberation dialogue advocated in the chapter, and sum-marizes ten conclusions reached in the chapter. These include the conclusion that deliberation dialogue can be classified into four subtypes: single-agent and multi-agent problem-solving, policy debate, personal and small group decision-making, and civic decision-making. It is also concluded that prac-tical reasoning needs to be seen as the main form of argumentation used in these kinds of deliberation dialogue.

6.1 The Printer Example

In this case (Walton, Norman, and Toniolo, 2015), Brian had a problem with his printer. Every time he printed a scanned document using the automatic document feeder (ADF) of his printer, a black line appeared down the middle of the page. To solve the problem he put these words into Google: "[name of model of printer] makes black line down the middle of page when using scanner." One of the findings the search produced was the manufacturer's manual for this type of printer. It contained a troubleshooting guide with a list of instructions, including the following ones. First, it gave this instruction: "if this problem happens when you print and when you copy/scan, the problem is in the print engine itself." If this was deemed to be the case, it gave the name of a site for troubleshooting help. However, the black line only occurred when he scanned pages from the ADF. In this case, the troubleshooting guide[1] gave the following series of instructions to solve the problem.

1. Open the Automatic Document Feeder cover and carefully check for any debris inside or on the rollers.
2. Open the scanner lid and examine the opening where the paper exits the ADF for any debris.
3. When scanning through the ADF the paper does not pass over the main glass area; there is a small strip of glass at the edge that it is passed over. Carefully clean this glass with a soft dry lint-free cloth.
4. On certain models the strip of glass is covered by a plastic piece; remove it and clean the glass underneath and the underside of the strip.
5. Try another scan/copy.

Brian followed the instructions and opened the scanner cover; he checked for debris, and found none. Next he located the strip of glass and cleaned it with a soft cloth. Then he scanned a document to see if this had solved the problem. He observed that the problem of the black line appearing down the middle of the printed page had not been solved. At that point he was not sure what to do, but he examined the small strip of glass once again. He saw that it there was a thin plastic film covering the strip of glass. He put his fingernail underneath the edge of the plastic film, and could see that it was flexible enough that it could possibly be removed. Although he was not sure that it was a good idea to meddle with it, he tried to pull at the edges of the plastic piece from different directions. The result of these efforts was that he managed to remove the plastic strip from the piece of glass. Having removed it, he could see that it had been secured under the frame around the glass by plastic clips. After examining the plastic piece more carefully, he found a small black mark at the bottom in the middle of the clear plastic. He tried cleaning the plastic to remove the black mark using a soft cloth and some optical cleaner fluid that is usually used for cleaning glasses.

He then scanned a test document. Again, the black mark was printed in the middle of the test document. Next he considered whether there might be some other way to remove the black mark. He showed the plastic piece with the black mark on it, which had resisted his cleaning attempts, to his wife Anna, to ask for advice. She took the plastic piece and applied a soft cleaning pad and some dishwashing detergent to the black mark. After careful rubbing, the black mark disappeared. Brian took the plastic part back to the printer and inserted it in its

---

[1] www.scribd.com/doc/227140958/Printer-manual-for-Samsung-SCX-3405FW%scribd.

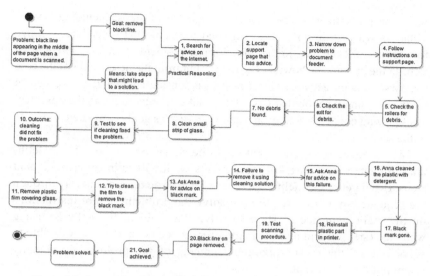

Figure 6.1: Sequence of Problem-solving in the Printer Example

original position so that it was secured over the narrow piece of glass in the printer. He once again went through the scanning procedure and found that there was no black line down the middle of the page. The page had printed in a normal manner. This final test showed that Brian's problem was solved. In this case the argumentation might be classified as problem-solving rather than deliberation.

The sequence of problem-solving actions is shown in Figure 6.1. As suggested by the hawk example in Chapter 4, problem-solving can be seen as a type of deliberation that uses practical reasoning. In Brian's case it was mainly a solitary problem of deliberation where a single agent had a problem and took action to solve it. However, other agents were involved as well.

This case should be classified as an instance of problem-solving deliberation where a single agent collects information, takes actions, and along with them seeks advice to help solve a problem. The sequence starts with the formulation of a problem, in this case the problem of the black line appearing in the middle of the page when a document is scanned. This is a problem because the printer is not supposed to print a black line in the middle of the page and it looks unattractive, interfering with the usability of the printed page.

Note that the sequence involves practical reasoning, as shown in the top right of Figure 6.1. Brian's goal is to remove the black line, and his problem is to find some satisfactory means to remove it. However, finding the right means to solve the problem involves a lengthy sequence of steps, including several instances where trial and error is needed to enable the procedure to move forward toward the solution of the ultimate problem. There are twenty-one steps in the procedure shown in Figure 6.1, but from the description of the case we can see that the actual sequence of steps is considerably longer, if we were to fill in every small action that Brian had to take in order to get to the next step. The carrying out of the actions that achieved Brian's goal culminated at step 21 in the sequence.

The sequence represents what might be considered to be solitary deliberation for the most part, but other agents are involved in some significant steps. Brian gets some help from other agents as he reasons his way through the sequence of actions required to solve the problem: he got instructions on the main sequence of steps to solve the problem from the Samsung webpage (step 2), and he asked Anna for advice (step 15). She was able to solve one of the most important elements of the problem by actually removing the black spot.

Advice-seeking and information-seeking intervals were important at other points in the sequence. In order to find out how to solve the problem, Brian spent some time searching on Google. To start with, he tried various combinations of keywords. For example, he tried searching using the expression, "black line down the middle of the page." These searches did turn up some interesting information and helpful hints. There were people who had posted hints saying that the problem had to do with the glass plate, and instructions were given to clean the glass plate with a soft cloth to remove any stains or marks that might be on it. This information by itself, however, did not solve the problem. It was important to realize that there was a narrow glass plate to the left of the large glass plate, and that the source of the problem was the plastic cover on the narrow glass plate. After trying various permutations and combinations, Brian finally managed to get the information that proved to be useful by adding the identification number of the type of printer, and including the word "scan" in the expression put into Google, as indicated above.

Thus, one important thing to remember about this case is that the deliberation dialogue that led to the solution of the problem was based on prior information-seeking and advice-seeking intervals, and it would not have been possible for the deliberation dialogue to reach a successful conclusion without these intervals. Moreover, it could also be noted that the information-seeking dialogue was interwoven with the steps taken during the sequence of practical reasoning in the deliberation dialogue. Brian had to record the precise instructions from the Samsung website and carefully go through a process of grasping what they meant and how they could be applied to the actions of finding and cleaning the glass plate in a way that would solve his problem. He had to explain the problem to Anna, including telling her about his attempts to solve it and how they had been unsuccessful. Before Brian found the instructions on the Samsung website, he had to search many websites using keywords, and to evaluate which of them showed promise of offering useful advice of the kind he required. The instructions that proved to be useful were stated on the website as a procedure that offers advice to the user on how to solve the problem.

6.2 The Real Estate Example

In the second case, first used in Walton (2011c), Alice and Bob moved from Edmonton to Windsor, and they are in the process of trying to find a house. They have narrowed their choices down to three homes: a condominium, a two-story house, and a bungalow. Currently, they are renting an apartment and would like to find a suitable house as soon as possible. In analyzing the case, it is significant to note that Bob and Alice share the values of health, saving costs, and preserving the environment. They sit down to discuss the matter and have a lengthy dialogue in which they examine all the pros and cons of each choice. Quoted below (with some minor changes) is a short segment of the longer dialogue from Walton (2011c, p. 3). This dialogue was also used as an example in Walton, Norman, and Toniolo (2015, p. 5).

BOB: The condo and the bungalow are in the same area, where I can ride to work on my bike in 35 minutes. The bike path goes right along the river straight to my office.

ALICE: The problem with the two story house is that it is twice as far away as the two other homes. It would take over an hour for you to ride the bike in from there.

BOB: If we lived there, I would have to drive the car to work most days.

ALICE: Riding the bike to work is more environmentally friendly. Also, you really like riding your bike to work, and it is good exercise.

BOB: Yes, and there is also the factor of the cost of gas. The cost of driving to work adds up to a significant amount over a year. Also, neither of us likes spending a lot of time in the car. It is wasted time, and getting exercise is a good way to spend that time. When you spend your whole day working on a computer, it is necessary for health to get some exercise.

ALICE: That is offset by the lower taxes of the two story house, because it is outside the city, even though it is a larger house.

BOB: I say let's make an offer on the condo.

One method that they could use to help them arrive at a decision is to identify all of the pro and con arguments for each option, and then compare them to see which one stands up best. In Walton (2011c), factors supporting and undermining the arguments in this example (actually a more lengthy variant of it) were compared to determine which option has the most positive and the least negative factors. However, here a different approach is taken that follows the general methodology of argument evaluation in CAS.

In this case, Alice and Bob have narrowed the decision down to three choices, and there are three values involved. A full argumentation model of deliberation would need to be broader in scope, in that it would also need to take into account the prior part of the discussion where Alice and Bob narrowed the proposals down to these three options. In Walton (2011c) there were three proposals in this model: to buy the bungalow, to buy the condo, and to buy the two-story house.

The argumentation method applied to the dialogue above builds a large argument map containing all the pro and con arguments put forward during the dialogue and then uses argumentation tools to judge which arguments are stronger and which arguments are weaker. For example, in the dialogue segment quoted above, there is a network of argumentation supporting the choice in favor of the condo or bungalow. Bob can ride to work on his bike from the condo or the bungalow in 35 minutes. Riding a bike to work is environmentally friendly. Bob likes riding his bike to work, and it is good exercise. Figure 6.2 is an argument diagram that represents the arguments for the condo. This diagram has been drawn in the style of CAS with the ultimate conclusion, the proposition that they should buy the condo, shown at the left.

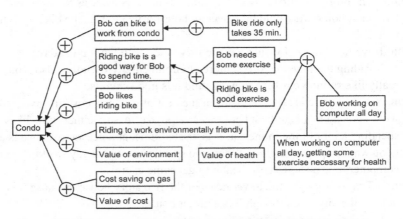

Figure 6.2: CAS Argument Map of Arguments Supporting the Condo Choice

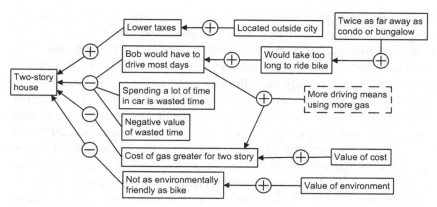

Figure 6.3: CAS Argument Map of Arguments against the Two-story Choice

There are five main pro arguments shown supporting the ultimate conclusion, and a premise in each of these pro arguments is supported by additional arguments.

There are also other arguments woven into the dialogue. For example, Bob adds that the cost of driving to work would be more for the two-story house because it is twice as far away as the other two homes. As shown in Figure 6.3, there are three con arguments attacking the proposal to buy the two-story house, and only one argument supporting it.

The three con arguments against the conclusion to buy the two-story house shown in Figure 6.3 all have pro arguments supporting them. On a casual inspection, it looks like there is not much of a contest. The arguments for buying the condo are overwhelming.

It is also possible to draw up a comparable argument diagram showing the pro and con arguments with respect to the option of buying the bungalow. However, having gone this far, it would also be possible to include the arguments for and against the third option and put the three argument diagrams together, building a much larger argument diagram showing the pro and con arguments supporting or rebutting each of the three choices. However, as we will go on to show in this chapter, it is not that easy. Determining the best choice also needs to identify some other features of the deliberation dialogue and take them into account.

It will be shown in the rest of the chapter that deliberation is best seen as a resource-bounded procedure that has an opening stage in which a choice has to be made, then goes through an argumentation stage where the pro and con arguments are considered and directed against each other. Finally, the procedure reaches a closing stage where the decision is arrived at on the basis of the pro and con arguments that interacted with each other in the argumentation stage (Walton and Krabbe, 1995). According to the MHP dialogue model (McBurney, Hitchcock, and Parsons, 2007), deliberation is a formal procedure that goes through several stages. At one point in the sequence, after a brainstorming process, competing proposals are put forward by parties to the discussion, and then there is an intervening stage where the parties support their own proposals with arguments and attack the competing proposals of the other parties using arguments. Many of these arguments would have the form of practical reasoning. In an argumentation-based formal model of deliberation dialogue, these matters would be brought in and considered during an argumentation stage where factual evidence of the circumstances (brought in from a knowledge base) is marshaled to support or attack proposals. Finally, there has to be a closing stage, where a decision is made that enough relevant information concerning the circumstances of a given case has been taken into account so that the pro and con arguments can be weighed against each other.

6.3 The Carneades Policy Modeling Tool

In the real estate example the main part of the discussion was carried on by the two principal participants, the husband and wife deciding which home to buy. Another type of discussion in which practical reasoning is used is the policy debate, where the participants are not arguing about which specific course of action to take in a given set of circumstances, but are discussing which of the several policies they are considering is the best. This is a different type of dialogue. It seems to be a kind of deliberation because the adoption of the policy has consequences, and hence the focus of the discussion is which of the policies has the best consequences, as opposed to the alternative policies being discussed. But in certain respects it also seems to be a persuasion dialogue because the participants are putting forward pro and con arguments with respect to all of the policies being discussed. Each participant puts forward pro arguments that support his or her own policy, and puts forward con arguments that attack the opposing policies. It is quite likely, of course, that in some parts it will combine both types of dialogue by shifting from deliberation on what to do to arguments about the factual circumstances of the case that are relevant to the policies being considered. In any event, policy debates represent a common setting in which practical reasoning is used.

CAS has a policy modeling tool that guides the user through the arguments on all sides of a policy debate.[2] This tool can not only help you to form your opinion by finding arguments both for and against it, but can also compare it to alternative positions. To use the tool the user must log in using a pseudonym, and begin by reading an introduction to the topic of the debate. The user then selects an issue of interest and answers a series of multiple-choice questions about the issue. There is an option to view quotations of arguments already formulated about the issue from source documents. The policy tool creates an argument graph comparing these opinions and the arguments for and against them. Anyone who wants to use the policy modeling tool begins by selecting an issue from a given set of issues that are taken to be of interest and for which concrete policies have been proposed. The policy modeling tool simulates the legal effects of the policy proposal on the facts of a given test case. The user can then browse the argument diagram constructed during the procedure to see how conclusions have been drawn by applying the policies to the facts.

How the argumentation scheme for value-based practical reasoning is used by the policy modeling tool can be shown by presenting a simplified version of an example of an argument on copyright policy.[3] In general outline, the example fits the scheme for value-based practical reasoning explained in Chapter 1. The goal is to achieve a state in which it is easier for researchers and students to work in more than one member state in the European Community. The action recommended is to harmonize the copyright exceptions. The values promoted are those of efficiency, legal certainty, scientific research, and education. The conclusion of this pro argument is that the permitted exceptions should be harmonized so that they are available in all member states.

However, in one respect, the value-based scheme used in the Carneades policy modeling tool is more complex than the one described in Chapter 1. There is an additional premise describing the circumstances of the case in which the decision has to be made. This version of the scheme is based on the action-based alternating transition systems model of Atkinson and Bench-Capon (2007). The circumstances given for the argument outlined above are that researchers and students increasingly work in more than one member state, and the patchy availability of exceptions makes their work more difficult. But to adapt the example to the simpler format of the practical reasoning scheme described in Chapter 1, the circumstances could be

---

[2] http://localhost:8080/policymodellingtool/home.html
[3] http://carneades.github.io/carneades/Carneades/

described as the problem that is confronted by the policymakers. Instead of setting out the circumstances as an additional premise, to process the example here we will use the simpler version of the scheme for value-based practical reasoning discussed in Chapter 1:

> Goal Premise: G is the goal to be achieved.
> Means Premise: Performing action A would realize G.
> Values Premise: Achieving the goal G would promote the value V.
> Conclusion: Presumably, action A should be performed.

The word "presumably" in the conclusion makes it clear that practical reasoning is defeasible, and is therefore subject to critical questions, such as the following ones:

CQ_1: Is there another action that would realize the goal G more effectively than A?

CQ_2: Is there another action that would promote the value V more effectively than A?

CQ_3: Would performing A have side effects which demote V or some other value?

Fitting the given argument to the requirements of the scheme produces the following reconstruction of its structure as an instance of value-based practical reasoning:

> Goal: to make it easier for researchers and students to work in more than one member state.
> Means: harmonizing copyright exceptions would make it easier for researchers and students to work in more than one member state.
> Values: efficiency, legal certainty, scientific research, and education are promoted by making it easier for researchers and students to work in more than one member state.
> Conclusion: copyright exceptions should be harmonized among the member states.

The analysis of this example produced by the Carneades policy modeling tool shows how the initial argument can be contested by two means. One is by a putting forward a counter-argument also based on value-based practical reasoning. The other is by the asking of a critical question.

First, let's consider the counter-argument, formulated below as fitting the scheme for value-based practical reasoning given above. The circumstances of the case that provide part of the background of the example are the proposition

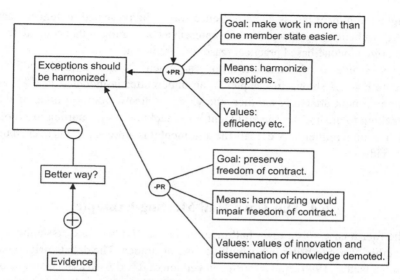

Figure 6.4: Structure of the Argumentation on Copyright Policy

that the current situation in which copyright exceptions are not harmonized facilitates freedom of contract:

Goal: drafting copyright legislation to recognize and preserve the basic principle of freedom of contract.

Means: harmonizing copyright exceptions would impair freedom of contract.

Values: impairing freedom of contract demotes the values of innovation and dissemination of knowledge.

Conclusion: copyright exceptions should not be harmonized among the member states.

When put in this form, the counter-argument above can be seen to be a rebuttal of the previous argument. The reason is that the conclusion of the counter-argument is the negation of the conclusion of the prior argument. The counter-argument is shown at the bottom right in Figure 6.4.

The second way to contest the original argument is to ask a critical question. Consider, for example, the following critical question:

CQ4: Are there better ways to promote the values of efficiency, legal certainty, research, and education other than harmonizing copyright exceptions?

This critical question could raise doubts by suggesting that there might be a better way to promote the values in the case. But by itself it would not defeat the original argument unless some evidence was to be presented to suggest that there is a better way. If so, it would represent a con argument that could defeat the original value-based practical reasoning argument.

The structure of the undercutting argument is shown at the left in Figure 6.4. As shown in Chapter 3, an undercutter is modeled in CAS as one argument attacking another, shown as an arrow from the node of the attacking to the node of the argument it is attacking. As for burden of proof, such an undercutter only defeats the argument it is aimed at if it is backed up by evidence.

6.4 The Town Hall Meeting Example

The fourth case was a town hall meeting in the Rhode Island Assembly on whether or not to bring in no-fault vehicle insurance. The debate originated from Lascher (1999), and a shortened version of it was used as an example of deliberation dialogue in Walton (1990a, 169). Reformers advocated bringing in a no-fault system similar to that being used in other states. The problem posed was the perception that insurance rates in Rhode Island were too high and had become increasingly burdensome for average citizens. The reformers argued that the change to a no-fault system would lower the cost of insurance. The opponents used two counter-arguments. One was that the no-fault system would fail to lower premiums. Another was that no-fault insurance would unfairly make good drivers pay for bad drivers. It is easy to see that the argumentation on both sides took the form of argument from consequences, possibly the most common form of argument in current political argumentation in democratic countries. Another argument against bringing in no-fault insurance was that encouraging competition is an important goal for the insurance industry. We can also see that goals and practical reasoning are parts of this argument. The argument is that encouraging competition is a goal, and that bringing in no-fault insurance would presumably go against the achievement of that goal, whereas staying with the current system of automobile insurance would promote the goal of competition in the insurance industry. This line of argument has to do with choosing actions that will fulfill worthy goals.

The printer example can be contrasted with the other three examples because it was a case of (at least mainly) solitary decision-making by a single agent, whereas the other three cases were group deliberations that involved argumentation between two or more main parties in the deliberations. The real estate example was relatively simple compared to the policy-making example because in the real estate example there were only two stakeholders involved in the decision-making. Other agents – for example, the real estate salesperson – provided information to Alice and Bob. The town hall meeting example was a deliberation on a much larger scale. It was a multi-agent deliberation that took place as a public assembly in a town hall meeting.

The literature in philosophy on practical reasoning at first concentrated on the single agent case, exemplified by the printer example, as shown in Chapter 1. As the real estate example showed, it is easy to generalize to a case where two agents are trying to decide what to do in a situation that affects both of them. The recent literature on practical reasoning in artificial intelligence, however, covers much broader kinds of cases of collective policy-making.

Practical reasoning is foundational to current research initiatives in computing, especially in artificial intelligence, including the project of designing systems for electronic democracy based on practical reasoning. In this regard, the third example can be taken as the best paradigm for building a model of deliberation suitable for such purposes. Practical reasoning is a fundamental argumentation structure for multi-agent systems, especially in systems of electronic democracy, where the purpose of the system is to look at ways and means of carrying out political goals based on intelligent deliberation in a democratic system. The capability of the system to pose critical questions for a proposed plan of action is vital for this application, as such deliberations are only useful if weak points in a proposal can be questioned. The capability of the user, or the system itself, to pose and reply to counter-arguments is important as well. However, a system to represent practical reasoning fully, and especially one that would take into account all the critical questions and opposed modes of argumentation that could be brought to bear, would be highly complex. Even so, it is necessary to build accessible systems that will resemble natural language argumentation and be easy to use.

Gordon and Karacapilidis (1997) undertook the research project of designing and implementing a mediation system to be used on the Internet to enable interested citizens and representatives of public interest groups to take part in electronic discussions with government officials planning public projects, such as zoning ordinances. The persons taking part in the discussion could include experts, such as city planners, as well as politicians and ordinary citizens who wanted to make their opinions known, or to interact in discussion with those implementing the system. In their study they reviewed formal models of argumentation that can be adapted to AI to represent knowledge and arguments in a way that could be used to assist the project. The problem they encountered is that arguments and other speech acts expressed by the parties in the dialogue had to be represented in a simple enough way that laypersons could use it. The system they developed to solve this problem, called the Zeno argumentation framework, was too difficult for laypersons to use effectively. There is danger of a "digital divide" (Gordon and Richter, 2002, 248), in which not all stakeholders have effective access to the process of e-democracy.

There seems to be little doubt that the possibility of developing widely useful systems of e-democracy requires a blend of argumentation theory, including argumentation schemes and typologies of dialogue, with formal models of reasoning of the kind that have been developed in AI. Constructing such systems doesn't seem to be the problem. The problem is one of making different systems that can be adapted to the needs of different implementations. In particular, for electronic democracy projects, the problem is how to design an argumentation-based AI system that is simple enough for laypersons to use in questioning a policy or task and arguing about it. There is little doubt that the model of practical reasoning that should be used needs to be simple enough for laypersons to easily use it without becoming frustrated by communication difficulties. These observations suggest that we need to begin with simple models even though we know that more fully adequate models will have various levels of complexity.

Atkinson, Bench-Capon, and McBurney (2004b) have devised a structure called the Parmenides System that can be used by a democratic government to solicit public input, viewpoints, and arguments on a contemplated policy. Once a specific policy is formulated, critics are allowed to pose a range of critical questions. The policy is formulated in the practical reasoning format, with a goal and proposed means to achieve the goal being stated. The system solicits criticisms of the policy by allowing justifications of the policy to be presented, and a succession of screens then allows the critics to present objections to the actions and goals that are part of the policy. The critical questions raise doubts about connections between goals and values, as well as connections between presumed consequences of the actions. They also allow for consideration of alternative actions to the one proposed, and the respondent can challenge the description of the fact situation.

6.5 The McBurney, Hitchcock, and Parsons Model

McBurney, Hitchcock, and Parsons (2007) utilize the concept of an action and the concept of a goal in building their formal deliberation system. An action is described as a sentence, possibly a speech act, which may be undertaken and recommended as a result of deliberation. The goal is described as a sentence representing a future world state external to the dialogue. The facts are described as sentences expressing some possible states of affairs external to the dialogue. The dialogue itself has an opening stage where the question is raised about what is to be done, and a closing stage where the sequence of deliberation is ended. This special question raised at the opening stage is called the governing question, meaning that this single question governs the whole dialogue, including the opening and closing stages. On the MHP model, the dialogue runs through a sequence of eight stages (McBurney, Hitchcock, and Parsons, 2007). As with all normative models of dialogue, the sequence of stages represented in the model does not necessarily represent the temporal sequence of how a discussion actually proceeds in a real case:

1. The Opening Stage. The governing question is raised.
2. The Inform Stage. There is a discussion of goals, and constraints on the actions or facts relevant to the discussion are considered.
3. The Propose Stage. Proposals for possible action are brought forward.
4. The Consider Stage. Comments on proposals, most notably arguments for and against the proposals, are put forward.
5. The Revise Stage. There is an opportunity to revise goals and the actions that have been proposed, as well as relevant facts that have been collected.
6. The Recommend Stage. At this stage participants can recommend a particular action and the other participants can either accept or reject this option.
7. The Confirm Stage. At this stage, all participants must confirm their acceptance of one particular option for action in order for the dialogue to terminate.
8. The Close Stage. At this point the dialogue terminates.

Looking over the whole sequence of dialogue, the following general outline can be observed. First, there is the opening stage, where the problem of what to do is posed by putting forward a governing question. This governing question is binding on the participants' arguments in all subsequent stages. What is or is not relevant at these subsequent stages is determined by the governing question set at the opening stage. Second, the facts that are relevant to the governing question are collected and made available to all participants, so that a body of data that is relevant to the governing question is then available to the participants. The factual data are not regarded as beyond questioning. Third, there is a stage where proposals for action are put forward. These proposals represent ways that the advocate of the proposal puts forward means to solve the problem posed in the opening stage. Fourth, there is a *consider* procedure, where arguments are brought forward both for and against the proposals.

It is important to recognize that arguments for or against propositions claimed to be factual are put forward at stage 5, suggesting a shift to a different type of dialogue. McBurney, Hitchcock, and Parsons (2007, 102) note that another type of dialogue – for example, an information-seeking dialogue or persuasion dialogue – may be embedded in the deliberation dialogue during this stage.

Naturally, during this stage the proposals are likely to be defended from the criticisms or counter-arguments that have been put forward. As noted by McBurney, Hitchcock, and Parsons, this procedure of attack and defense of the proposals will tend to take the form of a persuasion dialogue in which the factual evidence is used to supply premises to build pro and con arguments concerning the proposals. In such a case, two types of dialogue will be open at the same time: a deliberation dialogue and a persuasion dialogue. Hence, what happens at this stage is naturally modeled by describing it as a shift to a persuasion dialogue that is embedded in the deliberation dialogue during this part of the procedure. A natural aspect of considering both sides of each proposal is that proposals may be revised, or perhaps even retracted altogether. This does not mean, however, that all proposals except one will be eliminated. Several proposals may survive this procedure of attack and defense. Therefore, in order to reach the closing stage, there must be what McBurney, Hitchcock, and Parsons call the confirm stage, where the participants reach some agreement, based on the prior stage, on which proposal appears to be the best one to proceed with. There may be various ways to accomplish this agreement. For example, there may be a discussion of the pros and cons, and then a vote based on the discussion. Once this decision is made, the deliberation can be closed off.

At the opening stage of a deliberation dialogue an agent has to make a decision about a course of action to choose in a given set of circumstances in which a choice has to be made. Typically the choice has to be made because even doing nothing can be viewed as a choice. The deliberation dialogue always arises out of the problem posed by the question of what to do in any given set of circumstances. The issue to be resolved by such a dialogue is the question of what to do. This issue is the starting point of the dialogue and pervades the whole dialogue from the opening to the closing stage. For example, suppose there has been an emergency where a city has been flooded and a decision has to be made about what action to take. Should federal agencies such as the armed forces be called in right away? The choice to be made is whether federal agencies should be called in or not. Making this choice is the problem to be solved at this juncture. It is the decision to be made. It is the issue that defines the deliberation as a dialogue that has a goal. Simply put, the goal is for the participants to find the right decision on whether to call in the federal agencies or not. After the opening stage has been concluded, the dialogue moves to the argumentation stage.

The first step in the argumentation stage is to inform the agent(s) what the circumstances are. However, because an informed deliberation is better than one carried out in ignorance of the circumstances, and because in many instances knowledge of the circumstances may be considerable, there may be a need for a lengthy search to find information that is important for arriving at an informed decision. Hence, in a rational deliberation it is vitally important to collect as much relevant data as time and costs permit. Typically there is a significant trade-off between making a timely decision versus collecting more data. Delaying too long while collecting data can be procrastination that is very harmful to rational deliberation. On the other hand, making a decision in the absence of adequate knowledge of the situation can be an instance of the fallacy of jumping to a conclusion. For these reasons, in the model of rational deliberation proposed below, there needs to be an information-seeking dialogue embedded in the deliberation dialogue. Also, because the information relevant to the circumstances can be so vital to arriving at a rational decision, the collection of information on the changing circumstances needs to be seen as the key requirement for intelligent deliberation.

The information-seeking part is placed at the beginning of the middle stage, but this information needs to be updated during the entire argumentation stage, as shown in Figure 6.5. Another key feature in the argumentation stage is the putting forward of proposals by the participants, using the speech act of making a proposal. It is similar to the speech act of putting forward an argument, but different from it and needs to be seen as a distinctive type of speech act important for argumentation in its own right (Walton, 2005).

Once some proposals have been put forward, the dialogue reaches the third part of the middle stage. McBurney, Hitchcock, and Parsons divided this stage into two separate stages: the consider stage and the revise stage. During these stages each party raises critical questions and poses counter-arguments to the proposal. Typically one agent attacks another's proposal by claiming that implementing it would have negative consequences. In reply, the other agent may move by modifying or retracting the proposal. The agent may refine the proposal – for example, by making qualifications to it – so that its implementation is restricted in some way. Considering and revising naturally go together because they typically need to be based on counter-arguments or critical questions that show weaknesses in the proposal.

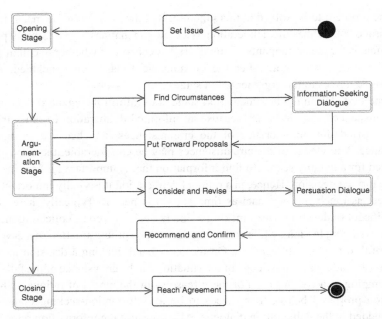

Figure 6.5: Outline of the MHP Model

The MHP model (2007) requires that unanimity of the participants is necessary for a decision to be taken to close the dialogue, but they add that this assumption is made for purposes of simplicity. However, in real instances of deliberation, for many reasons the dialogue, even though it has been useful, may arrive at no unanimous agreement on the best proposal. In such a case, in the MHP model the dialogue is a failure, because the argumentation in it has not unanimously resolved the issue set in the governing question. But an apparently failed deliberation of this sort could have been very helpful. It could have eliminated some proposals that were seriously being considered. The pro and con arguments might have brought out deficiencies in some of the proposals, showing that they would not work, and that they may even have unacceptable consequences.

It is interesting to note that McBurney, Hitchcock, and Parsons state that the only stages which must occur in every dialogue that terminates normally are the opening stage and the closing stage. It follows that in the MHP model every deliberation dialogue must reach the closing stage to be successful. In the MHP model, a deliberation dialogue is only successful if it terminates in a closing stage where a decision is unanimously arrived at on the best course of action to take.

This property raises some issues about the applicability of this model to real cases, and the inevitable limitations of the model to represent significant cases of political decision-making are discussed by McBurney, Hitchcock, and Parsons (2007, 19). They discussed a number of normative principles of formal dialogue systems generally, among which they include a discussion of something called the principle of rational mutual inquiry (Hitchcock, 1991). According to this principle, the primary goal of the dialogue is to secure rational agreements by the participants on how to answer a governing question specified in the dialogue. But the following subsidiary goal of such a dialogue is also acknowledged: if the participants cannot agree on an answer to the governing question, they may be able to achieve the more limited goal of reaching agreement on why they did not succeed in answering the governing question. This remark is a revealing comment on the general problem of formulating goals in formal systems of dialogue. It also affects the persuasion type of dialogue. In general, the goal of a persuasion dialogue is to resolve the conflict of opinions agreed upon as the issue at the opening stage. As has been shown, however (Walton and Krabbe, 1995), a persuasion dialogue can be very successful educationally in revealing the arguments and positions on both sides – even deepening them and enabling greater sophistication in expressing the positions of both. This goal of exposing the arguments and deepening the positions on both sides may be achieved even though the persuasion dialogue did not succeed in resolving the conflict of opinions by proving that the thesis of the one side is true and the thesis of the other side is false. So, this problem of determining the criteria of success of a dialogue in meeting its goal is a general one for formal dialogue systems, and is not unique to this model of deliberation dialogue.

As is usual in formal models of argumentation dialogues, there are protocols covering what moves can be made by each party, and how each party has to react to a particular type of move made by the other party. Hence, it is necessary in such a formal model to define the types of so-called locutions that can be made by each party in a particular move. Among the different kinds of locutions that represent permissible moves in MHP deliberation dialogue, the following ones should be noted. These types of dialogue moves are now commonly called speech acts in the literature on formal dialogue systems. They define the speech act of *propose* as a valid instance of the type of speech act containing a goal, a fact, and an action, including some other elements called constraint, evaluation, and perspective. They also have speech acts for making an assertion, preferring a particular option for action, asking the other party to justify an assertion, pronouncing on whether a proposal for action should be accepted or rejected, retracting a previous locution, and withdrawing from the deliberation dialogue. Additionally, they indicate which locutions are permissible at which stages of the dialogue.

To illustrate how their formal model applies to real cases, they offer the example of a deliberation about what action to take concerning potential health hazards from the use of cell phones. Here we merely offer a simplified account, somewhat modified, of how this kind of deliberation dialogue might be expected to play out in a particular case. The governing question, stated at the opening of the dialogue, is what to do about the health risk posed by mobile phones. The participants put forward arguments concerning the degree of risk, and move to an 'informed' stage to consider the factual data about the degree of risk posed by the use of cell phones. One participant puts forward an argument about the economic costs of medical harm caused by extensive use of cell phones. This could lead to factual issues, for example, concerning relevant medical statistics citing correlations between brain cancer and extensive use of cell phones. One proposal is to prohibit the sale of cell phones. Another proposal does nothing to prohibit the sale of cell phones. Another proposal is to limit usage. An argument put forward is that limiting usage is not practical. From these remarks the reader can easily get a rough idea of how a realistic case of deliberation could be modeled using the formal dialogue framework outlined above.

6.6 Speech Acts in a Deliberation Dialogue

In the well-known classification of speech acts of Searle (1969), the speech act of proposing lies between the speech act he calls a "directive," in which the speaker tries to get the hearer to carry out a course of action, and a "commissive," a speech act that commits the speaker to a particular course of action. It seems accurate to claim that the speech act of proposing commits the speaker to something. But does it commit the speaker to the particular course of action contained in the proposal? Suppose that Bob and Alice are deliberating on whether to make an offer on a house, and Bob says "I propose that we make an offer on the house." Does saying this commit Bob to the action of making an offer on the house? There may be some doubt about this. For one thing, Bob and Alice will presumably be making the offer jointly, as a couple. So just by making this proposal, Bob is not committing himself.

Instead, it seems more accurate to say that Bob is claiming that making an offer on the house seems like it would be a good idea as far as he is concerned, and he is asking Alice whether she thinks it would be a good course of action or not. Also, when Bob makes this proposal, if Alice accepts it, then Bob has committed himself to join with her in going ahead with the action of making an offer on the house. So, certainly commitment is involved. But Searle claims that the speech act of making a proposal lies between that of a directive and a commissive speech act. Hence, Searle may be saying that when the speaker makes a proposal for a course of action, it is not to say that the speaker is fully committed to that course of action. It seems, rather, that the speaker is making some sort of commitment indicating that he is recommending the action, unless the other parties involved can find something objectionable about the proposal.

In Searle's account of the felicity conditions for the speech acts of requesting and proposing (as summarized in the table given in Aakus, 2006, 409), the following characteristics of the speech act of proposing are worth mentioning. The first is that both the speaker and the hearer are able to contribute to the accomplishment of the action contained in the speaker's proposal. The second one is that it is not obvious to both parties that either of them can carry out this action on their own. The third one is that the speaker believes that carrying out the action will mutually benefit both parties, or at least the speaker believes they will be no worse off. The fourth condition is that the speaker's making a proposal needs to count as an attempt to enlist the hearer in mutually bringing about the action contained in the proposal.

Kauffeld (1998, 248) defines the speech act of making a proposal as making a statement of resolve expressing a determination or conclusion that the speaker has reached. In his view, when a speaker makes a proposal he or she must intend that her statement provides the hearer with reason to raise questions, doubts, and objections about the statement. This way of defining the speech act of making a proposal appears to mean that a speaker who makes a proposal has an obligation or burden of proof, if it can be called that, to defend it against any doubts or objections raised by the hearer. The issue of whether there is a burden of proof to the speech act of making a proposal will be taken up in Chapter 7.

The participants in a deliberation dialogue take turns making moves during the argumentation stage. Each move a participant makes must take the form of one of several distinctive types of speech acts:

- The speech act of making a proposal
- The speech act of retracting a proposal
- The speech act of making an assertion
- The speech act of retracting an assertion
- The speech act of putting forward an argument
- The speech act of asking a question

- The speech act of asking a critical question
- The speech act of articulating a goal
- The speech act of defending a goal
- The speech act of attacking a goal

The key to understanding the speech act structure of deliberation dialogue is to realize that the speech act of making a proposal has the structure of practical reasoning. When an agent makes a proposal, the proposal can be seen as having three parts, corresponding to the two premises and conclusion of the practical inference. The conclusion is that the participants in the deliberation should move forward by committing themselves to carrying out a particular action. One premise is that the group of agents in the deliberation share a particular goal. The other premise is a statement to the effect that the action designated in the conclusion is the best means to carry out that goal in the given circumstances. Thus, any instance of the speech act of making a proposal in deliberation takes the form of the following type of practical inference:

We as a group share goal G.
In the given circumstances carrying out action A is necessary/sufficient to fulfill G.
We should commit ourselves to carrying out action A.

To put this idea another way, the speech act of making a proposal has the structure of practical argument. Any proposal made in a deliberation recommends that the participants as a group should carry out a particular action A. This recommendation is based on the presumed goals of the group and the means that are held to be necessary are sufficient to implement these goals.

This observation about the practical reasoning structure of the speech act of making a proposal has two highly significant implications for the study of strategic maneuvering in deliberation dialogue. The first implication concerns basic ways to attack a proposal. It means that there are four ways to attack a proposal: you can attack the major premise, you can attack the minor premise, you can attack the conclusion, or you can attack the inferential link between the premises and the conclusion by putting forward an undercutter. According to the first way, the respondent, when confronted with a proposal, can argue that the proposal is not based on goals shared by the group composed of the agents that are taking part in the deliberation. According to the second way, the respondent can argue that the action being recommended is not really a means in the given circumstances to fulfill the goal. According to the third way, the respondent can present a new argument that supports the negation of the conclusion. According to the fourth way, the respondent can argue that even though the premises may hold, the inferential link leading to the conclusion fails to hold – for example, because there is an exception.

The second implication is that there is a standard method for giving advice to a respondent on how to attack a proposal by using the critical questions matching the argumentation scheme for practical reasoning. For example, one of the critical questions asks whether there are negative side effects of carrying out the action. Suppose a respondent does not have a really good idea ready at hand on how to critically question or attack a proposal that has been made by the other party in a deliberation, even though he has a lot of knowledge about the circumstances of the case. Is there some method or device he can use to search around in his knowledge base to come up with some information that might provide the basis of an objection to the proposal? On the theory advocated here, there is such a method readily available. The respondent can look around among the list of critical questions matching the scheme for practical reasoning to see whether one or more of these questions fits the evidential information in the knowledge base of the deliberation. This resource is a very handy tool for strategic maneuvering (van Eemeren, 2010) in a deliberation dialogue.

6.7 Revised Versions of the Model

There is a reason to separate the consider part from the revise part. The reason is that the consider part includes asking critical questions in order to find potential weaknesses in the proposal, and putting forward counter-arguments that attack the proposal. In the consider part these counter-arguments, as well as the arguments used to counter the counter-arguments, are based on factual evidence of the circumstances of the case, and factual projections on what might happen if the proposal were to be implemented. For these reasons the consider part is best modeled as a persuasion dialogue. During this consider segment there is a shift to persuasion dialogue, as the reasons for and against a proposal are critically examined in light of the circumstances of the case and the goals of the parties to the deliberation. As this persuasion dialogue segment continues, it may become evident to the group that some proposals are less susceptible to problems than others. The deliberation then proceeds to an evaluation stage where some of the proposals are weeded out, and the deliberation narrows down to a selected subset of the original set of proposals

In the fourth part of the middle stage, the two stages that McBurney, Hitchcock, and Parsons call "recommend" and "confirm" are combined. In this part of the dialogue, the participants give their reasons for preferring a particular proposal from among this narrower subset previously identified. For example, one participant might declare that she sees the proposal to deal with a flood disaster by bringing in federal forces as the best one because she thinks the flood should be classified as a disaster at the federal level. In other words, she uses argument from a verbal classification to support her conclusion that this particular proposal is the best one, and therefore it should be chosen as the course of action to solve the problem posed by the choice. In this fourth part of the middle stage, arguments are being put forward, which might suggest a persuasion dialogue. However, these arguments were already put forward during the third part of the middle stage, and during this fourth part they are merely being repeated and summarized.

At the closing stage, the participants in the deliberation use some method to come to agreement in selecting what they take to be the best proposal. Once the middle stage has been closed off, it is assumed that there has been acceptance by each member of the group that one proposal has been shown to be stronger than its alternatives. During the middle stage, it can generally be expected that there is still disagreement on which is the best proposal. But in order for the deliberation dialogue to be successful, there has to be agreement, based on the argumentation put forward in the first two stages, that there is one particular proposal that represents the best way to move forward and take action in the circumstances. The decision may need to be defeasible, should the circumstances change. Even so, because of the need to take action, some decision has to be made. And the decision has to be agreed to even by those who disagree with the proposal chosen. There can be many different methods for determining acceptance. However, in the most common kinds of cases the participants in the deliberation will take a vote, and a majority vote for one particular proposal will close the dialogue.

There are some additional problems with specific features of this model of deliberation. One problem is that the agents may have conflicting goals, but, as they exchange arguments, if these conflicts are reduced the quality of the deliberation could be improved. Also, there can be scheduling problems between time allocated for putting forward and considering proposals, and time allocated for searching for new information relevant to the circumstances that would influence the arguments for and against the various proposals being entertained. To deal with these problems, a new line of research on deliberation dialogue has taken a different approach.

Toniolo, Norman, and Sycara (2012) constructed a model of deliberation dialogue in which agents with individual plans to achieve their own goals collaborate together on a team project by discussing interdependent actions and goals in order to resolve conflicts between their plans. Their model used the argumentation scheme for practical reasoning to enable the agents in such a team to identify conflicts between their interdependent plans. They showed empirically that the use of practical reasoning in this kind of deliberation setting enabled more effective conflict resolution that helped the deliberation to move forward more constructively to achieve its collective goal of solving a problem or arriving at a good decision.

Their model (757) represents the procedure of deliberation as a tree structure where the root is the initial situation, nodes represent other situations, and the arrows joining the nodes represent actions that modify situations. A plan for an agent is defined as a path from the root node to other nodes that move toward the overall goal of the deliberation. Such a path represents a sequence of situations, each of which is scheduled on a time line. Also accounted for in their model are norms – external regulations about what actions an agent is obliged or forbidden to carry out. An agent can argue about the plans of other agents in the deliberation and can respond to criticisms of its own plan put forward by the other agents (758). Argumentation schemes are used to model these arguments along with sets of critical questions that match an argumentation scheme. The critical questions are used to guide an agent to identify counter-arguments that could defeat an opponent's view or support one's own position. For example, critical questions matching the argumentation scheme for practical reasoning can be used to ask whether an action proposed by another agent is possible, or whether a goal conflicts with another goal.

Speech acts used in the deliberation dialogue between agents include the following: proposing, rejecting, withdrawing, accepting, arguing, and asking a why question. The speech act of proposing is used to propose an action. The speech acts for accepting and rejecting are used for accepting or rejecting a proposal. The withdrawal speech act is used to withdraw the proposal. The why question challenges the performance of an action, requiring that the agent who proposed the action should present an argument to support carrying it out. Rules for these speech acts specify when each can be used in a deliberation and how each must be responded to as the dialogue proceeds.

The argumentation-based formal model of deliberation dialogue constructed by Toniolo, Norman, and Sycara (2013) uses argumentation schemes to deal with problems caused by conflicting goals and scheduling constraints in cases where two or more agents are planning together to solve the problem of what to do. A feature of their model is that it provides for the sharing of information between agents during the deliberation process. The problem is one of coordination of goals and actions between agents where a decision made by one of them may interfere with a decision made by others due to differences in goals or views of how things should be done. Although each agent's plan is internally consistent, in a typical case there may be conflicts between independent plans. Toniolo, Norman, and Sycara built a formal system for dealing with this problem using an argumentation method in which arguments can either defeat or support other arguments. The system deploys argumentation schemes, along with critical questions matching them, to allow agents to put forward arguments and counter-arguments. This model was also developed in Toniolo (2013) and has been further refined in Walton, Norman, and Toniolo (2015). To begin to show how the system works, it is best to use the main example from Toniolo (2013), which concerns an emergency response to a disaster situation.

The identification of plan alternatives is carried out using a three-step dynamic process that takes into account a timeline that identifies when each of the actions being proposed will take place. In the example, which can be called the water supply example, two agents are discussing the repair of the water supply in a disaster area. A key feature of the example is that it shows the need for dialogue enabling the agents to share information as the deliberation proceeds. They start the dialogue with no knowledge of each other's plans. One of the agents is the local authority. She proposes to stop the water supply in the location. She argues that the water supply is not safe because it is contaminated. The other agent represents a humanitarian organization. He proposes building a field hospital in order to deal with the casualties, and claims that a water supply is required for the field hospital. Here the agents have a conflict because of their different goals, even though they have the common goal of dealing with disaster. However, they can also consider other options. One is to build the field hospital in a different location. Another is to not use the water supply until after it can be guaranteed that it is safe to do so. They can replan by discussing the situation and find some options that they can both agree to. In general outline the dialogue moves ahead by the recognition of conflicts between the two parties, and by modifying their individual goals or proposed actions by dealing with the conflicts by two means. First, they can have sequences of argument exchanges. For example, one might use argument from negative consequences, and the other might question or attack the argument to cast doubt on it, based on the circumstances of the case. Second, as information about the circumstances of the case are exchanged between the two agents, the practical reasoning used in each of their arguments can be modified. This kind of argumentative discussion can help them to reduce the number of conflicts in their interdependent plans and make the deliberation dialogue move forward more efficiently by solving problems that are holding it up.

Another problem is that the set of rules that govern the sequence of speech acts used as moves in the turn-taking between agents in a deliberation dialogue need to be formulated. A good start was the basic sequence of argument moves between the two parties in the formal argumentation framework for deliberation dialogue of (Kok et al., 2010). This system is built around a set of rules (protocols) determining what kinds of moves can be made, a set of speech acts representing the types of moves, and a set of rules specifying the effects of putting forward a speech act by a party in the dialogue. There is a speech act for proposing an action, speech acts for accepting or rejecting a proposal, a speech act for withdrawing a proposal, and a speech act for presenting an argument that challenges a proposal.

Some of the available speech acts in the communication language for deliberation dialogue proposed in Kok et al. (2010, 79) are displayed in Table 6.1. The left column sets out a number of speech acts that can be used in a deliberation dialogue, the middle column sets out a number of attacks that can be made against the other party's speech act, and the right column sets out a number of surrenders that can be made in response to the attacks. Table 6.1 summarizes these three speech acts, and the three attacks that represent the appropriate responses to the putting forward of any one of the speech acts. The variable A stands for a proposition. The term 'implies' stands for the notion of defeasible implication defined in the formal argumentation system ASPIC+. To say that B implies A means that if B is accepted, then A also has to be tentatively accepted, subject to critical questioning. This notion of implication is defeasible, meaning that an argument based on it using defeasible *modus ponens* is open to defeat by exceptions that can be put forward by a critic.

Table 6.1: *Three Speech Acts in the Deliberation Dialogue Structure of (Kok et al., 2010)*

Speech Act	Allowed Responses
Propose A	*Why propose A?:* or *Reject A*
Reject A	*Why reject A?*
Why propose A?	*Argue B implies A*

This way of formalizing a deliberation dialogue is built on an abstract argumentation framework in which there are basically two kinds of moves: putting forward an argument, and attacking that argument by putting forward an opposed argument. The three speech acts shown in Table 6.1 merely illustrate how such protocols work. This method of setting out the allowable responses to the performance of speech acts in protocols was followed, with some changes, in the formal model of deliberation dialogue of Walton, Norman, and Toniolo (2015). But the use of a why question of the kind so carefully analyzed in Chapters 4 and 5 raises important issues about burden of proof. These issues are discussed in Chapter 7.

The water supply example used by Walton, Norman, and Toniolo (2015) showed that a deliberation dialogue structure needed to be built that can allow the agents to reconstruct the choices that they face as new information comes in describing the circumstances of the decision to be made. By devising a dialogue structure that makes exchange of information possible during all three stages of the dialogue it was shown that the number of conflicts between the agents' plans can be reduced. This model of deliberation recognizes that although deliberation is a collaborative enterprise, because the group of agents making the decision must set a collaborative goal at the opening stage, the agents will also construct their individual plans and proposals based on their own goals and the means they see as appropriate to achieve these goals. Hence, to engage in practical reasoning successfully in a model of deliberation dialogue for realistic applications, agents need to be able to discuss conflicts between their plans and to try to reduce these conflicts by using argumentation. For example, the agents will often need to exchange information about the changing circumstances of the case, and will need to use arguments such as ones fitting the scheme for argument from negative consequences to resolve the conflicts that arise. To make these capabilities possible, the system has to allow for argumentation within protocols built around speech acts enabling the disclosure of information.

The capability of the model to assist deliberation effectively was tested experimentally (Toniolo, Norman, and Sycara, 2012). The arguments used in the deliberation dialogue conform to an experimental design in which the agents were not given information about conflicts between their plans. Forty different initial plans were generated for each agent, with variations in time-scale, norms, goals, and beliefs (Toniolo, Norman, and Sycara, 2012, 759). Twenty-five pairs of plans were selected for each different conflict configuration among the 1600 initial plans that made up the deliberation. These plans were run experimentally and analyzed to measure the conflicts before and after the dialogue (Toniolo, Norman, and Sycara, 2012, 759). It was claimed that the outcome shown by the empirical modeling is that identification of conflict in plans led agents to form more feasible collaborative plans to move forward. An important feature of this mechanism was that it took into account new incoming information gathered during the course of the dialogue. The study provided evidence to show that the use of argumentation schemes enhanced the ability of the agents engaged in deliberation to resolve conflicts between their interdependent plans. It was shown that application of this procedure moved the deliberation dialogue forward to enable the agents to establish agreements on how to collaboratively act together to solve the initial problem.

These results and other comparable results from Toniolo (2013) were used in devising the protocols of the formal system of deliberation dialogue used in Walton, Norman, and Toniolo (2015). By running an empirical evaluation of the computational deliberation system it was confirmed that the rates of successful deliberation were increased by the use of protocols where agents were able to share information about their goals and the changing circumstances of the case, and to engage in argumentation with each other. In the experiment, the two agents started out with individual plans that shared some common goals and knowledge about the circumstances, but also had some conflicts. Argumentation between the two agents – which also included the sharing of knowledge about each other's plans and goals, and sharing of knowledge about the circumstances of the case – increased the efficiency of the deliberation in moving toward a successful outcome. The use of protocols that enabled the sharing of arguments and information between the agents resulted in a 25 percent increase in successful deliberation on average. This empirical research suggested the hypothesis formulated in Walton, Norman, and Toniolo (2015, 18) that the use of a protocol enabling agents to share information about their view of the circumstances of the decision during the course of a deliberation dialogue increases the number of successful outcomes between agents.

In the experimental work, three measures of success of a deliberation dialogue were applied. The feasibility of the plan refers to the extent to which one agent can act without impeding the goals of the other. The measure of feasibility was the increase in the number of conflicts solved. The third measure was the number of arguments exchanged. Future research proposed along these lines includes consideration of how to measure other criteria listed in the ten criteria for the success of a deliberation dialogue (see Section 9 in this chapter).

Building on these results, Walton, Norman, and Toniolo (2015) extended the MHP model of deliberation dialogue by adding an open knowledge base to the deliberation process. One purpose of introducing this new feature was to make it possible for agents to continually gather and revise information about the circumstances during the course of the dialogue from the opening to the closing stage. This feature is especially important to model the kind of deliberation typified by the water supply example, where the agents have individual goals but also have interdependent plans. As indicated earlier, in such cases, there can be conflicts between the plans – for example, conflicting goals or norms – and it is useful for the agents to use argumentation to deal with these problems. During this argumentation phase, knowledge of the circumstances can be important for each agent to communicate to the others. In the water supply example, two agents might need to discuss options such as building the hospital in a different location, and so facts concerning the circumstances about which locations might be feasible for such a project might be relevant.

Protocol for this revised model of deliberation dialogue comprises the stages of the deliberation and the speech acts that define the moves and responses sides as the dialogue proceeds through the argumentation stage. After the opening stage, a proposal is brought forward by one of the agents, and the proposal is then discussed. Central to the discussion is the bringing forward of pro and con arguments on whether the course of action that has been proposed is a good one for them to accept. But during this stage the agents may also need to modify their plans as new information about the circumstances comes into the dialogue. This may lead to alternative proposals recommending different actions as ways to solve the problem posed at the opening stage. Another thing to notice is that the problem itself may need to be reconfigured in light of new information that comes in during the argumentation stage. The dialogue reaches the closing stage when the problem is solved or when the agents are satisfied that there are no further issues to be discussed at this point.

A distinctive feature of this revised model of deliberation dialogue is that the exchange of information about the circumstances during the sequence of argumentation in the dialogue enables the agents to modify their plans, reconfigure the alternative proposals by dropping some and modifying others, and thereby reduce the conflicts in their plans. To make this possible the agents use argumentation schemes, especially the scheme for practical reasoning and the argument from negative consequences that represents one of the critical questions matching this scheme. It might be noted as well that explanations as well as arguments are important to this part of a deliberation dialogue; one agent typically needs to explain how its plan is supposed to work to enable another agent to realistically evaluate the plan and to deal with potential weaknesses in it.

When one agent puts forward a plan, the question of whether there is any action to be discussed will be raised. This discussion automatically leads to deliberation dialogue and then to an argumentation phase during which the plan may need to be modified, and which may also raise the question of whether there is an alternative plan to be discussed (Walton, Norman, and Toniolo, 2015, 14). During this argumentation phase the agents need to take turns putting forward arguments and other speech acts and responding to the arguments made by the other agent. If the participants reach agreement on a plan they both accept, the dialogue can be closed. If not, they may have to modify their plans, including some of their goals, and this can be accomplished by going through the argumentation phase again.

The protocols were selected in order to solve as many conflicts as possible. This line of research suggested that the existing protocols in the literature need to be modified, but it also showed that the deliberation framework in which these protocols are to be used needs to be revamped and expanded by taking a different philosophical view of deliberation dialogue. It also suggests the need to rethink how deliberation dialogue is related to persuasion dialogue and information-seeking dialogue during dialectical shifts.

6.8 Deliberation with an Open Knowledge Base

In a widely accepted model of persuasion called the critical discussion (van Eemeren and Grootendorst, 2004, 59–61) there are four stages: an opening stage, a confrontation stage, an argumentation stage, and a closing stage. In the confrontation stage, it becomes clear that there is a difference of opinions, and in order for the discussion to proceed this difference of opinions needs to be expressed explicitly. In the opening stage, the parties try to find some common ground that can serve as a starting point of the discussion. At this stage the parties also define their roles as protagonist and antagonist. In the argumentation stage, the protagonists advance their arguments. Each tries to defend his own position and to cast doubts on or to refute the position of the opposing party. During the argumentation stage, participants put forward speech acts, like the speech act of making an assertion, and the protocols (dialogue rules) systematize the effect of putting forward a speech act. For example, if one party puts forward a speech act of making an assertion, the proposition asserted is automatically inserted by the system into that party's commitment store. After the argumentation stage has played out, the dialogue reaches the closing stage, where a decision is reached on which party has been victorious and the dialogue is terminated. In the concluding stage, as it is called by van Eemeren and Grootendorst (2004, 60), the parties establish what result has come out of their argumentation. The criterion for closing the dialogue is that both parties have to reach agreement that the proposition argued for by one side is acceptable and so the doubt of the other side must be retracted. Another feature of this model is that there is a set of propositions identified as the common ground determined by both parties at the opening stage. In computational terminology, this set of propositions can be defined as a knowledge base containing a set of commitments that both parties recognize as representing factual information that can be used as common knowledge for them to employ as premises in their arguments.

In this model, the knowledge base is represented as fixed at the opening stage. In a persuasion dialogue this way of framing the discussion seems reasonable. For example, if we are having a debate on some controversial issue, we cannot start from nowhere. If we do not have at least some agreement as a basis for argument, the conflict will never be resolved. To provide this basis for agreement, it can be settled at the opening stage that we will accept some source – for example, an encyclopedia or some database on the Internet – we both accept as factual, and agree not to dispute the set of propositions. Other propositions could be included here as well. For example, we might agree not to dispute propositions that are generally accepted as common knowledge and that are not in dispute within the framework of this particular persuasion dialogue on some issue. We might not be able to dispute a statement like 'Some dogs are black,' for example. Such propositions could be disputed, perhaps at a meta-level, but it simplifies the basic model if the participants are required to have some basis of agreement that is not subject to dispute during a particular persuasion dialogue that is underway in a given case.

In a deliberation dialogue, however, the issue set in place at the opening stage is a problem of deciding what to do in a particular set of circumstances requiring a choice of actions. Therefore, in parallel with persuasion dialogue, deliberation requires the agents who are deliberating to share some common knowledge of the circumstances of the choice they face. A knowledge base comprising these circumstances therefore needs to be set in place for all agents at the opening stage of a deliberation. As circumstances can change rapidly, it is necessary for the practical reasoning agents to take any changes into account. Because it is so important for intelligent deliberation to be informed and flexible, one of the worst errors is for a practical reasoning agent to fail to take changing circumstances into account.

For this reason, deliberation as a framework for rational argumentation clearly needs to have a different structure from the simple model of persuasion dialogue described above. Propositions need to be added to the knowledge base and deleted from it during the argumentation stage

For these reasons the MHP model of deliberation dialogue needs several revisions to bring it in line with the other features of deliberation studied by Toniolo, Norman, and Sycara (2013) and Kok et al. (2010). In the revised model, there needs to be a knowledge base set in place at the opening stage that defines the choice that is to be made or the problem to be solved. That is the governing question in the MHP model.

However, once we reach the argumentation stage, this knowledge base needs to be opened so that if the situation changes and information about these changes becomes available to the agents making the deliberation, this can be taken into account during this stage when proposals are put forward and considered.

In the computational model of Walton, Toniolo and Norman (2014, p. 9), as shown in Figure 6.6, there is a cycle of proposing, considering, and revising.

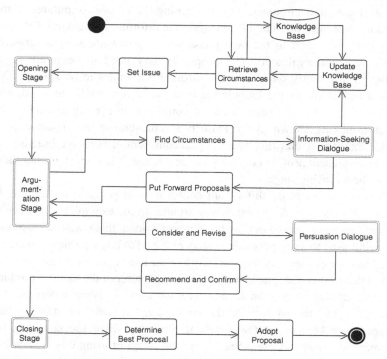

Figure 6.6: Revised Model of Deliberation Dialogue

This argumentation cycle can be influenced by the changing circumstances of the case as new information about the circumstances comes in from the knowledge base. For these reasons the new model has an opening stage that includes an open knowledge base that allows for new information to come in during the whole sequence of deliberations. Based on this incoming knowledge, proposals can be revised, reconsidered, and re-evaluated. One can see, as shown in Figure 6.6, that during the argumentation stage there is a cyclical flow of argumentation as new knowledge comes in that affects the argumentation for and against proposals that are affected by the new information. For example, it may become evident that a particular proposal is completely untenable because of new factual information showing that implementing the proposal might have catastrophic negative consequences.

In the MHP model there were dialectical shifts during the argumentation stage. There need to be shifts from deliberation dialogue to information-seeking dialogue, permitting new knowledge of the circumstances to enter the deliberations. And there need to be shifts to persuasion dialogue so the agents can resolve problems arising from their conflicting goals. As shown in Figure 6.6, new circumstances concerning the choice formulated in the opening stage must be shared by the agents in information-seeking dialogue. Then there is a shift to the next phase where proposals are put forward, considered, and evaluated. The proposals may need to be modified or evaluated differently once this new information comes to be known. The revised model shows the knowledge base being continually updated, and the knowledge that has been retrieved continuously cycling around in the decision-making shown in the main box representing the argumentation stage. The danger that this cyclical procedure could continue indefinitely is an ever-present problem of deliberation. Hence, it is important that there should be a closing stage.

There also have to be shifts from deliberation to persuasion dialogue. In Chapter 2 we saw shifts the other way around. In the examples of the health product messages studied in Chapter 2, it was evident that practical reasoning was being used to try to persuade readers of the ad to buy a particular medication. Thus, we can say that the framework of the use of practical reasoning is a kind of persuasion dialogue in which the manufacturer of the medical product, or the advertising agency the manufacturer has hired, is trying to persuade the audience to buy the product. At the same time, the reader of the ad is also engaged in a kind of internal practical reasoning when she considers the argument in the ad and examines the pros and cons of using this medication. We can see from observing how these ads are used that practical reasoning is sometimes used in a relatively simple setting where an agent is making a decision on what course of action to take based on its goals, while in other cases it is used in a more complex setting where several agents are involved. In a more complex setting one agent is communicating with another, and in order for the communication to take place and to be successful, both agents have to use practical reasoning.

There is also the danger (mentioned above) that this cyclical process of collecting information and using it to continually build further proposals and arguments could lead to delay, or even to failure of the deliberation to reach its goal. For practical reasons of time and cost, a decision often needs to be made even though there is not enough time for further research. For these reasons it is necessary to have protocols to determine closure of a deliberation dialogue.

6.9 Closing a Deliberation Dialogue

As indicated above, there are also some important issues remaining about how to set up criteria to implement a good procedure for the closing stage. What if it cannot be determined, on the available evidence, which is the best proposal? Or what if there is a tie? What if two or more of the proposals appear to be equally good, based on the outcome of the argumentation stage?

Let's go back to our example where Bob and Alice are deliberating on whether to make an offer on the house, and Bob says "I propose that we make an offer on the house." Suppose that Alice then replies, "Okay, I agree with your proposal, let's go ahead and do it." Should that be the end of the deliberation, or might Bob still respond by saying, "Well, it seems like a good idea to both of us, but we still have a little more time to make a decision. Maybe we should try to discuss the pros and cons a little more." This sort of move might be possible, because the circumstances of the case might leave some time for collecting more information, for reflecting on the decision by mulling it over, or by further brainstorming by having a discussion in which the considerations on both sides are re-examined. Even so, procrastination is a significant kind of failure in a deliberation dialogue. Making a decision in a timely fashion is often very important as well, in order to avoid delay in taking advantage of conditions that are in a state of change. The bottom line is that decisions often have to be made under conditions of lack of knowledge. So when can practical reasoning be closed off?

Answering this question requires an awareness of a form of argumentation called a lack of knowledge inference, a commonly used and reasonable kind of defeasible reasoning. It fits the argumentation scheme below (Walton, 1996, 254):

Major Premise: If A were true, A would be known to be true.
Minor Premise: A is not known to be true.
Conclusion: A is (presumably) false.

Even though a knowledge base is incomplete, the argument from ignorance can be a reasonable defeasible form of argument, holding tentatively as the search through the knowledge base proceeds. Three appropriate critical questions match the argumentation scheme:

CQ$_1$: How far along has the search for evidence progressed?
CQ$_2$: Which side has the burden of proof in the dialogue as a whole? In other words, what is the ultimate *probandum* and who is supposed to prove it?
CQ$_3$: How strong does the proof need to be in order for this party to be successful in fulfilling the burden?

CQ$_1$ concerns depth-of-search in the knowledge base. Argument from ignorance is a necessary type of reasoning, for example, in law, and in deliberation in all areas of practical life. Nevertheless, it can also be dangerous.

In some cases the closed world assumption can be invoked artificially, or without real justification, in order to silence opposition and force a wrong conclusion. In cases where no real search of the database has been made, and yet the closed world assumption is made, the argument from ignorance may be fallacious. The classic case is that of the witch hunt, or the McCarthy trials, where a database is closed off peremptorily, when it should remain open. Such fallacious cases are notorious where a charge, such as being in league with the devil, is vague and hard to refute by factual evidence. In most cases of practical reasoning, the database should be seen as open and the argument defeasible. In evaluating lack of knowledge inferences, there is always the question of how reasonable the assumption of closure of the database is. Whether the assumption should hold is an important critical question.

Consider once again the case of Alice and Bob's decision-making about which house to buy. Theoretically their decisions should only be made when they have collected enough information about the real estate market, and they have evaluated all the pro and con arguments on both sides of every available option that was proposed. But there is always the possibility of finding a better deal if the search continues, because the housing market is in a continual process of change depending on supply and demand. A lot may depend on how they individually feel. If they find one house that is within their budget and they both really love, they may want to act fast because they don't want to miss out on the possibility of getting this house. Clearly, once they have arrived at this point the deliberation should be concluded and an offer should be made, even though the deliberation could be re-opened – for example, if the seller will not agree to their asking price. Still, at the point where they have agreed to go ahead with the offer, and it is reasonable to conclude that the strongest pro and con arguments have been given a good hearing, the decision should be made. The deliberation dialogue should be closed.

But there is also the possibility that they may have to shift to a different type of dialogue. For example, suppose that the condominium is very close to Bob's workplace, and he dearly loves riding his bike to work. Alice, on the other hand, has always had a cherished vision of living in a large house in the suburbs. It may be clear that their values differ, and so here we might have to move to the value-based variant of practical reasoning. Or it may be that one of them is simply asked to compromise, because he or she is strongly committed to the happiness of the other party. But still, it is only possible to arrive at this point by first of all discussing in sufficient depth all the pros and cons of all the proposals that are currently being considered. If it is a tie between two of the choices being considered, then at least they can say that they have looked at all of the options very carefully so they are satisfied with that part of the procedure, and they can move ahead to make a final decision based on some other factor. In some cases, this final stage could involve shifting to a negotiation dialogue.

The bottom line is that in order to properly close a deliberation dialogue there has to be an argumentation sequence in which reasons pro and con all the proposals being considered are gone into in sufficient depth. In the argumentation stage, all the relevant arguments need to be collected and evaluated based on the evidence available from the knowledge base. The important thing, then, is what happens during this argumentation sequence.

A general outline of how to frame the segment of the deliberation dialogue in which proposals are put forward and evaluated by a deliberation is shown in Figure 6.7. At the first step, in the text box at the top left, a participant in the deliberation puts forward a proposal for a particular proposition representing a course of action. If the other parties simply accept it, without further questioning, as shown in Figure 6.7, the deliberation process stops. However, if the other participants are not willing to accept the proposal, then they are obliged to present arguments showing why they object. This move naturally leads to a dialogue sequence in which the proponent of the proposal has to respond to the criticisms showing how the

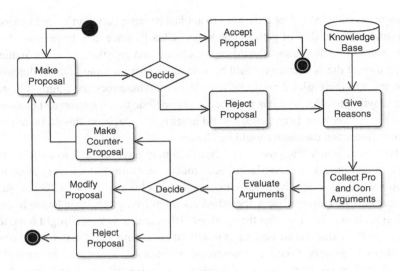

Figure 6.7: How the Speech Act of Making a Proposal Fits into a Deliberation Dialogue

objections can be met. Alternatively, the discussion can stop there if the proponent finds the objection to this proposal so convincing that he simply gives up and says, "You are right, I agree that the proposal is not a good one." In such a case the dialogue sequence would be a short one. In a typical case, however, the dialogue sequence would go through several pro and con moves. For example, when the proposal is attacked by somebody offering a reason against it, the participant making the proposal then responds to the con arguments by offering con arguments against them.

This dialogue interval is concluded when there are no further moves to make. Based on the arguments for and against that are brought forward and criticized during the dialogue sequence, a reasoned decision can now be arrived at on what to do. There are four options. The original proposal can be accepted, in which case the deliberation stops. The original proposal can be rejected, in which case the deliberation also stops. Or there are two other options. The proposal can be modified, to take into account the objections made during the dialogue, or a counterproposal can be brought forward. In either of the latter two cases, the procedure of formulating a proposal goes around the cycle again, except that this time a new proposal has been formulated in place of the one that was not accepted.

The decision of when the deliberation has reached its closing stage cannot be made by any current model of deliberation. However, research by Walton,

Norman, and Toniolo (2015) has built a computational framework based on the model of deliberation dialogue advocated in this chapter. In this framework, the following ten criteria that determine the extent to which a deliberation has been successful have been set out (Walton, Norman, and Toniolo, 2015, 10). It is these criteria, quoted below, that need to be applied to any given case to determine when a deliberation dialogue should be closed:

- Whether the proposals that were discussed represent all the proposals that should be considered, or whether some proposals that should have been discussed were not.
- The accuracy and completeness of the information regarding the circumstances of the case made available to the agents during the opening stage.
- How well arguments were critically questioned or attacked by counter-arguments.
- How well the agents followed the procedural rules by allowing the other agents to present their proposals and arguments openly, and how they responded to proposals.
- How thoroughly each of the proposals that were put forward during the deliberation were engaged by supporting or attacking argumentation.
- Whether any arguments that should have been considered were not given due consideration.
- How good the arguments were supporting or attacking each of the proposals, depending on the validity of the arguments and the factual accuracy of their premises.
- Whether the argumentation avoided personal attacks, or was unduly influenced by opinion leaders or personalities who dominated discussion during the argumentation stage.
- The relevance of the arguments put forward during the argumentation stage.
- The taking into account of the values of the group of agents and engaged in the deliberation.

Relevance in a deliberation dialogue is determined by how the sequence of practical reasoning connecting the agents' goals to the means leads to the outcome determined at the closing stage (Walton, 2004b, 143). Relevance of an argument is determined by how the sequence of practical reasoning, combined with arguments supported or attacked by evidence that comes in through the knowledge base, connects to the problem or choice of action set as the issue of the deliberation at the opening stage. Relevance can only be judged by the information that is available on the problem that the parties are deliberating, so their goals can be integrated with the actions they are planning to take (Walton, 2004b, 143). In order to reach a thoughtful and well deliberated decision on when the closing stage has been reached in a given case, the party judging the dialogue should use the ten criteria given above. Only by this means will it be proved, to the appropriate standard of proof, that one proposal is better than another. In real cases, however, there is always the problem of constraints of time and resources. It may be necessary to reach a timely and practical decision even if ideally it would be better to collect more information and continue further with the argumentation pro and con the various proposals.

In an emergency, the closing stage may have to be reached quickly. In other cases, the determination of when the closing stage has been reached may depend on costs or on practical matters of how much time there is for discussion. In theory, the closing stage should only be reached when the arguments and proposals considered on all sides have been discussed thoroughly enough that it is clear that all relevant factors have been taken into account. At this point, an evaluation of all the argumentation that has taken place through the argumentation stage should be evaluated thoroughly enough that it is clear that all the potentially usable proposals have been discussed, and which proposal is the best. But in practice, in the circumstances a decision may have to be made within time constraints, and so a determination of which proposal is best may still be subject to pro and contra argumentation. In such cases, the argumentation stage will need to be closed off and some means taken to arrive at a decision – for example, taking a vote. Practical reasoning is therefore at the core of the decision-making on when to close off the deliberation dialogue. Time and costs of continuing a deliberation are relevant practical factors that need to be taken into consideration.

6.10 Conclusions

This section begins with a summary of the main properties of the new model of deliberation dialogue proposed throughout the chapter. After that, it summarizes the general conclusions of the chapter, indicating how the findings of the chapter describe features of the new model that extend the current formal models of deliberation dialogue.

The new model of deliberation put forward in this chapter has three stages: an opening stage, an argumentation stage, and a closing stage. At the opening stage, the participants agree on the problem to be solved, and they agree roughly on the choice to be made, although as refinements are made during the argumentation stage, the framing of the choice into two or three options, for example, may need to be reconfigured. Also during the opening stage, the participants need to share quite a bit of knowledge about the circumstances that pose the problem. They also need to be expected to share common knowledge – for example, knowledge about what might be taken to be the normal circumstances of carrying out a type of action. But the knowledge base is incomplete. Some of the agents may know things that the others do not know, and it is important that the knowledge base be left open during the argumentation stage so that new relevant information can come in that might affect proposals and commitments. For example, before the dialogue can proceed to the argumentation stage all the agents involved in the deliberation need to know that the power supply has been disrupted by a disaster in a particular location. They all need to know further specifics about the type of disaster, the extent of it, why it is a problem, and so forth. For there to be a deliberation, they do not need to know at this stage that something needs to be done.

In order for a deliberation to be successful, it has to be assumed that the participants are willing to cooperate and that they share some goals. However, it is by no means the case that the agents need to be expected to share all goals. It is to be expected that they will have different goals and that they will have differences of opinion about the means to fulfill them. It is also to be expected that they will have differing perceptions of the circumstances of the case.

During the argumentation stage, the agents take turns putting forward speech acts, such as asking questions, putting forward arguments, criticizing arguments previously put forward, making proposals, criticizing proposals previously made, and so forth. During this stage, some agents will have knowledge that others lack, and therefore one important type of speech act is that of presenting a proposition that is taken to represent factual knowledge in order to inform the other agents involved in the deliberation process. Also during the argumentation stage, new information can come in that will alter the structure of the choice being made – for example, by suggesting a new option. During the opening stage the choice may be basically one of making the repair in the water supply in one of two ways. But it may emerge during the argumentation stage that there are other options.

During a deliberation dialogue proposals are put forward to solve a problem or to take action on a choice that needs to be made. The choice or problem is formulated at the opening stage. During the argumentation stage, proposals are put forward for an action to take in order to solve the problem or make a good choice for a prudent course of action. A proposal essentially takes the form of an argument from practical reasoning, based on the goals of the agents who are involved, the circumstances of the choice situation, the means to be considered that might contribute to the goals, and the circumstances of the situation in which the decision is to be made.

The judgment of the success of the deliberation can be evaluated in two ways. As indicated earlier, the participants can reach a consensus that one proposal has been shown to be superior. This is called an internal evaluation. The other way is an external evaluation carried out at a meta-level. Once a deliberation has been carried out in a given case by a group of agents, another group of agents can then keep a record of the argumentation in the deliberation – for example, by keeping a transcript of the discussions that were made during the deliberation. Then they can analyze and evaluate the argumentation in the deliberation dialogue and arrive at an evaluation of how successful the dialogue was according to the ten criteria set out above.

During the closing stage, an evaluation is made of the argumentation carried out during the argumentation stage to see if this sequence of argumentation has been successful in meeting the goals set at the opening stage. As indicated above, there are ten criteria that determine whether a given instance of deliberation dialogue has been successful in fulfilling its goal. Satisfying these criteria implies that enough proposals have been thoroughly discussed and evaluated (as instances of practical reasoning) so that further discussion is unlikely to turn up anything new or useful for making a good decision or solving the problem. That does not mean that the dialogue cannot be re-opened if it turns out that the proposed solution does not work once it has been tried. However, because of time or cost limitations that do not permit the collecting of more evidence from the knowledge base by adding to it, the deliberation may have to be closed off prematurely. This decision has to be made on a basis of practical reasoning. For example, further discussion might mean delay, and that might have negative consequences that interfere with the goal of the deliberation dialogue. This solution to the closure problem, while not yet implemented in a computational system, is useful for the project of improving the current models.

This final part of Section 10 summarizes ten general conclusions reached in the chapter. The first conclusion is that practical reasoning does not only involve fitting goals to actions that are taken to be the means to carry out these goals. In order to engage in intelligent practical reasoning, the rational agent needs to also have knowledge of the circumstances in a given case where a decision is to be made. In typical cases of any realistic kind, to gain knowledge of the circumstances the agent has to make some serious effort to consult with other agents, or go to sources of information – for example, the Internet.

These characteristics of practical reasoning were shown graphically in all four examples (Sections 1–4).

The second conclusion of this chapter is that deliberation dialogue can be classified into four distinctive subtypes, illustrated by the examples treated in Sections 1–4: problem-solving, policy debate, personal and small group decision-making, and civic decision-making. This four-way classification is not meant to be exhaustive of all the different types of deliberation, but represent some prominent and important types that have distinctive characteristics.

The third conclusion is that during the process when practical reasoning is put forward by a proponent and criticized by a respondent, the respondent needs to ask critical questions to probe into the weak points in the practical reasoning. The knowledge of the circumstances can change; therefore, the knowledge base supporting the argumentation in a case of practical reasoning typically needs to be open to new incoming information concerning the changing circumstances of the case. This conclusion poses several problems for when to close off the knowledge base. If the knowledge base may be regarded as complete, meaning that the agent knows everything there is to know about the circumstances of the situation, the practical reasoning that leads to the conclusion on the best course of action could, in principle, be deductive in nature. However, the three examples studied in this chapter suggest that deductive closure is possible only in simple, artificial cases such as the blocks world example, and cannot generally be presumed to obtain in realistic examples of deliberation.

The fourth conclusion of this chapter is that, for the above reasons, practical reasoning is normally best seen as a defeasible form of argumentation (or explanation) that leads to a conclusion that is merely a presumption or hypothesis, based on what is known and what is not known at a particular juncture in an investigation or set of circumstances that is ongoing.

The fifth conclusion of this chapter is that the four examples show that typically an agent is not acting in isolation, but often has to communicate with other agents not only to find information, to act within the constraints of a group that shares common goals, even though the individuals in the group may be expected to have their own separate goals. Hence, the MHP model of deliberation frames deliberation in a setting where agents in the group put forward proposals for discussion. Recent work in artificial intelligence has moved in this direction because researchers in this field see practical reasoning as a useful argumentation tool in different settings where many agents take part, even computational settings such as those required for electronic democracy projects (as shown in Section 3 of this chapter).

The sixth conclusion is that there are two levels required to analyze and evaluate practical reasoning as used in realistic cases. At the first level, practical reasoning is seen as a form of argumentation – or, in some instances, a form of explanation – that can be visually represented using an argument diagram, along with a different type of diagram used to model explanation schemes. But in this chapter we saw that this level is not sufficient by itself to provide the resources for us to evaluate practical reasoning as successful or not in any given case. To accomplish that task, we have to look at the framework of dialogue on how practical reasoning is being used for some purpose – for example, persuasion or deliberation.

The two concepts of practical reasoning and deliberation have been shown in the four examples discussed in this chapter to be so closely intertwined that one cannot be adequately understood without taking the other into account. Practical reasoning is the inferential process of arriving at a conclusion to take action through which deliberation serves as a rational method of decision-making based on an agent's knowledge of its circumstances. Thus, rational deliberation cannot be understood without the fabric of practical reasoning that holds it together. Wooldridge (2002, 66) divides practical reasoning into two component activities:

1. the process of deciding what state of affairs to achieve, called deliberation, and
2. the process of deciding how to achieve these states of affairs, called means-end reasoning.

The end result of means-end reasoning is a plan (Wooldridge, 2002, 66). Thus, practical reasoning is closely related to the technology of planning, a field well developed in artificial intelligence.

The seventh conclusion of this chapter is that the MHP model is basically the right type of framework to represent how practical reasoning is used in realistic cases. It was shown that according to this dialectical model there is an opening stage where the choice to be made is formulated, setting the issue. Next, there is an argumentation stage containing shifts to information-seeking in persuasion intervals. During this argumentation stage, proposals are put forward by the concerned parties, and pro and con arguments are put forward in order to evaluate each proposal as relatively weak or strong. Finally, at the closing stage, the strongest proposal is selected as a basis for reaching agreement on what to do, or what policy to go forward with.

The eighth conclusion is that the MHP model needs to be revised, especially in relation to cases where the agents taking part in the deliberation have conflicting goals. For this reason, the revised version offered in the chapter provides for the sharing of information between agents during the deliberation process so that goals and actions can be coordinated. The extended model enables the agent to take advantage of knowledge about dynamic changes of circumstances required to achieve more successful dialogue outcomes. In this model it is possible to establish whether a dialogue is successful even if the decision on what to do was not made. Ten criteria were given to determine whether a deliberation was successful. These criteria give useful insights for the closure problem of other types of dialogue

The ninth conclusion of the chapter is that the revised version of the model also has to take into account a dialectical analysis of the speech act of making a proposal with a practical reasoning structure. What this means is that when an agent puts forward a proposal to another agent in a deliberation, what the first agent is essentially doing is putting forward a sequence of practical reasoning. In this sequence the first agent is asking the second agent to go forward with a course of action, based on the assumption that the practical reasoning is founded on premises that represent the common goals of the two agents.

The tenth conclusion is the solution provided to the closure problem of practical reasoning provided in the chapter. The closure problem is the problem of determining when practical reasoning ends. It can be formulated as a question. When should a sequence of practical reasoning end? When can the searching for knowledge about a case be closed off so that the premises of the practical reasoning can be taken to provide an evidential base sufficient to prove the conclusion? Or, to put the question another way, when is the burden of proof for an instance of practical reasoning fulfilled? To solve this problem, the concept of a dialogue structure with three stages – an opening stage, an argumentation stage, and a closing stage – has been brought in. The closure problem for practical reasoning has now been reformulated as a problem of determining closure for a deliberation dialogue. So recast, it concerns the conditions for closure of practical reasoning in deliberation dialogue. When can the deliberation be closed off so that further discussion and searching for information is curtailed? A deliberation may have to be closed off and a decision taken based on the pro and con argumentation put forward for practical reasons, typically time and money. A decision by majority vote may have to be taken to meet the practical demand for closing of the discussion. However, the depth, comprehensiveness, and thoroughness of the pro and con argumentation brought for a proposal considered is the most valuable feature of a deliberation leading to an adequately supported conclusion offering a well-reasoned decision for action. So, from a normative point of view of determining when a deliberation can be declared successful enough to solve the original problem or dispute set at the opening stage, the criteria for successful closure of the dialogue are formulated in the ten requirements.

7

Goal-Based Argumentation in Different Types of Dialogue

The most basic problem that led to the other problems studied in the book was posed in Chapter 1. If you try to model the given instance of practical reasoning as a sequence of argumentation only by an argument map, you are led to a state space explosion. Throughout the subsequent chapters we have moved toward a solution to this problem by embedding practical reasoning in an overarching procedural framework in which any given sequence of practical reasoning should be viewed as a part of a deliberation dialogue having an opening stage and a closing stage. This problem led to Chapter 6, where criteria for the proper closure of a deliberation dialogue were proposed. As shown in Chapter 6, practical reasoning is most characteristically used in deliberation dialogue – goal-directed dialogue in which a choice for action needs to be made or problem needs to be solved. It was also shown in Chapter 6 that that deliberation dialogue is often mixed in with information-seeking dialogue as new evidence of the circumstances comes in. Also, as early as Chapter 2, it was shown that practical reasoning is used in persuasion dialogue – for example, in ads for medical products.

Atkinson et al. (2013) showed that there are also many shifts in a deliberation dialogue to persuasion dialogue intervals. Typically, for example, a proposal that has been put forward as part of a deliberation dialogue is attacked by a critic who shifts to a persuasion dialogue in order to attack the arguments that were used to support the proposal that was made in the deliberation dialogue. It is important to see that there is nothing inherently illegitimate about such shifts.

However, a general problem arises from the variability of different communicative multi-agent settings in which practical reasoning is used. As seen in the examples from Chapter 6, deliberation dialogue is the most important and central setting in which practical reasoning is used, and the true colors of practical reasoning as a form of argumentation really begin to emerge once we embed it into this setting. Nevertheless, we also need to confront the underlying problem that in the argumentation in natural language examples where practical reasoning is used, there so often appear to be dialectical shifts from deliberation dialogue to persuasion dialogue.

Chapter 7 also confronts a special issue related to this problem. Burden of proof is generally a requirement for making a claim or putting forward an argument in a persuasion dialogue. But should it also be taken as a reasonable requirement on the speech act of making a proposal in a deliberation dialogue? Because the persuasion dialogue is blended in with the deliberation dialogue in the argumentation that one might find, for example, in an actual text of discourse, it is tempting to think that the same notion of burden of proof that is operative in the persuasion dialogue should also be applied in the deliberation dialogue. But should be a burden of proof be imposed on an agent that makes a proposal in a deliberation dialogue? This chapter will argue that while there is a burden of advocacy in deliberation dialogue, there is no burden of proof of the kind found in the persuasion dialogue protocols.

This chapter can be summarized as follows. The first five sections are taken up with reconsidering the closure problem posed in the four examples studied in Chapter 6, and with analyzing two new examples. These six examples are shown to pose several problems for AI systems that are supposed to be applicable to real examples of argumentation that occur in deliberation and other settings of the kind representing natural language discourse and decision-making. The last five sections are taken up with discussing how to move research efforts forward toward solving these problems. Some of the issues, such as the one about burden of proof, are highly controversial and need further discussion and continued research.

7.1 Reconsidering the Closure Problem in the Examples

In the printer example studied in Chapter 6, Section 1, Brian confronted the problem of the black line appearing down the middle of the page on any document he scanned. Brian's goal was to make the scanner do its job properly, without producing the black line down the middle of the page. This goal did not change during the whole sequence of argumentation that Brian went through. What changed during the argumentation stage was that Brian went through a succession of possible solutions he found on the Internet, and then with some help from Anna he was able to implement one of the solutions he found. However, when Brian found a particular solution, there was no burden of proof on him to prove to himself or anyone else that this was the right solution. He merely tried it out, and if it didn't work, he searched around to find some information that would help him move forward with a different solution. This pattern of argumentation is quite different from the normal one in the persuasion dialogue, where arguments are presented on one side and then attacked by critical questioning or the posing of counter-arguments by the other side. Each side tries to support its thesis set in place at the opening stage, and the one that meets its burden of proof set at the opening stage wins the dialogue.

Let's reconsider this solution to the closure problem in the printer example more carefully. This solution to the closure problem makes it seem easy to solve it. For one thing, the example requires only instrumental practical reasoning. The problem is solved when Brian fixes the printer, or at least finds a solution to the practical problem of how to fix it. But if the example is extended, values may come into it. What happens if Brian keeps trying different proposed solutions but can't find one that actually makes the black line down the middle of the page disappear in time to allow him to continue his work? He still has a problem. What should he do next? Should he keep trying, or give up? If he has to give up, what is an alternative? An alternative might be to hire a technician to fix the problem. Or if the printer is still under warranty, another alternative might be to try to get the vendor or the manufacturer to fix the problem. But that may take a lot of time and effort. Brian may then have to balance the costs of not having a working printer against the costs in time and money of getting a new one.

What these considerations suggest is that the solution to the closure problem depends on the framing of the original problem or decision that Brian was confronted with. Was he simply trying to solve the problem himself without handing it over to someone else? Or was his goal to get rid of the black line down the middle of the page by any means available, even if it meant giving the printer over to somebody else to deal with the problem? Or was his goal to get a working printer within a reasonable time-frame, even there were costs involved?

These remarks in turn suggest a more general insight that the solution to the closure problem in this particular case depends on the framing of the particular problem that Brian faced in his practical reasoning when he began to search for some way of removing the black line from the scanned pages so that the scanner would work properly. What is set in place at the opening stage of a deliberation dialogue is a set of circumstances requiring a choice or posing a problem that needs action, and the goal of the participants in the deliberation dialogue is to find the best proposal for action and thereby solve the problem posed. As shown in Figure 6.1, the deliberation dialogue is closed when this goal is achieved. But in evaluating the practical reasoning used by an agent in any particular case and trying to determine when the reasoning should be closed off, it is necessary to be very clear about how the decision to be made or the problem to be solved was formulated at the beginning of the dialogue. This does not mean, of course, the temporal beginning of the dialogue in the sequence of practical reasoning in the given case. It refers to the logic of the sequence of the practical reasoning in relation to the ultimate goal it is supposed to move toward, defined by the goal of dialogue in which it is embedded.

A deliberation dialogue is similar to a persuasion dialogue in this particular respect. There is some sort of issue or problem set at the opening stage, and the dialogue is closed when this issue has been resolved. However, what is different is that there are two different ways of resolving two different kinds of issues, and differences in the issue or problem set at the opening stage. These differences, in turn, will affect the closure requirements of the dialogue that needs to be formulated. These requirements will therefore affect matters relating to burden of proof.

In the real estate example set out in Chapter 6, Section 2, Alice and Bob have, at the opening stage, narrowed down their choices to three homes: a condominium, a two-story house, and a bungalow. The example is a simplified one compared to many typical deliberations because the other options are not considered. For example, they don't consider the option of rejecting all three choices and continuing to search for others. Also, they don't consider the option of moving to a different city because all the choices available in the city where they are searching for accommodation are far too expensive for their budget. According to the example, none of these options are being considered, or have been ruled out at the opening stage. So the fact that there are only three options makes the case appear similar to a persuasion dialogue where there are only two options: accepting or rejecting the thesis set as the issue at the opening stage. However, even here, the options can be modified as the argumentation proceeds during the argumentation stage. For example, suppose Alice and Bob decided to make a very low offer on the two-story house, because they like it the best even though it is way over their budget. They know that this offer is unlikely to be accepted, so they also adopt a back-up strategy of making an immediate offer on the bungalow as soon as they find out that the low offer on the two-story house has not been accepted. They might arrive at this decision while ruling out the possibility of negotiating a higher price for the two-story house as they don't want to delay too long in order to get the bungalow because they know that this is the best option of the three in their price range. They are taking a risk on delaying the offer on the bungalow, but they agree that this risk would be justified if they could get the two-story house at the price they want. In such a case, they reconfigured the options during the argumentation stage. This pattern is different, at least from the standard case of persuasion dialogue where in the ideal model, the issue is set at the opening stage and needs to be fixed during the argumentation stage because it determines which side wins at the closing stage. Trying to change the original issue by arguing for something else is associated with fallacies of relevance in a persuasion dialogue.

The same point can be made with regard to the policy modeling tool set out as an example in CAS. As shown in Chapter 6, Section 3, the structure of the argumentation in this case is based on the value-based scheme for practical reasoning. The goal is to achieve a state in which it is easier for researchers to work in more than one member state. The action is to harmonize the copyright exceptions. The values promoted are those of efficiency, legal certainty, scientific research, and education. The conclusion is that the permitted exceptions should be harmonized so that they are available in all member states. In this case it looks like there should be a burden of proof operable, because the conclusion is a proposition that is stated to be true. Also, the premises correspond to the normal premises and the argumentation scheme for value-based practical reasoning. What this shows, characteristic of all the examples studied in Chapter 6, is that when the speech act of making a proposal is put forward in deliberation dialogue, it conforms to the structure of the argumentation scheme for practical reasoning – in this instance, the scheme for value-based practical reasoning. So it looks like what we have in such a case is a conclusion that is a course of action being recommended based on premises that are arguably supported by the evidence in the case.

But this could be a misleading way of looking at the argumentation in the case. The argumentation illustrated in this case has the form of value-based practical reasoning, but presumably it is one argument in a larger context of deliberation that has the aim of changing current policy in order to solve what is taken in the given circumstances to pose a problem. The problem is posed by the circumstances. One is that copyright exceptions have not been standardized in the different member states in the European Community. The other is that it has become difficult for researchers and students to work in more than one member state. These circumstances pose a problem, and the solution being advocated by this particular proposal is to harmonize the copyright exceptions in the member states. In this particular example, only the one proposal for solving the problem is being considered, as far as we know, but the way is open to consider other proposals.

In the case of the town hall meeting, the decision was whether to lower the cost of insurance rates in Rhode Island. The problem was that the existing rates had become increasingly burdensome for average citizens. During the argumentation stage, the reformers argued that changing to a no-fault system would lower the cost of insurance, while the opponents argued that the change to a no-fault system would fail to lower premiums and would unfairly make good drivers pay for bad drivers. In this case, as in the other examples, the initial issue seems to be similar to that of a persuasion dialogue where there are only two options: lowering the cost of insurance or not. But this may not necessarily be the case, depending on how the argumentation went during the argumentation stage. A different proposal, might have been put forward – for example, someone might have argued that the system of lowering rates currently being considered could be modified so that it would more effectively lower the cost of insurance. Or, it could be argued that a different system could be put forward that compromises to some extent with the existing system by still having some mechanism that would prevent good drivers having to pay for bad drivers. In short, the proposal set in place at the opening stage can be modified during the argumentation stage in order to meet objections put forward by the other side. Things don't work that way in a persuasion dialogue or an inquiry dialogue. Retractions can be made, and often need to be made, during the argumentation stage of both these types of dialogue. But in neither instance is a participant allowed to change the issue that frames the dispute set at the opening stage. Of course, in realistic examples people often try to do this. It is known as the strategy of reframing the issue, and is a popular argumentation strategy in political rhetoric, for example. But, strictly speaking, according to the normative model of the persuasion dialogue, it is not allowed. If you reframe the issue by changing the proposition to be proved or disputed, you have in effect moved to a different persuasion dialogue where the global burden of proof has changed.

7.2 An Example of Persuasion Dialogue Mixed with Deliberation

The following example of an argument is quoted from an article[1] in the *Economist*. The article begins by posing a problem about the American economy, and then goes on to discuss alternative solutions to the problem. Certainly, the argumentation in the article involves deliberation about the current situation that many perceive as a highly significant economic problem in the American economy. Right at the beginning (quoted from page 10), the article poses the problem to be solved:

> America's president sees himself as the champion of a fairer society. He decries an economy in which 95% of the gains of the recovery have flowed to the

---

[1] No author given, How to be a Progressive, *The Economist* (March 1, 2014, 10–11).

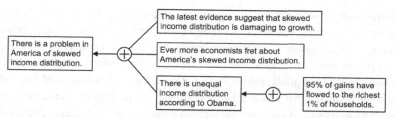

Figure 7.1: Arguments Posing the Problem of Skewed Income Distribution

richest 1% of households, and in which social mobility has stagnated even as inequality has widened. He wants to narrow income gaps and build "ladders of opportunity" for those at the bottom. By and large, those are admirable aspirations. Ever more economists fret about America's skewed income distribution: the latest evidence suggests it is damaging to growth, whereas moderate redistribution is not.

This part of the article poses the problem presented by the skewed income distribution in America, and presents some argument backing up the contention that it is a serious problem that needs to be solved. This part of the argumentation is summarized in Figure 7.1.

There could be different ways of interpreting the argument, as will be shown in the discussion of its extension below, but so far, it can be seen as stating the problem, and offering some arguments to show why it is a problem. But the article is highly political in nature and, as one might expect, combines deliberation with partisan political arguments. Having posed the problem, it goes on to discuss solutions. But there is an evident shift to a different type of dialogue when the author goes on to criticize what he or she describes as the solution to the problem offered by Barack Obama in the next part of the text (quoted from page 10).

The problem lies with Barack Obama's solutions, which are too timid and reliant on left wing rostrums, such as a big increase in the minimum wage and more spending. He lambasts [sic] a tax code that benefits special interests, but has not pushed for tax reform. He wants to invest more in the poor, but has shown no appetite to overhaul America's welfare state, many elements of which – from disability insurance that discourages work to ineffective training schemes – do nothing to boost economic opportunity, and often undermine it.

Instead of going on to engage in a deliberation dialogue to make a proposal about how to solve the problem of skewed income distributions in America, the argumentation in the article has, at this point, shifted to a persuasion dialogue in which Obama's proposed solutions to the problem are attacked. Indeed, this part of the text even begins with the statement that the problem lies with

Obama's solutions, described in highly negative terms as being "too timid and reliant on left-wing rostrums." The next sentence in the text even accuses Obama of inconsistency. On the one hand, he is said to be against a tax code that benefits special interests. The statement articulates what the author takes to be one of Obama's goals: reforming a tax code that benefits special interests. But then it alleges that Obama, because he has not pushed for tax reform, has shown no evidence of carrying out actions required for tax reform. The article goes on to back up the claim that Obama has not pushed for tax reform by arguing that he supports the welfare state that often undermines the economy rather than boosting opportunity.

From there the author of the article states what he thinks Mr. Obama should do. He argues that Obama needs to get tougher with the Democrats in Congress, and he needs to reach out to Republicans. The author then argues that the main problem with the tax code is not a lack of progressivity but the disproportionately large amount of income taxes paid by the wealthy. So what the author is doing in these latter parts of the article is presenting an alternative account of the problem that needs to be solved, and presenting his or her version of the solution to the problem.

In the beginning parts of the article, there is evidence that the text can be categorized as having hallmarks of a deliberation dialogue. A problem is posed, and it is described as a serious problem of the current American economy that demands a solution by the American people. It offers evidence by claiming that many economists are worried about America's skewed income distribution. Evidence is given that this is a serious problem by citing negative consequences of the skewed income distribution, namely that it is damaging to growth. Here we have argument from negative consequences being used to support the allegation that skewed income distribution is a serious problem. Anything that would be damaging to the growth of the economy would be taken as a serious problem because the current failure of the economy to grow as fast as many would like is widely perceived in America to be a serious problem that requires a solution.

7.3 The Dialectical Shift in the Example

So far so good, but the tricky part comes in when we consider the shift between the first part of the text quoted above and the second part. In the second part, the real problem is said to lie with Obama's solutions. This is an interesting shift because it reconfigures and restates the problem, shifting the focus onto what the author takes to be Obama's solutions. The text in the second part quoted

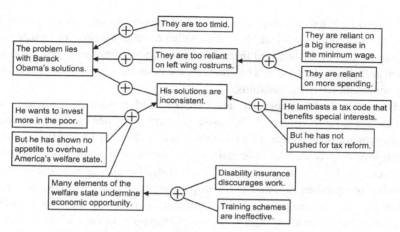

Figure 7.2: Structure of the Argumentation in the Second Text

may look to the reader to be continuing the deliberation dialogue based on the problem set in the first text. However, the argumentation in the second text shows strong evidence of having shifted to a persuasion dialogue, in that it is attacking what the author takes to be Obama's political arguments that he has directed to the American public. It goes so far as to argue that there is an inconsistency between the position on tax reform that Obama has advocated and his actions, which are said to do nothing to boost economic opportunity (and even to undermine it). This argument, which claims to find a practical inconsistency between Obama's stated goals and the actions he has taken to try to achieve these goals, is a negative attack on Obama and his alleged political positions.

The network of argument in this second text is displayed in Figure 7.2. The problem, shown at the top left, is stated in a way different from the way it was in Figure 7.1.

The use of the word "problem," as shown in the top left text box in Figure 7.2, might suggest that we are still involved in a problem-solving deliberation of the kind shown in Figure 7.1. However, what the statement in the top left text box implies is that Obama's solutions are wrong, and that the author is about to offer some arguments that will show why. First, there are the two arguments at the top. One states that his solutions are too timid. The other states that they are too reliant on left-wing rostrums, and backs up this claim with two premises in a linked argument supporting the claim. These two arguments are certainly pointing out problems alleged to be present in Obama's solutions. But, more than that, they are also arguing that his solutions won't work. What this suggests is that the argumentation has shifted to a persuasion dialogue in which there is a conflict of opinions between two points of view – that of the left, and that of the right. These arguments are attacking what are taken to be Obama's solutions on the basis that they are too timid and too reliant on left-wing rostrums.

But it is when we come to consider the third argument, based on the premise that his solutions are inconsistent, that it becomes most evident that the argument is no longer a collaborative deliberation where the two parties are trying to solve a problem or make a good decision on what they should do collectively. Instead, it has become an adversarial exchange where there is a conflict of opinions dividing the dialogue into two sides – the pro and the contra – and the presenter of the argument is trying to show to a wider audience that his point of view is right while the point of view of the opposed side is wrong. This third argument, alleging that his solutions are inconsistent, can be identified as fitting the argumentation scheme for argument from inconsistent commitments.

The scheme for argument from inconsistent commitment (Walton, 1998b, 252) takes the following form where a is an agent:

Initial Commitment Premise: a has claimed or indicated that he is committed to proposition A (generally, or in virtue of what he said in the past).

Opposed Commitment Premise: other evidence in this particular case shows that a is not really committed to A.

Conclusion: a's commitments are inconsistent.

Argument from inconsistent commitment is defeasible, because even if an arguer being attacked admits he has committed himself to an inconsistency in his commitment set, he might still be able to resolve the conflict somehow.

Argument from inconsistent commitment is closely related to another form of argument called the circumstantial *ad hominem* argument (Walton, 1998b, 253), represented by the following scheme:

Argument Premise: a advocates argument α, which has proposition A as its conclusion.

Inconsistent Commitments Premise: a is personally committed to the opposite (negation) of A, as shown by commitments expressed in her/his personal actions or personal circumstances expressing such commitments.

Credibility Questioning Premise: a's credibility as a sincere person who believes in his own argument has been put into question (by the two premises above).

Conclusion: The plausibility of a's argument α is decreased or destroyed.

Argumentum ad hominem has sometimes been assumed to be identical to argument from inconsistent commitments. However, on the model of *ad hominem* schemes proposed in Walton (1998a, 106–111), only arguments in which one party uses a personal attack (an attack on the opponent's ethical character) to attack another party should properly be considered as *ad hominem* arguments. An attack on a person's integrity falls into this category. It should also be noted that *ad hominem* arguments are frequently put forward based on innuendo and suggestions that are not very well supported by objective evidence. This indirect aspect can make them easier to refute, but sometimes makes them harder to refute (Walton, 1998a).

So, what about the argument in the example? When it is argued that Obama's solutions are inconsistent, this move provides evidence that the argument fits the scheme for argument from inconsistent commitment. But why should this argument be considered a circumstantial *ad hominem* attack on the character of Obama? To see the answer we have to look at the other three arguments shown along the bottom of Figure 7.2. The one on the left claims that he wants to invest more in the poor, but also that he has shown no appetite to overhaul America's welfare state. This argument does not pick out an obvious inconsistency, but consider what happens when we add the additional premise that many elements of the welfare state undermine economic opportunity. Now there is evidence of a conflict in the elements on the additional assumption that undermining economic opportunity will presumably make everything worse for everybody in America, including the poor. Thus, when you put these premises together they suggest an inconsistency that suggests that Obama's view is either illogical or insincere.

Next let's look at the other argument supporting the claim that his solutions are inconsistent. It is based on the premise that he lambasts a tax code that benefits special interests, but he has not pushed for tax reform. This argument suggests an inconsistency (i.e., that he is against a tax code that benefits special interests but that he has not pushed for tax reform). In other words, since he has not tried to carry out the means required to change the tax code, it is implied that his expressed wish to change it is not sincere. This allegation implies that he is not really sincere in his commitment to trying to change the tax code that benefits special interests. This apparent inconsistency suggests that he does not practice what he preaches. In terms of practical reasoning, it suggests that his goals are not commensurate with his actions in a way that suggests a lack of integrity. Comparable to the previous argument considered above, the argument suggests a character defect and can therefore be classified as an *ad hominem* argument.

Just after the second part quoted above, the author even writes: "if he wants to counter America's economic stratification rather than just rail against it,

Mr. Obama needs to think again." On the surface, this sentence appears to be offering advice to Obama on how he could rethink his current political position to bring it into line with what the author considers to be the real problem about income distribution in the American economy. But at a deeper level, the argument is an *ad hominem* attack against Obama, suggesting that he does not really want to counter America's economic stratification, but only wants to "rail against it" in order to try to fulfill his real political and economic goals. This part of the argument can be described as an *ad hominem* attack because it is alleging that Obama is insincere. The reason given is that it is suggested that he may not really want to counter America's economic stratification, but only to rail against it, perhaps for purely rhetorical political purposes, rather than for the practical purpose of solving the problem of economic stratification posed in the first text quoted above.

The article is an interesting political commentary, and is a legitimate expression of the author's views on the American economy and on the current political situation in light of the important problem of skewed income distribution. Practical reasoning is used throughout the article because clearly it is a case of problem-solving based on goals such as narrowing income gaps, values such as social mobility, and consideration of actions that should be taken in order to try to fulfill these goals, such as raising or lowering taxes. So, one might think that it is possible to evaluate the sequence of argumentation by placing it in a context of deliberation dialogue to see how the sequence of practical reasoning links the goals, the values, and the solutions to the problems that are posed. Yet clearly this would be a naïve approach, because it fails to take into account the shift from what appears initially to be a deliberation dialogue to a persuasion dialogue in which one political position is pitted against another.

It is interesting to compare this example with the examples in Chapter 2 of practical reasoning used in commercial ads for health care products. In these cases, it is obvious to the reader that the ad is a commercial message, and that the company who produces the medication is using practical reasoning to try to get the reader to buy it in order to solve the perceived health care problem of the reader. What is interesting here is that practical reasoning is used in so many of these commercial advertisements, and indeed can even be said to be the typical kind of argumentation used in such commercial ads. Thus, the primary setting in which practical reasoning is used in such cases appears to be that of persuasion dialogue. Nevertheless, it was shown in Chapter 2 that deliberation is involved, basically because the reader of the ad has some problem he or she is trying to solve, and the ad is conveying the message to the reader that the way to solve this problem is to take the action of buying the product. Thus, the companies who write the ads have to craft their persuasion argumentation around this deliberation framework in which both the writer and the reader of the ad are using practical reasoning. The writer of the ad has to grasp the practical reasoning used by the reader of the ad, and then apply her knowledge about what she takes to be the reader's goals and perceptions of actions that might fulfill these goals within the framework of a persuasion dialogue.

In the examples in Chapter 2, it is obvious from the outset that the basic context of use of the argumentation is that of persuasion dialogue. The situation is different in the case of the article about economic opportunity. It might appear that the article is about the economics of income distribution because it initially appears to be about the problem of skewed income distribution in America. Therefore, the reader might be led to reasonably expect that once this problem has been formulated in the article, in the first text quoted above, that the rest of the article will be a deliberation dialogue that employs practical reasoning to discuss proposals about how the goal of equal economic opportunity can be achieved by taking action to solve the problem of skewed income distribution. But there is another problem with the case as a whole, and that is that there are different views about how to solve this problem; and, in fact, in America these views are split into two opposed positions, essentially the left and the right positions: the Democratic and Republican political positions. So, the article quickly shifts from its formulation of the problem to attack the position of the left by using arguments accepted by the position on the right. In other words, as the article goes along there is a gradual shift from deliberation dialogue to persuasion dialogue.

7.4 The Social Progress Example

An article[2] in the *Economist* that discusses how to sustain recent social progress in Latin America raises two issues about how CAS can apply the notion of audience in order to evaluate arguments based on practical reasoning. The same example also raises the issue of how evidence can be factored into the kind of argument evaluation method used in CAS. The article poses the problem of how to sustain recent social progress in Latin America and discusses several means that might be implemented to achieve this goal. Since social progress may be classified as a value, the kind of practical reasoning involved in this example is value-based practical reasoning. Let's call the

---

[2] *The Economist*, March 1, 2014, 12. The word "Bello" appears with the title, indicating an unnamed author.

article the social progress example. The article supports the existence of the problem by offering statistical evidence cited in the World Bank report stating that in 2012 only a quarter of Latin Americans were in the poor category, but recent figures showed that economic growth in the region has slowed (12):

> Growth has certainly slowed, to below 3% in the past two years compared with an annual average of 5% in 2003 to 2008. But poverty continues to fall. In a report released this week, the World Bank reckons that in 2012 only a quarter of Latin Americans were poor, a category defined as those living on less than four dollars a day at purchasing power parity (see chart).

The article uses this evidence (along with a statistical chart tracking poverty statistics) to support the statement, "this still leaves Latin America as the world's most unequal region, along with sub-Saharan Africa." In this instance we have statistical evidence based on an expert source – the World Bank – presented to support the claim that there is a problem of social progress in Latin America. We also have an instance of use of argument from values in the claim made that Latin America is the world's most unequal region, except for sub-Saharan Africa.

Next the article (34) goes on to present statistical evidence from another expert source (Nora Lustig), who basically agrees:

> Nora Lustig, an economist at Tulane University in New Orleans, has crunched the household-survey numbers for individual countries. She thinks the fall in income inequality is continuing in many countries, and has accelerated in Argentina, Bolivia and Ecuador – though not in Mexico, where it seems to have reversed in 2010. But she, too, thinks that there is a risk of the fall in inequality petering out.

She is said to think that income inequality has decreased in Argentina, Bolivia, and Ecuador, but not Mexico. As quoted above, she is also said to think that there is a risk of inequality petering out. Here we have another use of evidence based on the argumentation scheme for argument from expert opinion.

The sequence of argumentation in this part of the article can be modeled by the argument diagram shown in Figure 7.3. The ultimate conclusion, shown at the far left of Figure 7.3, is the statement that there is a problem of how to sustain social progress in Latin America. The rest of the diagram shows arguments supporting the claim that there is such a problem. Looking over the diagram, it can be seen that four of the arguments fit the argumentation scheme for argument from expert opinion. The argument at the bottom toward the left has a pro argument from expert opinion used to support the ultimate conclusion, based on the premise that Nora Lustig is an expert in Latin American economics and the premise that she thinks that there has been a fall in income inequality in three of the Latin American countries.

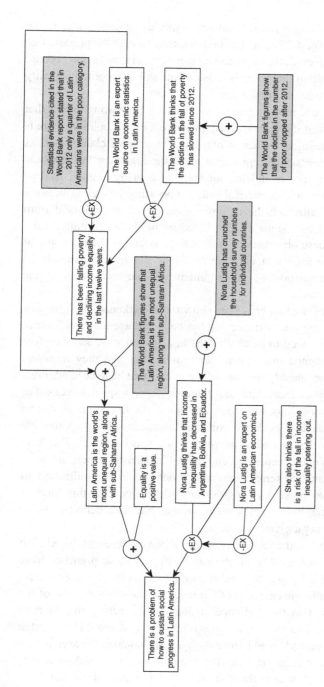

Figure 7.3: Argument Diagram for the Social Progress Example

This argument is attacked by a con argument acting as an undercutter to the prior argument from expert opinion. The undercutter also uses the premise that Nora Lustig is an expert on Latin American economics, but it takes into account Nora Lustig's qualification that there is a risk of the fall in income inequality petering out in Latin American countries.

As one looks over the argumentation in this case, it is interesting to note that even though quite a bit of it is based on argument from expert opinion, there is also quite a bit of statistical evidence presented to support claims used as premises in the arguments. The representation of the argument in the whole text of the example is not complete, but there is actually a good deal of statistical evidence given with numerical values supporting the claims throughout the article. Thus, although the arguments are based on argument from expert opinion, they are presumably also based on hard data compiled from statistical findings. These observations raise the question of whether some of the text boxes in the argument diagram could be classified separately as constituting evidence supporting the arguments at various points in the sequence of argumentation.

In Figure 7.3 four of the text boxes are shown with darkened backgrounds, indicating that they represent evidence that has been collected. The difference is that these text boxes need to be challenged in a special way, and therefore should also be represented in a special way, indicating that they represent evidence. Evidence presumably consists of statements that have been admitted as being supported by external data, and therefore have a special status. For example, in this instance, since the article appears in the *Economist*, it can be assumed that the statistical evidence collected and assessed by appropriate experts, such as statisticians and economists, has a special status. This kind of evidence is not beyond questioning, and indeed in the article there are some discussions about how the term "poverty" is defined in the collection of evidence about issues of social progress and inequality. But this kind of evidence is still special because it is recognized as having a definitive value in proving or disproving a given claim.

Note that in Figure 7.3, the four propositions taken to represent this kind of evidence have been darkened, indicating in CAS that these premises have been accepted by the audience. So, that is another characteristic of evidence. If something is put into the category of evidence, in the general sense of the word, it is indicated that the audience is prepared to accept this kind of evidence generally, and so the propositions representing it should be inserted into the system as accepted, even before the system evaluates the argumentation. This will have effects on how the argumentation is evaluated. For example, suppose the statement that the World Bank figures show that Latin

America is the most unequal region, along with sub-Saharan Africa, is taken as an evidence statement. Then, the text box in which the statement appears is darkened, as shown in Figure 7.3. Automatically, the system will calculate that the conclusion that this premise supports – the statement that Latin America is the world's most unequal region, along with sub-Saharan Africa – will also automatically be shown in a darkened text box. Assume also that in this case the premise that inequality is a positive value is accepted. The outcome will then be that, other parts of the diagram being equal, the ultimate conclusion that there is a problem of how to sustain social progress in Latin America will also be accepted. So, its text box will automatically be shown with a darkened background.

7.5 The Second Stage of the Social Progress Example

The article goes on to discuss a number of factors that play a role in reducing inequality, concluding that the big change has been in wages, influenced by the expansion in education. Stating that gains from this source have now largely run their course, the article poses the question: "What can governments do to keep progress going?" One means offered to the goal of keeping progress going is to undertake the structural reforms required to boost economic growth. Another means to keep the falling inequality going is to launch a crusade to improve the quality of education. But then it is said that accomplishing this task means raising taxes. One way to do this might be to raise taxes on consumption, but the article argues against this by saying that this action would risk aggravating inequality rather than reducing it.

The deliberation in the article compares the considerations for and against each of the three proposals, but it does not postulate an exclusive choice between the three by arguing that one is better than the other two alternative proposals. However, it certainly does evaluate the three proposals comparatively by means of argumentation, pointing out pros and cons of each of the proposals. The first proposal – that of undertaking structural reforms – is considered below, using statistical evidence on fluctuation in poverty rates:

> The most important answer is to undertake the structural reforms required to boost economic growth as the commodity boom wanes: 70% of the fall into poverty rates in 2003–12 was due to a rise in incomes from employment, not from social programs according to the bank.

Here again, the article cites statistical evidence from the World Bank. Hence, assuming that social problems fall under the category of structural reforms, this part of the article is rejecting the structural reforms necessary for an effective solution to the problem, at least by themselves.

Finally, the article comes to the third solution to the problem: "Keeping the fall in poverty and inequality going may require a squeeze on the rich – but done cleverly, so as not to deter growth enhancing investments." The solution is supported by the premise that rich Latin Americans pay less than their fair share of taxes.

A careful analysis will show that practical reasoning is woven throughout the argumentation in this segment of the text of the article. To sum up, the argumentation in this part of the article proposes three means being considered as ways of fulfilling or working toward the goal of sustaining the recent social progress in Latin America. The first proposal is to undertake structural reforms. The second proposal is to take action to launch a crusade to improve the quality of education. The third proposal is to increase taxes on the rich. These three proposals are compared by considering arguments for and against each of them in turn. This sequence of argumentation is shown in Figure 7.4.

The ultimate goal of sustaining recent social progress in Latin America is shown at the top of Figure 7.4. Below it, the three proposals put forward as possible means of achieving this goal are displayed. Each of them is configured as an instance of the use of practical reasoning. Supporting the first proposal of undertaking structural reforms, there is a pro argument with two premises. The one premise is that a boost in economic growth might play a role in reducing inequality. The other premise is that undertaking structural forms is required to boost economic growth. This argument too would seem to be an instance of practical reasoning. So, what we have here is a typical chain of arguments based on practical reasoning, one linked to the other.

The next argument is based on two premises. One is that expansion in education has been a big factor in reducing inequality. This premise suggests that it is the value-based variant of practical reasoning that is at work here. The other premise is that launching a crusade to improve the quality of education could be a means to reach the goal of sustaining recent social progress in Latin America. Supporting the former premise is the claim that launching a crusade to improve education requires raising taxes. Here we have inserted the implicit premise that improving education is a goal, since it has already been indicated that expansion in education has been a big factor in reducing inequality. Adding this implicit premise makes the argument also an instance of practical reasoning. Raising taxes, in general, is seen as something to be avoided, and therefore this argument might also be classified as a value-based kind of practical reasoning. However, we should not try to take this into account in the diagram, for fear of making it too complicated to be very useful as an

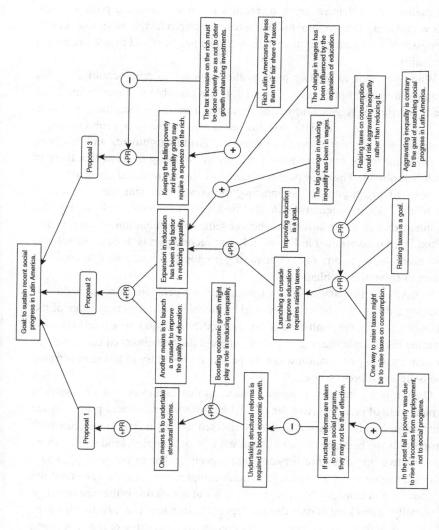

Figure 7.4: Proposals and Practical Reasoning in the Social Progress Example

example. Also, the negative value of raising taxes will be taken into account in the next argument.

The next argument in the sequence has the premise that one way to raise taxes might be to raise taxes on consumption. But then a con argument against this premise is that raising taxes on consumption would risk aggravating inequality, rather than reducing it. From a practical reasoning point of view this would make the proposal to raise taxes counterproductive when considered alongside the ultimate goal of sustaining social progress and thereby reducing inequality.

When you look at the two parts in the sequence of argumentation in this example displayed in Figures 7.3 and 7.4, it is possible to observe that there are two different stages. During the first part of the argumentation, as shown in Figure 7.3, the ultimate conclusion is that there is a problem about sustained social progress in Latin America. All the arguments and evidence in the sequence of argumentation are directed to trying to show that there is such a problem. The vast preponderance of the argumentation in the case consists of pro arguments supporting the conclusion that there is such a problem. The argumentation in this first part has to do with setting the problem that is to be solved in the subsequent deliberation, shown in the second part diagrammed in Figure 7.4. The second part is directed to solving this problem, or, at any rate, considering proposals for actions that could be taken to solve the problem.

In CAS, the first stage – that of formulating a problem to be solved or of framing a decision to be made – would be modeled in the opening stage of the dialogue. Setting the conflict to be resolved or the decision to be made is called framing the issue in rhetorical studies, where it is often observed that there can be contest of argumentation when the parties involved try to frame or reframe the issue in different ways.

On the other hand, the argumentation shown in Figure 7.4 represents a typical case of practical reasoning in deliberation where several proposals are put forward and the argumentation is directed toward trying to decide which proposal is the best one to move ahead with. In the simplest kind of case there are just two proposals put forward, and a decision has to be made on which course of action to take. However, in more complex cases there can be multiple proposals, and considerable disagreement about which one is the best one. It is especially in this kind of case that the argumentation model is valuable because it can look at the pros and cons of only arguments supporting or attacking each proposal, and then compare the solutions depending on the values of the audience, the strengths and weaknesses of the arguments, and how the arguments are connected to each other.

The dialectical framework of this example needs to be compared with that of the printer example, where a decision needed to be made about what the goal of the dialogue should be. Should the goal simply be to remove the black line that was appearing down the middle of the page, or should it include alternatives such as enlisting a technician to fix the problem as opposed to Bryan's trying to continue to do it himself? Both examples show the importance of the framing of the decision to be made or the problem to be solved at the opening stage.

Another interesting aspect of the social progress example is the answering of the question of who the audience is supposed to be. In the standard type of deliberation dialogue, there is a group of parties who are acting together to solve a common problem or make a decision that affects all of them, and they are looking at the arguments pro and con each proposal. However, the dialectical framework in the social progress case is quite different. The author of the article is presenting the problem of social inequality in the Latin American countries and discussing possible solutions to it. As noted above, in the first part he is arguing to try to prove there is such a problem, and in the second part he is examining the proposals by considering the pro and con arguments supporting or attacking each proposal. This looks very much like deliberation. But note that it is not the author who is making the decision to take action or not and who has to decide which proposal represents the best course of action. This decision is up to the Latin American countries themselves, either individually or collectively. So, the framework of the dialogue is not precisely that of a deliberation. The real audience is the readers of the *Economist*. We do not know who they are. So it can be conjectured that the dialogue could possibly be classified as a type of persuasion dialogue in which the author is trying to persuade the readers that the problem exists, and is trying to marshal some evidence from economics to show that some of the more plausible proposals for a solution can be evaluated, by examining the pro and con arguments based on this evidence. Or, at least, the author is trying to enlighten readers by pointing out that the problem exists and discussing the worth of some of the proposed solutions to it by examining some of the evidence available from economics.

7.6 Is There a Burden of Proof in Deliberation?

In the examples studied in the first five sections of this chapter, there does seem to be something like a burden of proof operative in deliberation dialogues as the argumentation moves forward. After all, when a proposal is put forward by a participant in deliberation, it is expected that the other parties will put forward arguments either supporting or attacking the proposal, and since the proponent of the proposal is advocating or suggesting the right course of action for the group to take, she will be expected to defend the proposal if it is attacked by any of the other participants.

As shown in Chapter 6, in the formal model of deliberation dialogue built by Kok et al. (2011), there are speech acts for putting forward a proposal and protocols allowing or requiring a respondent to present an argument against carrying out the proposal. When the respondent challenges the proposal by asking the why question 'Why propose A?,' the proponent is required at the next move to put forward an argument supporting A. It would appear that, in this model, making a proposal in a deliberation dialogue carries with it a burden of proof on the proponent who made the proposal to defend it if the other party challenges it. Failure to defend the proposal means that the proponent should immediately have to retract it. This is the familiar burden of proof protocol in persuasion dialogue requiring any participant who makes a claim to immediately defend it by presenting evidence to support it when the claim is questioned by the other participant. But should the speech act of making a proposal in a deliberation dialogue be treated in the same way with respect to burden of proof as the speech act of making an assertion (claim) in a persuasion dialogue? There are two sides to this issue.

According to the analysis by Kauffeld (1998, 248), there are three essential requirements characteristic of the speech act of making a proposal. The first requirement is that the speaker must present what Kauffeld calls a statement of resolve, "and act as if this statement expresses a determination or conclusion that the speaker has reached." According to the second requirement, "the speaker must openly give it to believe that she is speaking with the intention of answering doubts and objections regarding the statement put forward." According to the third requirement, the speaker must "overtly intend that her statement and commitment to advocacy provide the hearer with reason to raise questions, doubts, and objections with regard to the proposition." Kauffeld also has the idea that the speech act of making a proposal commits the speaker to something. In this third requirement the speech act of making a proposal represents commitment on the part of the speaker to advocacy. In Kauffeld's description, this kind of commitment provides the hearer with reasons to raise questions, doubts, or objections with regard to the proposition being advocated. The idea seems to be that the speaker has a commitment to defending the proposition, or at least the intention of inviting the hearer to raise critical questions about the proposition so that the speaker can answer them.

Both of the accounts of the speech act of making a proposal of Searle and Kauffeld are dialectical, in that both presuppose a framework in which two or more parties are taking turns making moves that put forward statements that allow for the questioning of the statements by the other party. The dialectical nature of the analysis is most clearly expressed in the second and third conditions put forward by Kauffeld, which explicitly involve answering doubts and objections and providing the other party with reason to raise questions, doubts, and objections. These requirements even imply that the speaker who puts forward a proposal for a proposition incurs a burden of proof, or at least a responsibility to reply to objections or critical questions with respect to that proposition. However, despite these initial appearances, reasons can be given to support the thesis that there is, strictly speaking, no burden of proof on the participant in a deliberation dialogue who brings forward a proposal for action.

Deliberation dialogue works differently from persuasion dialogue, inquiry dialogue, and some other types of dialogue. In persuasion dialogue and inquiry dialogue, there is a single proposition set in place at the opening stage, and the goal of the dialogue is either to prove this proposition or to show that it cannot be proved by the evidence that is available. Parenthetically, it needs to be said that there is always a twist with the persuasion type of dialogue because there are two basic types of dialogue: the dispute and the dissent. In the dispute the proponent has a thesis to prove and the respondent has to prove the opposite or negation of that proposition. In the dissent, the proponent has a thesis to prove and all the respondent has to do in order to emerge victorious is to show that the evidence is insufficient to prove this thesis. For these reasons, there is a global burden of proof set in place at the opening stage in a persuasion dialogue or an inquiry dialogue, and this burden of proof governs the argumentation as it moves back and forth from one side to the other during the argumentation stage. In the closing stage, the global burden of proof determines which side won or lost the dialogue.

In CAS the notion of burden of proof is linked to standards of proof of the kind used in legal argumentation. For example, the preponderance of the evidence standard (also known as the balance of probabilities), the standard applicable in civil cases, is that the proposition at issue is proved if the pro arguments are stronger than the con arguments. The beyond reasonable doubt standard, the highest standard used in Anglo-American jurisprudence and the standard applicable in criminal law, requires that the arguments supporting the claim must not be amenable to any opposing arguments or critical questions that can leave any reasonable doubt open on whether the argument is acceptable. This standard does not require the proof to show that a conclusion is true with absolute certainty. It is not a standard of beyond all doubt. It only needs to be strong enough to overcome any reasonable doubt that can be raised by arguments or questions put forward by the defense. The clear and convincing evidence standard, which lies between the other two standards, is higher than the preponderance of the evidence standard but not as high as the beyond reasonable doubt standard. The substantial evidence standard requires that there be at least some reasonably strong arguments supporting the claim, in contrast to the scintilla of evidence standard, which requires only the smallest bit of evidence to have been brought forward by supporting arguments. These are just some examples of standards of evidence that are applicable in legal argumentation. The kinds of standards of evidence that might be applicable in everyday conversational arguments might not necessarily be perfectly coextensive with these standards. In any trial a so-called burden of persuasion is set at the opening stage, and then there is a localized notion of burden of proof called the evidential burden that shifts from one side to the other as the speech acts are put forward by both sides during the argumentation stage. A legal trial of this kind can be classified as a species of persuasion dialogue.

The speech act of making an assertion in a persuasion dialogue has two components. One is the proposition contained in the assertion. The other is the stance or attitude taken toward the proposition claiming that the proposition is true, or at least can be supported by evidence that shows that it should be accepted. These two components taken together imply that when a participant makes an assertion, there is a burden of proof attached to it, meaning that the participant must provide some evidence to support the acceptability of the proposition if it is questioned by any other party in the discussion, otherwise the participant must retract his assertion.

To discuss the question of whether there should be a burden of proof requirement in deliberation dialogue comparable to the kind of burden of proof in a persuasion dialogue, some differences between the two types of dialogue have to be made clear. The goal of a deliberation dialogue, set in place at the opening stage, is for the participants to decide what to do in a situation that requires choice, based on their knowledge of the circumstances of the particular case they confront. The goal of a persuasion dialogue, set in place at the opening stage, is for the participants to use rational argumentation to resolve a conflict of opinions on a contested topic. Each opinion is represented by a proposition that each side holds to be true (or false). Suppose an agent puts forward a claim in a persuasion dialogue and another agent questions it or puts forward a counter-claim. If the claimant agent fails to defend its claim by immediately presenting an argument to back it up, he or she should have to retract it. In the case of a persuasion dialogue an assertion is a claim made that needs to be defended if questioned. The nature of deliberation dialogue is different. Participants in a deliberation dialogue generally have different plans in mind, and these plans may conflict. But a conflict of plans is different from a conflict of opinions. Even though plans can conflict, the disagreement between them is different from a conflict of opinions. Although the two agents may have a common goal of arriving at a way of solving the problem or making a decision they set out to discuss, even though they have not formed a plan yet, they may have their own plans partly based on their own interests and their own perceptions and knowledge about the circumstances of the case. However, their individual goals and plans will have to be integrated if they are to arrive at a solution to the problem they all think will work in order to solve it. What they will mainly need to argue about is how their individual plans can be integrated to provide a feasible solution to the problem, as shown by the four examples of deliberation dialogue presented in Chapter 6.

One important criterion for feasibility of the plan proposed in Walton, Norman, and Toniolo (2015) is the increase in the number of conflicts resolved between the two plans. When a why question is asked in a deliberation dialogue, its purpose is not to demand evidence to back up a claim by the other party. Instead, the why question needs to be seen as a request for the other party to explain her plan, or to give reasons why the parts of her plan hang together and are supported by a review of the circumstances of the case. The speech act of questioning a proposal should be set up in such a way that it allows the respondent to clarify its plans, its goals, and what it takes to be its knowledge of the circumstances.

When a why question is asked in a deliberation dialogue, one agent asks the other 'Why do you want to perform this action?' The speech act (Arg_{sup}) defined in Toniolo (2013) is a request for the other agent to explain parts of that other agent's plan, including its presumed knowledge of the circumstances, and also to deal with changes in the circumstances as new knowledge has entered into the dialogue. In such a case, the respondent might be partly in agreement with the proposal made by the other party, but might think that it needs to be modified or updated by some new information about the circumstances that the other party lacks. This juncture might lead to a further conversation about how each plan can be modified, or how some other parties in the discussion might have further information about the factual circumstances in which the decision needs to be made. Such a discussion could be a very positive direction. It is therefore important that the protocol designed for responding to a why question should be flexible enough to allow for explanations, and for presenting and re-evaluating information about the circumstances of the case. For these reasons, it would be an error to construe the speech act of asking the why question in a deliberation dialogue as carrying with it a sharp burden of proof requirement comparable to the way the speech act protocols work in a persuasion dialogue.

Hence, there is no comparable burden of proof attached to the speech act of making a proposal in a deliberation dialogue. When an agent puts forward a proposal and another participant questions whether that proposal is acceptable, even if the agent fails to immediately defend a proposal by presenting a supporting argument, it does not mean he has to retract the proposal. It is always possible that some other party in the deliberation might present arguments in favor of the proposal. But if nobody defends the proposal, as the deliberation continues it is likely that a better proposal will be found, and that this proposal will simply fall by the wayside. It still stands as a proposal, but unless all of the competing proposals have strong arguments against them, it is unlikely that this proposal will get any consideration for acceptance at the end of the argumentation stage.

Hence the sequence of argumentation operates in quite a different manner in a deliberation dialogue. As shown in Chapter 6, there are four types of deliberation dialogue, including the problem-solving deliberation, which is often a solitary process, and the decision-making type of deliberation dialogue, where some sort of action is called for on the part of an agent or group of agents making a choice on what to do in a given set of circumstances. In the latter type of case a familiar sort of situation is a dilemma or two-option choice, where an agent has to decide how to move forward by taking a fork in the path, choosing to take one course of action or another. The dilemma is often taken to represent the typical type of deliberation dialogue. But in this regard, appearances can be misleading. For one thing, in a deliberation dialogue, it may be an oversimplification of the circumstances to think that there are only two options when in fact there may be multiple options. This feature of deliberation is more obvious in the group deliberation cases studied in Chapter 6. In a deliberation dialogue, the whole structure of the argumentation as the proposals are made and evaluated during the argumentation stage is fragmented into multiple courses of action that now constitute new proposals in their own right as the argumentation proceeds. Factual evidence concerning the circumstances of the case composes much of the argumentation that typically comes to the forefront when evaluating the practicality of such proposals. Burden of proof is operative when evidence to support or attack a claim is brought forward, but when this happens, there has been a shift to a persuasion dialogue.

7.7 Speech Acts and Burdens in Deliberation Dialogue

For all that, there needs to be a device comparable to burden of proof in a deliberation dialogue that achieves the same function of linking the opening stage of the dialogue to the closing stage in a way that it can be used to evaluate the arguments put forward during the argumentation stage. Such a device can be set in place as follows. During the opening stage of a deliberation dialogue, circumstances are described that pose a problem or require a choice to be made by taking some action. However, these circumstances can change as new knowledge comes in during the argumentation stage. These circumstances can change the nature of the problem or choice to be made as the argumentation stage proceeds. Hence, they should not be fixed at the opening stage. One of the important things about deliberation dialogue using practical reasoning is that flexibility is very important. The existing plan of action may have to be given up altogether or severely modified once knowledge of new circumstances comes in. If the argumentation stage is not open to such severe modifications, this can be a major obstacle to the completion of a successful deliberation that will really deal with the circumstances appropriately to solve the problem. One of the worst failures of deliberation is sticking to the plan even though it has become evident that the plan will fail unless modified.

When a participant in deliberation dialogue puts forward a proposal, and someone else challenges the proposal – for example, by citing negative consequences of it – it is not an obligation of the particular party who put forward the proposal to immediately defend it. The participant could reply by conceding that the proposal she put forward has these negative consequences, but she can maintain that even though it is open to having these negative consequences, since nobody has put forward a better proposal, the proposal she put forward still stands. There is, however, a burden of responding constructively that can apply. If the opponent can put forward a better proposal that does not have these negative consequences, then that will be an argument in favor of his proposal against her proposal.

In Table 6.1 it was shown how Kok et al. (2010, 79) formulated speech acts in their communication language for deliberation dialogue by indicating the attacks an agent can make when replying to the other agent's speech act. When the first agent makes a move of putting forward a proposal for A, the second agent has only two options for reply. He can either ask the question 'Why propose A?,' or he can say 'Reject A.' The way the structure of burden of proof is set in this protocol, the proposal will be defeated unless the proponent can give some argument to support it. In other words, the response of asking the why question shifts the burden of proof onto the side of the proponent of the proposal. The reason is that in this system, one based on an abstract argumentation framework, a why question can only be answered satisfactorily by presenting an argument that supports the proposition questioned. However, this way of framing the procedural rules for responding to speech acts does not fit with the approach to deliberation taken in previous chapters, where a why question can also be interpreted as a request for an explanation. Another factor stressed in the model of deliberation built in the previous chapters is that it was emphasized that it is important in deliberation dialogue to encourage the putting forward of proposals. When a proponent puts forward a proposal, it should be open to the other parties to support the proposal by putting forward pro arguments.

The protocol for deliberation dialogue of Walton, Norman, and Toniolo (2015, 15) is set up in such a way as to allow the agents to identify plan conflicts, to argue about and explain such conflicts, and to work toward settling the conflicts. To understand how the protocol works, and defines a distinctive species of deliberation dialogue it is necessary to explain two speech acts P_{cir} and P_{ncir}, used in the argumentation stage. P_{cir} is used by the agents to exchange information about their individual circumstances. P_{ncir} is used to argue against carrying out some negative consequences of an action. There are seven speech acts allowed by the protocol: proposing, rejecting, withdrawing, accepting, arguing, asking a why question, and disclosing. When a proposal to carry out an action is put forward, the respondent can either accept it or attack it. In order to attack it, the respondent can either ask the why question about the action or present an argument rejecting action. Both responses must use P_{cir} or P_{ncir}. When an argument is put forward, it can be attacked by asking a why question or by presenting a counter-argument. The original argument or the counter-argument can be withdrawn or accepted by the other agent.

Hypothesis 1 put forward by Walton, Norman, and Toniolo (2015, 16) is stated as follows: "The use of the protocol where agents are able to share information about their view of the circumstances of the decision during the course of deliberation increases the number of successful outcomes between agents." The experimental evidence collected showed that the percentage of successful deliberation dialogues was higher by about 25 percent in protocol P_{cir} than in protocol P_{ncir} (Walton, Norman, and Toniolo, 2015, 16). This result was taken to show that a deliberation dialogue that enables agents to disclose information about circumstances as the dialogue proceeds will show a significant improvement in the likelihood of success for the dialogue at the closing stage. What is required to enable the implementation of P_{cir} is an open knowledge base that permits evidence about the circumstances of the case to be introduced to the participants during the course of the deliberation. These findings suggest some advantages of making further changes to the protocol relating to burden of proof.

One suggestion is that when the speech act of making a proposal is carried out by a proponent three speech acts should be allowed as responses to it by any respondent in the deliberation dialogue:

1. *Accept A*, and optionally *Present Argument pro-A*;
2. *Reject A*, and optionally *Present Argument con-A*; and
3. *Propose B?*, and optionally *Present Argument pro-B*.

In this approach, when the proponent puts forward a proposal, there is no so-called burden of proof in place so that at the next move, if any respondent puts forward a why question challenging the proposal, the proponent has to present an argument supporting the proposal. The proponent should respond to any argument put forward that challenges the proposal, but she does not have to respond to a mere question that does not present an argument for thinking that the proposal is not a good one. When the proponent puts forward a proposal, anyone taking part in the deliberation should be free to present arguments for or against it, and there is no specific requirement for the participant who made the proposal to be the one who defends it. In general, however, there is an expectation that if somebody puts forward a proposal, they are advocating that proposal, and therefore there is an expectation that they are able to give reasons that explain why the proposal is a good one for the group to move forward with.

However, it needs to be said that setting up the rules for the making of speech acts and reacting to them in a deliberation dialogue requires some notion comparable to burden of proof as it works in deliberation. For this purpose, the burden of responding constructively is useful. When the proponent puts forward a proposal, it is presumed that she is suggesting to all the other participants in deliberation dialogue that they should follow this proposal as a way of solving the problem or making the decision originally formulated at the opening stage. It is inappropriate to require that she has to prove this proposal, and hence the notion of burden of proof is out of place. But there should be a requirement that, since she is putting forward this proposal for the whole group to follow, she should be able to explain how it can help the group move forward to its goal. Hence, it is a requirement that at the next move after the proposal has been put forward by the proponent, if the respondent demands that the proponent give an argument to support the proposal, the proponent can reply that she is not required to do that, and if the proponent wants to raise the issue of whether the proposal is acceptable one, he needs to present some argument showing why he thinks it is not acceptable. Once he presents such an argument, she can reply to it in the usual way, either by retracting the proposal, or by responding to his argument by presenting a counter-argument. So there is what can be called a requirement of responding constructively attached to the making of a proposal in deliberation dialogue, but it does not operate in the same way that burden of proof works in a persuasion dialogue.

When a participant in deliberation dialogue puts forward a proposal, and a respondent challenges the proposal – for example, by citing negative consequences of it – the proponent should be allowed to reply as follows: can you put forward a better proposal that does not have these negative consequences? This kind of reply by the respondent should not be regarded as an illicit attempt to get off the hook of having to deal immediately with the argument from negative consequences. It is not an obligation of a party who has put forward a proposal to immediately defend it. The participant can concede that the proposal has these negative consequences, but maintain that since no better proposal has been offered, her proposal should stand. Even so, a burden of responding constructively can come into play. If the respondent can come up with a better proposal, the system should automatically put that one in place, thereby defeating the original proposal.

Much less should the proponent be required at her next move in the deliberation dialogue to provide an argument to support a proposal she has made if the respondent says, "Prove your proposal by backing it up with evidence to show it is a good proposal." If the proponent is directly asked by the respondent to show that the proposal she just made is a good one, as noted above, it should be left open as her next move in the deliberation dialogue for the proponent to ask the respondent to give some reason why he thinks the proposal is not a good one. This kind of attempt to turn the tables would be regarded as illicit in a persuasion dialogue, a type of dialogue where there is a burden of proof on an arguer to back up any claim that has been challenged by an opponent. But it should not be regarded as illicit in a deliberation dialogue.

7.8 Advising Dialogue

Typical examples of offering advice to someone trying to decide which car to buy can be found in abundance in the magazine *Consumer Reports*. For example, an article called "5 Steps to the Best Deal: Money-saving Tips from our Car-buying Pros" (April 2014, 26) offers advice to someone who is in the position of having to buy a car on the best way to solve the problem. The reader is guided through five steps:

1. Choose your exact car.
2. Set up your financing in advance.

3. Get dealers to compete.
4. Get the most for your trade-in.
5. Just say no to dealer extras.

The article offers detailed advice on how the reader can proceed by taking specific steps to move toward the ultimate goal of getting the best price on the car that she has chosen, presumably based on the information and advice given in the other articles in the same issue of *Consumer Reports*. For example, several specific steps are described in the procedure required to get dealers to compete. The reader is told to call or e-mail several dealers in the area and request a quote through their websites, telling them the exact car that you want and letting them know that you are shopping around. The reader is also advised to get other quotes from automaker websites or other sites that give information on standard car prices. The article advises the reader that the more quotes you get, the better is your position for negotiating with other dealers.

Consumer Reports tests new vehicles currently being offered on the market, tells the reader about how each of the vehicles performed in the tests, and passes along additional information about how each of the vehicles performed in safety tests made by other agencies. When *Consumer Reports* comparatively rates each of the cars, it offers this kind of information to the reader, using it as evidence to support the advice it gives. For example, in rating a particular all-wheel-drive car (*Consumer Reports*, April 2014, 42), the report first stated that all-wheel drive provides extra traction in slippery conditions. This statement passes general information to the reader on how all-wheel drive works. But then the text advises the reader that if he or she wants all-wheel-drive in a moderately priced sedan, options are limited. It then goes on to describe some competing vehicles that are also available with all-wheel drive, but are more expensive.

Typical articles in *Consumer Reports* can be seen as a blend of different types of dialogue, but prominent among them is advising dialogue. Basically, the authors of the car ratings and other articles published in the magazine offer their readers advice on all matters relating to the purchase of the vehicle. The different vehicles are compared and then, based on assumptions about what goals a reader might have in buying a car, the articles give advice on which vehicle might be the best one to achieve these goals. Some readers might want a sports car, while others might want an SUV. Some readers might want an economical car that will be environmentally friendly, while others might want a luxury car that offers comfort and style. The ratings divide the vehicles into categories, such as compact cars, luxury cars, and so forth, and then typically they comparatively evaluate the cars in a category. They do this by putting the cars in a particular category in a linear order depending on how each car has been rated, based on the tests that all of the cars have been subjected to and other information on the properties of the cars. They also select the car or cars they take to the best in a particular category.

Advising dialogue was involved in all three of the examples of practical reasoning we looked at. In the printer example, Anna not only gave Brian advice on how the black line could be removed, but in the end she helped him to remove it by using the method she recommended. Brian found the advice he needed to get the solution to this problem by searching on the Internet. He eventually got what he took to be the best advice, after much searching, once he found the Samsung website. In the real estate example, the real estate sales agent would presumably be required to give the couple advice on how to pursue their goals. For example, if the buyers have given her information about their preferences – for example, one of them prefers a quiet location, while the other prefers to be near the shops and cafés downtown – the real estate sales person would be expected to advise them on which locations would suit these requirements. On the other hand, the real estate sales agent makes her living by selling properties on a commission basis, and therefore the buyers should not always accept the advice she offers as being entirely unbiased.

What these observations about the real estate example indicate is that advising is a circumscribed part of the dialogue. The dialogue structure of the relationship between the real estate agent and her two clients is complex and often shifts from one type of dialogue to another. Much of the time, for example, they would be engaging in an information-seeking dialogue in which the real estate agent informs the couple about aspects of the city they are moving to, locations of properties, and so forth. Basically the structure of the dialogue is deliberation in which a family is trying to decide which house or condominium to buy, but along the way they may need advice from many other parties, such as building inspectors, lawyers, and so forth.

One clarification is that the speech act of advising needs to be seen as different from the speech act of warning. The latter speech act has the following four requirements, reformulated but based on the list of conditions in Searle (1969, 67):

Propositional Content Condition: The propositional content of the speech act poses some future event that may affect the hearer.

Preparatory Condition: The speaker has reason to believe that this event will be against the interests of the hearer.

Sincerity Condition: The speaker believes that the hearer will benefit from knowing in advance that this event may occur.

Essential Condition: The action of telling the hearer about the event is taken to offer to the hearer a way of avoiding its coming about or affecting him.

The first preparatory condition postulates that some event might affect the interests of the hearer. The second preparatory condition states that the occurrence of this event will have negative consequences for the hearer that can be avoided. The sincerity condition requires that the hearer can benefit from knowing about the event in advance. The essential condition is that telling the hearer about the event is taken to offer him a way of avoiding it.

Now let's compare the speech act of warning with the speech act of advising. The following set of four requirements for the speech act of advising are based roughly on the four conditions of Searle (1969, 67), but modified to fit argumentation theory:

Propositional Content Condition: The propositional content of the speech act describes some future problem or choice the hearer is confronting.

Preparatory Condition: The speaker has reason to believe that choosing one way or another can affect the interests of the hearer.

Sincerity Condition: The speaker believes that the hearer will benefit from knowing in advance about means to solve the problem or make the best choice.

Essential Condition: The action of telling the hearer how to proceed is taken to offer to the hearer a way to solve the problem or make the best choice.

By comparing the two sets of requirements it can be seen how the speech act of warning is different from the speech act of advising. The speech act of advising, as defined above, strongly suggests a context of use in deliberation where one party is trying to make a choice or solve a problem and the other party is trying to suggest a good way to proceed. The advisor is not the party who has to make the decision and is therefore external to the deliberation, but nevertheless takes part in it by offering the decision-maker some helpful counsel on how to move ahead in an expeditious way and take steps toward solving the problem.

These speech act analyses are useful, but what is even more useful is to fit them into a broader framework. Advising needs to be seen as not only a speech act, but as a speech act that is a distinct type of locution or move that is central to a distinctive type of dialogue in its own right. Let's call it advising dialogue, or perhaps it could also be called advice dialogue.

In the simplest case, advising dialogue has two parties. In formal dialogue models, one party is usually called the proponent and the other the respondent. We will call the proponent the advisor and the respondent the advice receiver. The advisor's goal is to offer advice to the respondent, and the respondent's goal is to benefit from this advice. The respondent needs to consider the advice, and ultimately to accept or reject it. In a normative model of dialogue, the respondent should only accept the advice if it is good advice. The purpose of the dialogue as a whole is to help the respondent attempt to make a decision on what to do in a situation that requires choice, or to solve the problem he is confronted with. Hence, advice dialogue is typically embedded in a larger structure of deliberation dialogue where a single agent or group of agents is trying to solve a problem or decide what to do in circumstances that require a choice of actions.

Advice dialogue is similar to persuasion dialogue in some respects, but it is not the same thing. In persuasion dialogue, there is a difference of opinions that needs to be resolved. One party accepts that a certain proposition is true, while the other party is of the opinion that this proposition is false, or at least has doubts that it can be proved to be true. In advice dialogue, one party confronts a problem or choice of actions, while the role of the other party is to furnish information relevant to the circumstances of the decision or problem that will guide the other party or help them move ahead to make a good decision based on adequate evidence. Advice dialogue definitely fits the form of argumentation, because the advice given takes the form of pro and contra arguments – arguments that support or attack the recommendation given by the advisor – displaying the evidence on both sides of the decision for the advice receiver to consider.

There are three stages in an advising dialogue: an opening stage, an argumentation stage, and a closing stage. The advice seeker opens the dialogue by formulating a problem using the scheme for practical reasoning to frame it. He tells the advisor that he has a goal and poses the problem of how to find an action that is the best means to carry out the goal. He asks the advisor if she sees any way of finding such a best means in the given circumstances.

During the argumentation stage the advisor asks for more information about the circumstances. She may also ask for further information about the advice seeker's goals and discuss some ways to achieve these goals. If she offers advice, the advice seeker needs to ask for explanations and further information about the advice. During the argumentation stage the advice seeker should question any weaknesses in the plan of action proposed by the advisor.

The closing stage is reached once the advisor is satisfied that the advice given to him has shown him a good way to solve this problem. Even if he is still not satisfied that the plan she has recommended is the best means to carry out his goals, the dialogue could be terminated successfully if the advisor has presented some way of working toward a good way of addressing or solving the problem. In this instance, the next step for the advice seeker might be to seek further advice from other advisors.

7.9 Moving Research Forward on Practical Reasoning

There are two strands to the continuing research program on practical reasoning. One is the project of building formal, computational models of argumentation that prominently contain practical reasoning as a type of argument. This research provides, and is based on, a logical structure that is extremely helpful in providing a clear and precise model of how practical reasoning should work in computational environments. The other program is fitting these abstract and formal computational models to our practical reasoning as used in settings such as human decision-making, legal reasoning, international affairs, policy-making, economics, practical affairs of daily life, and many other settings that provide examples of how practical reasoning really works in realistic argumentation. However, these two strands are closely connected because these software programs to aid computational tasks, and such practical tasks as rational decision-making, for example, are meant to be applied to real cases. It is the argument of this book that these two tasks need to be carried forward in tandem, each supporting the other.

In the first six chapters of the book, some formal argumentation models from artificial intelligence, such as CAS, were applied to examples of real or realistic cases of practical reasoning used in different argumentation settings. This work had already begun with the previous research that had established some relatively clear and precise models of both types of practical reasoning – the instrumental type and the value-based type. CAS was applied to examples of practical reasoning of both types, and it was shown how this form of reasoning can be evaluated as a type of argumentation in the system. Research on CAS continues at the time of writing this book, and the results are coming in on its foundations, the abstract logical structure it is based on, and on its representational capabilities to deal with forms of argumentation such as practical reasoning. One project that has been set as a topic for research on CAS is the problem of how to model deliberation dialogue.

However, as shown in Chapter 6, there are formal computational models of deliberation dialogue now being developed that can already take into account how information-seeking dialogue needs to be embedded into deliberation dialogue in order to achieve a formal model of deliberation dialogue in which practical reasoning can play a central role as an argumentation method for solving problems and supporting rational decision-making. It has been shown how the recent research of Walton, Toniolo, and Norman (2015) has provided a model of deliberation dialogue that is both useful for developing autonomous systems and multi-agent computing and that can support human practical reasoning. It was shown that real instances of natural deliberation contain circumstances on which practical reasoning needs to be based, which can change rapidly. It was shown how an extension had to be made to the current models of deliberation in artificial intelligence by incorporating a knowledge base into the dialogue sequence that captures dynamic changes of circumstances as the sequence of practical reasoning carries on during the dialogue. Moreover, it was shown empirically that an argumentation model which can consider group settings in which the arguments of one side are continuously interacting with those of the other side produces superior results because the conflicts between the two sides can make a collaborative deliberation proceed more efficaciously.

Another problem that needs to be taken up is how to reframe the protocol for posing and responding to a why question in a deliberation dialogue. To solve this problem, the ambiguity of the why question needs to be taken into account, and more room needs to be introduced for the use of explanations in the model. It was shown in Chapter 6 that it is important for the agents to disclose information about the need for plan elements, and it would seem that the best way for this to take place is to allow the agents to ask for explanations of each other's goals, intentions, and plans. Accordingly, for these purposes a different way of configuring the protocols for the speech act of making a proposal is required. A broader approach is required to make these kinds of moves possible.

The dialogue protocol for the Walton, Toniolo and Norman deliberation system is also made up of protocols governing putting forward and replying to speech acts. The first one is the asking of the why question by an agent, when one agent asks another why it wants to perform a particular action. According to the protocol of this model, when an agent asks a why question, such as 'Why do you want to perform this action?,' the other agent can only respond by offering an argument supporting the proposal for action. But surely the other agent should also be able to reply by explaining some elements of its plan and goals? For example, following the contours of the argumentation scheme for practical reasoning, the agent may communicate some goal that it has to the questioner, offering this as the reason for its preference for a certain action.

Such a goal provides a reason for the agent to think that carrying out this particular action is something that should be done. This kind of response combines argument and explanation. The answerer's reply might typically introduce some new information about the circumstances as well as offering an explanation to clarify the agent's goals or intentions.

This observation shows that models of deliberation dialogue should be expanded to include the possibility of explanation being interwoven with argument in the protocols of the system. It shows how the process of a deliberation dialogue needs to be assisted by each agent having the capability to ask another agent to explain its motive for an action by stating its goal, along with some circumstances. This explanation has a practical reasoning structure, because the components of the goal, the circumstances, and the means available in these circumstances, combine to furnish the structure of the argumentation. It is a practical reasoning structure that combines argument and explanation.

Thus, at the theoretical level of improving formal computational models, research on deliberation is rapidly moving forward to provide a model of the structure in which practical reasoning is used in its central setting, that of the deliberation dialogue. But more work also needs to be done by those in the more practical areas of argumentation study to work with real examples of the use of practical reasoning in different kinds of discourse. The real traction in coming to understand the structure of practical reasoning and learning how it works in diverse settings comes from the synergy between these two areas of research.

7.10 Conclusions

This chapter has shown that solutions to the closure problem and the burden of proof problem for practical reasoning in any given case depends on the framing of the particular problem to be solved or the decision to be made at the opening stage in the formal model of dialogue representing the multi-agent setting of practical reasoning in that case. In evaluating the practical reasoning in the examples discussed in this chapter, great care has to be taken to identify what type of dialogue the practical reasoners are supposed to be engaged in. For example, whether the dialogue is supposed to be part of a persuasion dialogue or a deliberation dialogue will make a big difference to a reasoned judgment of whether the practical reasoning is strong or weak.

This chapter concludes that there is no global burden of proof in deliberation dialogue in the way that there is in persuasion dialogue. Unlike the persuasion dialogue, where the burden of proof (called the burden of persuasion) is set at the opening stage of the dialogue, there is no global burden of proof of this sort set at the opening stage of the deliberation dialogue that continues over the other two stages (the argumentation stage and the closing stage). However, there is a burden of proof of a kind comparable to the so-called evidential burden (or burden of production of evidence) in law, which requires provision of evidence for a claim to move forward under questioning. This burden only applies, however, during the shift to the persuasion dialogue interval during the argumentation stage where proposals are backed up by arguments.

Great care needs to be taken in particular cases of the very common sort where an argumentation analyst is trying to analyze and evaluate argumentation based on practical reasoning used in a given text of discourse such as the ones in the examples from the *Economist*. In such cases, inevitably there is a mixing of persuasion dialogue, information-seeking dialogue, and deliberation dialogue woven through the argumentation. Such a mixture is inevitable because practical reasoning in any deliberation needs to take into account changes in circumstances during the sequence of practical reasoning, but knowledge of the circumstances is typically imperfect, and therefore arguments, ideally based on evidence, need to be brought forward to sort out the factual issues of the case.

This mixing generally occurs because there are disagreements in a typical deliberation dialogue in which there are differences of opinions on how to solve a problem using practical reasoning. In particular, there are conflicting goals among the parties to the decision-making, and conflicts about the best means to achieve these goals. In order to deal with these conflicts and help the deliberations move forward, incoming information from an open knowledge base that represents the changing circumstances of the case needs to be considered. Also, there can be conflicts of opinion between the stakeholders in the deliberation, and for this reason persuasion dialogue (or even negotiation dialogue) is helpful, and can be supported by factual evidence of the circumstances of the case brought in from an open knowledge base. This way of placing practical reasoning in a setting of this sort, with an open knowledge base providing information about the circumstances of the case, has been supported empirically in Walton, Norman, and Toniolo (2015), and enables the deliberation to move forward to a solution to the problem in a more expeditious manner. These aspects of practical reasoning in deliberation show that it cannot be emphasized strongly enough that intelligent practical reasoning needs to be based not only on goals, and on means to carry out the goals, but on knowledge of the relevant circumstances in which the decision is being made.

It has been shown how modeling practical reasoning as an argumentation scheme, and analyzing and evaluating instances of practical reasoning in realistic cases, are tasks that can be carried out within CAS. But the outstanding problem posed in the previous chapter was that of formulating the closure requirement for any instance in which practical reasoning is used as a form of argument to prove something that is subject to doubt or questioning. The closure problem depends on standards of proof, and it has been shown that in principle it is possible to formulate standards of proof within computational argumentation systems such as CAS. But the remaining problem is that in order to apply the model to real examples of practical reasoning, it has to be determined which standard is appropriate, depending on the type of dialogue in which the practical reasoning has been embedded. Chapter 6 concentrated on the deliberation type of dialogue, because surely this is the central one for practical reasoning. However, this chapter has shown that other types of dialogue – such as information-seeking dialogue, persuasion dialogue, and advising dialogue – are typically embedded within a deliberation dialogue, and are vitally important to the structure of the deliberation dialogue if it is to be used as a goal-directed type of argumentation in which practical reasoning represents a rational way of solving a problem.

Many readers of this book will wonder what lessons it has on the philosophical question of how the notion of rationality should be understood generally, given that it has now been shown that practical reasoning has such an important place in rational thinking and decision-making. The general consensus of opinion, stemming from the Enlightenment and the rise of natural science, is that rational thinking is of two kinds – deductive reasoning, exemplified by formal mathematical logic, and inductive reasoning, of the kind associated with probability and statistics. Recent work in artificial intelligence and argumentation has challenged that assumption, by emphasizing the importance of defeasible reasoning – a kind of reasoning that has proved to be resistant to reduction to exclusive application of deductive and inductive models of rationality. So what, if anything, does this tell us about the concept of rationality? Has it changed? Has it reverted to ancient Greek dialectical theories, such as that of Aristotle, who recognized the importance of this kind of reasoning in his study of topics and his dialectical framework of argumentation? These philosophical questions will be discussed in Chapter 8. They do not yet have precise answers, but they do bear speculation, given that the advent of the argumentation approach to practical reasoning put forward in Chapters 1 to 7 suggests an approach to the concept of rationality that is quite different from the one that is still dominant in many influential circles in philosophy at this point in history.

8

Practical and Epistemic Rationality

This chapter discusses the theoretical questions that are raised as one navigates across the storm-tossed seas of philosophical controversies about rationality. The analysis of the structure of practical reasoning advanced in the previous chapters has raised the question of whether it can be used to frame a new philosophical definition of rationality, but it also poses some problems. One of them is how to define the other kind of rationality that is apparently left over once practical reasoning has been shown to represent some notion of practical rationality. Some (pragmatists) think that nothing is left over, and that all rationality is practical rationality. Some call what is left over theoretical rationality, while others call it epistemic rationality.

The four examples of the use of practical reasoning in deliberation studied in Chapter 6 showed that intelligent deliberation needs to be based on knowledge of the circumstances of the case that is continually streaming in to an agent (or group of them) from an open knowledge base. This view of how practical reasoning is used requires a different approach to the notions of epistemic and practical rationality. The two notions need to be defined separately as distinctive concepts, but they also need to be seen as concepts that are combined in practical reasoning. Practical reasoning needs to be based on an agent's goals and values, but also on its knowledge of the circumstances. However, because the circumstances are continually changing, both human and machine agents, even when working together, are fallible. This means we are continually subject to bias, misperceptions, and errors of judgment. As we saw when defining the list of characteristics of a rational agent, one of the most important characteristics is the capability for error correction based on feedback as new information streams into the agent's knowledge base.

The central feature of knowledge in this view is that it has to be based on evidence, rather than requiring the truth of its findings. This fallibilistic conception of knowledge is contrasted in this chapter with the traditional veristic conception, which holds that a proposition cannot be knowledge unless it is true. In the evidence-based conception, scientific inquiry is seen as a social process of knowledge construction in which conclusions drawn are subject to later retraction once new evidence comes in. Based on this view, epistemic rationality is defined as reasoning that uses defeasible argumentation based on the evidence available in a case.

Practical rationality is defined as thinking based on an agent's goals, the means at its disposal in its given situation, knowledge of its circumstances in that situation, and its values (in cases of value-based practical reasoning). According to this view, practical reasoning requires an intelligent agent to act on knowledge of its circumstances, knowledge of what is possible, and other kinds of knowledge. Thus, practical rationality presupposes epistemic rationality.

Both practical and epistemic rationality, as defined in Sections 1–5 of this chapter, are shown to be typified by defeasible reasoning employed within a fallibilistic theory of knowledge. In this approach, the negative notions of error, irrationality, and fallacy are important, and are explored in Sections 6 and 7, where it is shown why irrationality is different from fallaciousness. Section 8 reviews the examples of the four different types of deliberation identified in Chapter 6 to show that practical rationality needs to take into account the setting in which practical reasoning is used. Section 9 presents a dialectical theory showing how practical and epistemic rationality are combined. Section 10 offers a summary of the key characteristics of the dialectical model of practical and epistemic rationality, and offers suggestions about directions for further research on how to extend the model to yield a clearer and more precise account of the distinction between practical and epistemic rationality that can be applied to problematic cases.

8.1 Practical Versus Theoretical Reasoning

Rescher (1988, 1) defines 'rationality' as "the appropriate use of reason to resolve choices in the best possible way," adding that "to behave rationally is to make use of one's intelligence to figure out the best thing to do in the circumstances." This definition is a good start, because it defines rationality in relation to a framework of deliberation in which the practical reasoning is being used to try to make a choice on the best course of action in a given set of circumstances. It requires a framework of rational deliberation, but Chapter 6 provides one. However, it leaves no room for contrasting categories of rationality, such as theoretical rationality or epistemic rationality. Indeed, the definition of 'reasoning' offered in Section 4 allows for instances of reasoning that do not have to be cases of practical, goal-directed reasoning. According to the account given there, theoretical rationality and irrationality can also be properties of reasoning, even when reasoning is not tied to goals, circumstances, and actions. It seems reasonable to assume from what has been argued so far that there is a purely cognitive kind of reasoning that is not practical reasoning, and does not (directly or essentially) involve practical reasoning. What should this kind of reasoning be called, and how should it be characterized?

We might try to get around this problem by tying the definition to changing standards. Theoretical reasoning might just be defined in relation to whatever canons have been adopted by science at any particular time to evaluate inferences as structurally correct or incorrect, according to the then accepted standards. For a long time, the theory of the syllogism reigned supreme as the accepted standard. Now, I would say, three standards of what is a structurally correct argument are generally accepted (the third one albeit only recently, and still not all that widely outside of computer science). The first, and best established standard, is that of deductive inference, represented these days by classical, first-order logic – essentially the modern propositional calculus with the theory of quantifiers built onto it. The second standard is that of inductive inference, represented broadly by the methods in use by the science of statistics at any given time. The third standard is that of reasoning based on defeasible argumentation schemes, species of nonmonotonic reasoning that are not inductive in nature.

Theoretical reasoning could initially be seen as the chaining together of inferences of one or more of the above three types. While practical reasoning concludes to a prudent course of action, theoretical reasoning concludes to a proposition as true, probable, or tentatively acceptable as true. Theoretical reasoning, in this view, does not require an agent to carry it out, while practical reasoning does. Theoretical reasoning is not an inherently dialectical notion. It can be defined in abstraction from the dialectical framework required by multi-agent practical reasoning. Practical reasoning also seems non-dialectical at first, but reveals significant dialectical aspects once it is explored. These differences seem to offer a basis for drawing a contrast between practical and theoretical reasoning.

Beyond these differences, there is room for controversy. Some would say that practical reasoning is characterized by deliberation on what to do, while theoretical reasoning is characterized by questions of what is true or false and what can be proved as scientific knowledge. These issues have implications for the question of whether the methods of scientific investigation are a model of rational argumentation that are also applicable outside science.

Both Clarke (1985) and Audi (1989) contrast practical reasoning with what they call theoretical reasoning. Clarke (1985, 2) distinguishes between theoretical and practical reasoning in terms of the goal each type of reasoning is directed toward, and the means used to move toward that goal: "theoretical reasoning is directed towards matters of fact and is employed in ascertaining what states of affairs obtain; practical reasoning, in contrast, is directed toward conduct and is a means for determining how the states of affairs are to be altered by the intervention of agents." This approach is curious, because it defines both theoretical and practical reasoning using practical reasoning itself in the definition. Audi's definition of practical reasoning (1989, 24–28) is hard to pin down since he bases it on interpreting Aristotle's remarks on the subject, and, of course, these are subject to interpretation and tend to be subject to disputation by scholars. At any rate, what seems common to both definitions is that practical reasoning is directed toward action, or at any rate a conclusion about what action should be taken, and it is based on premises that express a means for altering circumstances to achieve a goal. In contrast, theoretical reasoning is directed toward a conclusion that is a proposition about matters of fact, and is employed to determine whether a proposition is true or false. This way of articulating the contrast, while it represents a way of reformulating and combining both accounts of the distinction between practical and theoretical reasoning, may represent a helpful clarification. At any rate, it seems to be a good starting point.

We are already familiar with practical reasoning through the discussions and analyses in the previous chapters, where it has been defined as an argumentation scheme or form of argument, and a reasoning structure that can be modeled in CAS. So, we have a pretty good idea of what that is. But what is theoretical reasoning?

The first point to be made is that it is misleading to name the category of reasoning that Clarke and Audi contrast with practical reasoning by using the expression 'theoretical reasoning' because it may not always be theoretical in nature, where the term 'theoretical' suggests some high-level abstraction. The reason is that this kind of reasoning, whatever you call it, is often about whether a proposition about particulars is true or false, and therefore in such instances it is a concrete kind of reasoning. For example, we may be arguing about whether Pamela has blue eyes or green eyes, and bring forth a witness who says that she definitely has blue eyes. This inference is not about abstractions or generalizations, but it is a kind of reasoning directed to determine whether a proposition is true or false, and therefore it falls into the category opposed to practical reasoning.

According to the online entry (Wallace, 2014) entitled Practical Reason in the *Stanford Encyclopedia of Philosophy*, practical reasoning asks the question of what one ought to do, or what it would be best to do when an agent is presented with a set of alternatives for action. According to the article, because of its normative nature, practical reasoning is "concerned not with matters of fact and their explanation, but with matters of value, of what it would be desirable to do." In this article, on this basis, the contrast between practical and theoretical reasoning is drawn as a contrast between norms for the regulation of action and norms for the regulation of belief. The account of practical reasoning put forward in the previous chapters of this book is not consistent with this way of drawing the distinction between practical and theoretical rationality. The main reason for the inconsistency between the two accounts of practical rationality is that in the model presented in this book, practical reasoning needs to be concerned with matters of fact and their explanation, as well as with matters of value, and with agent's goals, because intelligent practical reasoning always needs to consider factual information about the circumstances of the case in which a decision is to be made.

In short, we need a better way of reframing the distinction between practical reasoning and the other kind of reasoning it supposedly contrasts with. We can use the term 'epistemic reasoning,' but it too may be misleading, in that it seems to imply that this kind of reasoning is exclusively about knowledge. It seems better to say that this kind of reasoning is about proving or disproving a proposition that is at issue, or is not known to be true or false. We could call it proof-directed reasoning, but this could be slightly misleading in some respects too. As a hypothesis to move forward tentatively, let's call it epistemic reasoning.

According to the previous chapters of this book, it is a necessary part of the analysis of practical reasoning that it should be at least partly defined in relation to the agent's knowledge of the circumstances of the case in which a decision is to be made on what to do. Is the same kind of knowledge characteristic of epistemic reasoning, or is it something different?

8.2 Two Views of Knowledge

According to Aristotle, practical wisdom (*phronesis*) is different from the more abstract kind of rationality (*episteme*) characterized by the way reasoning is used in theoretical science. Epistemic scientific rationality, the paradigm being Euclidean geometry, is based on necessary demonstrations (deductive reasoning from axioms). Practical reasoning is based on a presumptive assessment of how to reason in a particular given case, by applying generalizations to it that are open to exceptions in special cases, and that requires judgment to be used in fitting the particular to the general. But this contrast between practical and epistemic rationality, so nicely displayed by Aristotle's account of epistemic reasoning, was lost to subsequent generations. Most notably, his theory of syllogistic reasoning became the dominant model of rational thinking. The notion of practical reasoning languished after Pascal's successful ridicule of casuistry (Jonsen and Toulmin, 1988), and the success of the Enlightenment program that held up scientific and theoretical reasoning (including the newly developed theory of probability) as the only kind of correct argumentation worth paying serious attention to. It was not prominently taught as part of logic, or seen as important generally. Aristotle's account was fragmentary anyway, and was never developed by him as a formal calculus in the way that propositional calculus has been developed today. But he did have the idea of a practical inference, the basic idea of means-end reasoning to a conclusion by an agent, using a goal as the major premise. And this Aristotelian notion of the practical inference was the basis of the structure of practical reasoning worked out in the pioneering accounts of practical reasoning of Anscombe (1957) and Hare (1971), followed up in later developments by Clarke (1985), Bratman (1987), Audi (1989), and Walton (1990a).

But times have changed and Aristotle's vision of demonstration as the model of epistemic rationality as an inquiry that proves by deductive reasoning from axioms is no longer accepted as the paradigm of epistemic rationality (Hamblin, 1970). The traditional view of rationality that is still the dominant view in graduate schools in philosophy in North America views science as an empirical process in which true premises based on observations lead by deductive reasoning to a conclusion that can be said to be known to be true, for that reason. This view has now been challenged – for example, in computer science – by the advent of acceptance of defeasible reasoning, suggesting a different model of rationality in which knowledge is obtained by premises based on evidence leading to a conclusion that is tentatively acceptable but subject to retraction in the face of new evidence. Retraction may be necessary even though the conclusion may be established to a high standard of proof appropriate for a scientific field. On this latter view of scientific rationality, science is seen as a social process of knowledge construction recognizing that observations are theory-laden.

An important feature of knowledge on this epistemological view is that scientific conclusions and theories need to be seen as defeasible and open to challenge as scientific progress is made. Science is never at an end that has resulted in the absolute truth, even though it makes advances that get it closer to the truth.

Underlying these two views of rationality, there is a deep and persisting philosophical conflict between two opposed views of knowledge. The one view, currently the dominant view in epistemology, is shown to be characterized by four defining principles, stating that:

1. Knowledge bases contain only truths.
2. Knowledge bases are consistent.
3. Knowledge bases are closed under deductive implication.
4. Knowledge bases contain the assumption that if a proposition is known, then it is known that it is known.

The first principle, called the veracity principle by Rescher (2003), is so widely accepted that traditional epistemologists feel that it would be unthinkable to reject it. According to Rescher (2003, 10), holding that the linkage between knowledge and truth is merely contingent "inflicts violence on the concept of knowledge as it actually operates in discourse." He claims that the locution 'an agent knows that proposition p but p is not true' is "senseless." The opposed view holds that a proposition can be established as knowledge during the course of an inquiry, but later rejected as knowledge once new evidence has falsified it.

This opposed view was advocated by Charles S. Peirce. In his view, the real aim of an inquiry that yields knowledge is not that of actually reaching the truth, and knowing that it has been reached, but only that of a firm settling of opinion. Peirce (1984, 354) wrote that the "only legitimate aim of reasoning is to ascertain what decision would be agreed upon if the question were sufficiently ventilated." The limitation pointed out by Peirce is that scientific research represents a kind of inquiry that takes place in a finite amount of time with limited resources for collecting evidence. On this epistemological view, setting the requirement that truth has to be the result of an inquiry would "block the path of inquiry because our minds would be closed, and hence, we would never be motivated enough to inquire" (Peirce, 1931, 6.3). This view of scientific inquiry, and of knowledge generally, is called fallibilism (Cooke, 2006).

The skeptical roots of the fallibilistic view of knowledge are traceable back to the variant of Academic Skepticism progressively developed by philosophers such as Arcesilaus, Carneades, Philo of Larissa, and Cicero. As reported by Cicero, the Greek skeptic Arcesilaus adopted the view, appropriated from the Socratic dialogues, that nothing can be apprehended with certainty by the senses or the mind. Socrates did not claim to have knowledge, in some strong sense of the term, but only claimed that he was wise because he was aware that he did not know what was indisputably the truth. Arcesilaus characterized this fallibilistic view of knowledge by the saying "Truth is submerged in the depths" (Thorsrud, 2002, 6).

Greek skeptical attacks on conventional notions of knowledge were based on the observation that inferences from an appearance to a conclusion about the contents of that appearance are fallible. The lessons of these attacks have not been fully taken advantage of in modern epistemology, and the only way to accommodate them is to move to a fallibilistic epistemology. It has been shown in the analyses of examples in the previous chapter of this book how two defeasible forms of argument – argument from appearance and abductive reasoning – are defeasible argumentation schemes representing epistemological forms of evidential reasoning.

To sum up, there are two different conceptions of knowledge. According to the veristic conception, something cannot be knowledge unless it is true. In this conception, knowledge only comprises true propositions, and therefore a sharp contrast is drawn between knowledge and mere opinion. Opinions are variable, and can sometimes turn out to be true and sometimes false, whereas genuine knowledge can never turn out to be false. If something we take to be known to be true later turns out to be false, then in this sense of the word 'knowledge' it is incorrect to say that it was known to be true. It merely seemed at the time that it was known to be true, but then later, when we found out that it wasn't true, we found out that it wasn't really knowledge after all.

According to the fallibilistic conception, a proposition does not have to be true in order to be really classified as knowledge. In this view, if we take something to be known to be true and later it turns out to be false, it could still be correct to say that it was known to be true at the earlier time, even though at the later time we can say that it is no longer part of knowledge. In this view, the proposition in question was correctly classified as knowledge at the earlier time, even though it ceased to be knowledge at the later time. Hence, a proposition not conclusively established as true, and that may be subject to doubt, can still properly be classified as knowledge. Even a proposition that has been refuted, or replaced by a hypothesis that supersedes it, could be called knowledge. Knowledge discovery, in this view, begins with a more fluid stage for the acquisition of knowledge, prior to an aimed-at product stage where closure of an investigation has been reached.

Chapter 6 explained the importance in building formal deliberation models of explicitly taking into account changes in circumstances during a sequence of practical reasoning. The solution to this problem advocated in Chapter 6 was to include a knowledge base that can be updated as new information comes to light. But what is also stressed in the earlier chapters on practical reasoning is that circumstances are continually changing in the situation where a practical reasoner has to arrive at an intelligent decision based on the evidence about the present state of the circumstances in a case. Practical reasoning, in this way of framing it, needs to be based on the agent's knowledge of the circumstances, but since the circumstances are changing, the knowledge that the agent uses to guide its actions must be flexible and adaptable to those changes by getting its evidence from an open knowledge base.

The account of practical rationality given in this book is not reason-based, but evidence-based. In this account, knowledge is not defined as justified true belief, or by using any of the many variations on this approach. In this alternative theory, practical reasoning is based on knowledge that comes in as evidence to the agent making a decision on what to do in a given set of circumstances. The knowledge is provided by the agent's capability to perceive its circumstances and collect information about them by other means, such as witness testimony, expert opinion testimony, and other forms of argument. These resources provide the factual evidence that needs to be meshed in with the agent's goals and other commitments using the practical reasoning scheme that enables the agent to arrive at a rational decision on what to do. Such a rational decision depends not only on the agent's goals and what it takes to be the means to carry out these goals, but also on the evidence-based knowledge that the agent possesses or obtains in a given case. Based on its goals and this incoming evidence on the available means – something that is constantly changing in realistic decision-making situations – a rational agent carefully weighs the arguments on both sides, arriving at an intelligent and thoughtful decision. The rational agent uses its evaluation of these arguments to arrive at its decision on which path to take.

In this theory, an agent can be a machine, a human, or some combination these. What is especially distinctive in this model of practical rationality is its capability for modeling practical reasoning by groups of agents who act together to try to achieve a common goal even though they have differences of goals between them, and differences in their knowledge about how to achieve these goals. In a typical deliberation of the kinds studied in Chapter 6, there are proposals that need to be expressed, and the decision on what course of action to take needs to be based on the arguments for and against each proposal. These arguments need to be based on the evidence continually streaming in during all three stages of the deliberation procedure.

8.3 Epistemic Rationality Defined

In the traditional view, in order to qualify as being knowledge, a proposition must be true. This means that if a proposition taken at an earlier time as known to be true was later found to be false, it is no longer correct to have said at the earlier time that it was known to be true. This principle is sometimes called the veristic principle, meaning that knowledge deductively implies truth. As opposed to this traditional view, argumentation theory requires a defeasible conception of knowledge that is evidence-based. In the evidence-based model, a proposition can be classified as knowledge if:

1. it has been proved in an investigative procedure called an inquiry,
2. to the proof standard appropriate for the inquiry,
3. based on the evidence marshaled during the inquiry, and
4. using the kind of evidence that is relevant in the inquiry.

However, an inquiry of this sort, in order to properly represent a scientific investigation based on a hypothesis that has been proved by evidence, has to be open to retraction if evidence should come in showing that the hypothesis is no longer tenable. Hence, in this fallibilistic theory of knowledge, a proposition can be properly said to be shown to be true, even though later on, when new evidence came in, it was shown to be false. In this view, the argumentation scheme for arguing from evidence to a scientific hypothesis is regarded as defeasible and open to critical questioning. The old view of knowledge was based on deductive logic, whereas the new argumentation-based view of knowledge is based on defeasible argumentation schemes.

The theory of knowledge as a defeasible concept that is evidence-based but is also subject to falsification by further investigation does not require an external criterion of truth, even though it does require input from an external reality. This is because the evidence supporting a claim to knowledge comes from external evidence – say, from a factual investigation or from experimental findings. It is a requirement for this use of the term "evidence" that the body of evidence taken to support a claim to knowledge can be tested by comparing it to other evidential data and by testing it experimentally. The evidence-based model holds that a proposition can be established as knowledge during the course of an inquiry, and is knowledge at that time even if it turns out later to be rejected as knowledge once new evidence has falsified it (Walton, 2011c).

The notion of transmission of knowledge, either in an educational setting or in a legal trial, where evidence is presented by a scientific expert in court, is vitally important. When a scientific expert makes a claim that a particular proposition is known to be true, and has been shown to be true by scientific investigations, the argument from scientific testimony conveyed to the audience must be regarded as a defeasible type of argument fitting the argumentation scheme for the argument from expert opinion. Hence, it always has to be regarded as a defeasible form of argumentation. But even within the scientific discipline itself, where the proposition in question has been proved by scientific methods of inquiry, the argument from evidence to a hypothesis must also be regarded as a defeasible form of argument.

In short, the view of knowledge that best fits with the argumentation theory described earlier in this chapter is a fallibilistic one (Hannon, 2014). According to this theory, in order for a proposition to properly qualify as being part of knowledge, it does not have to be true for all time. It can be knowledge now, in the current state of scientific investigations, but at some later point, as new evidence comes in, its status as knowledge may have to be retracted. When a scientific theory or finding is presented by a teacher in a classroom setting, it is important to stress that the proposition classified as knowledge, although it may be evidence-based and even proved to a high standard of proof in a scientific discipline, should always be regarded as open to critical questioning. This principle is called falsifiability by Popper (1963). One of the most essential properties of scientific knowledge is that of falsifiability, meaning that a scientific hypothesis – no matter how well it has been tested, and how well established it is by scientific evidence – must always be subject to continual testing, and must be retracted if the evidence shows that it can be falsified. In short, scientific reasoning of the kind that is the paradigm of epistemic rationality must be both evidence-based and falsifiable.

The models of argument, explanation, and knowledge presented in this chapter form an argumentation-based theory of epistemic rationality that has ten general characteristics:

1. It analyzes and evaluates argumentation for a claim on a balance of evidence where there is evidence for it as well as against it, using standards of proof.
2. It views rational argumentation as a dialogue procedure, implying that two heads are better than one when assessing claims on what to accept based on evidence.

3. It uses critical questioning as a way of finding weak points in an argument, and it can represent critical questions as special types of premises in an argument map.
4. It views argumentation as procedural, meaning that proving something is taken to be a sequence with a start point and end point, as represented on an argument map.
5. It is commitment-based. It uses a database of commonly accepted knowledge that includes previous arguments and commitments expressed in them.
6. It is dynamic, meaning that it continually updates its database as new evidence comes in that is relevant to an argument being considered.
7. It is defeasible, meaning that an argument being considered is subject to defeat as new relevant evidence comes in that refutes the argument.
8. It is presumptive, meaning that in the absence of evidence sufficient to defeat it, a claim that is the conclusion of an argument can be tentatively accepted, even though it may be retracted later.
9. It has the capability to model explanations and to use this model to show how argument, explanation, and evidence are combined.
10. It does not see knowledge as a set of fixed propositions that must be accepted beyond all doubt, but recognizes the fallibility of evidence-based scientific knowledge.

The central feature of scientific knowledge in the fallibilistic view is that it is based on evidence, rather than requiring truth of its findings, and on how evidence can be used to support arguments for and against competing theories. For that reason it is appropriate to call this view evidence-based epistemology. In the literature on epistemology it is currently called evidential epistemology, but more recently it has also been called the epistemology of scientific evidence, or the ESE view (Walton and Zhang, 2013). The best name for this general type of approach is evidence-based epistemology, or EBE. In this view, being evidence-based is a requirement of knowledge, in place of the requirement of the opposed view that being true is a requirement for a proposition to qualify as knowledge. This meaning of the term comprises the kinds of evidence collected in different disciplines, including science and law, archaeology, forensic evidence, medicine, and authentication of works of art and other artifacts.

Epistemic rationality is defined, to fit the requirements stated above, as reasoning that uses defeasible argumentation schemes, as well as deductive and inductive forms of inference, to draw reasoned conclusions based on premises supported by the evidence, as evaluated by the evidence collected at a point in time. The evidence is evaluated by the pro and con arguments available at that time. Epistemic scientific rationality needs to be defined in the setting of an inquiry where evidence is collected in a restricted and well-defined domain of science with established methods and standards of proof. The paradigm model of scientific investigation is that of the inquiry dialogue framework.

The goal of an inquiry is to prove that the statement designated as the hypothesis, the ultimate *probandum* to be evaluated, or otherwise to support the negative finding that there is insufficient evidence to prove it (Walton, 1998a, chapter 3). The goal of the inquiry is to prove or disprove something by a high enough standard of proof to make the possibility of the retraction of a finding as remote as can be achieved. According to the account in Walton (1998a, 70), inquiry dialogue is *cumulative*, meaning that once a statement has been accepted at the closing stage of the inquiry, it has been accepted as scientific knowledge, and as such it is established so that it should never need to be retracted unless new findings, not yet known, require this. However, inquiry dialogue is more constrained than persuasion dialogue or information-seeking dialogue on allowing for retractions.

Black and Hunter (2007) developed a formal model of inquiry dialogue and applied it to medical investigations. Their model defines cumulativeness as a form of acceptance of a hypothesis based on evidence collected and applied during a dialogue, firmly fixed but open to revision by new evidence as the investigation proceeds. In subsequent work (Black and Hunter, 2009) they distinguished two subtypes of inquiry dialogue. Argument inquiry dialogues allow a group of agents to share knowledge to jointly construct arguments. Warrant inquiry dialogues are used to allow a group of agents to share knowledge so that they can construct dialectical trees to collect evidence which can then be used to prove an ultimate conclusion, or alternatively to show that it cannot be proved on the basis of the evidence.

Their system includes a dialogue protocol for each subtype of inquiry and also an argument construction strategy that selects one of the moves to make at any given point in the dialogue. Although earlier work, such as Walton and Krabbe (1995), was only concerned with modeling the different types of dialogue, a new trend in artificial intelligence is to use a knowledge base to advise the user which one of the legal moves should be made next any given point in the dialogue. This capability is called argument construction, and is associated with the traditional rhetorical task of argument invention first developed by the ancient authors in rhetoric and philosophy. The model of inquiry dialogue of Black and Hunter works in the standard way of designating a proposition at the opening stage of the dialogue that the participant agents are jointly trying to prove, and tracking the sequence of argumentation put forward for this purpose during the argumentation stage. The argumentation stage takes the form of a dialectical tree, roughly comparable to the examples of such trees displayed in the argument diagrams in previous chapters of this book. The goal of this type of inquiry dialogue is to enable agents to jointly construct arguments based on premises that none of the individual participants can construct from their own belief sets. They exchange beliefs to acquire better arguments that can be used to determine whether a conclusion can be proved on the basis of the evidence or not.

8.4 Practical Rationality Defined

The words 'rational' and 'irrational' are used in all kinds of ways in common speech. That is to be expected, because the word 'irrational' has now come to be a technical term in psychology, psychiatry, and related disciplines. But the target of analysis appropriate for this investigation is not common usage, or technical usage in the social and medical sciences. To get a grasp of the meaning sought here, think of a task such as solving a technical problem like fixing a computer part (a problem comparable to the printer problem studied in Chapter 6), or taking a meaningful part in a town hall meeting. That is the central meaning of 'rationality' aimed at here. But around this central meaning are peripheral meanings. We don't just say that reasoning is rational or irrational, or that arguments are. We say that actions have these properties, and that agents have them. We can say that speech acts other than arguments, such as beliefs or explanations, are rational or irrational. But in relation to the kinds of doubts so often recently expressed about rationality, the notions of reasoning and argument are central.

As the four examples in Chapter 6 revealed, understanding practical rationality requires a context in which agents interact with other agents, even in instances of what appears to be solitary reasoning. As shown in Chapter 6, new theories and techniques of multi-agent reasoning now used in artificial intelligence research in computer science bring out this lesson very well (Wooldridge and Jennings, 1995; Wooldridge, 2002). What these developments suggest is that rationality should not be seen according to the model of an agent acting alone in nature. A better approach is to see rationality in a framework in which agents act in a coordinated way by communicating with each other as they act. Rationality needs to be defined as a dialectical concept, and not just an abstract logical concept that is a property of propositions, abstracted from their use in a conversational exchange. The dialectical view of rationality follows in the footsteps of the unjustifiably neglected account of rationality in Bartley (1962), an account that also sees reaction to criticism as an important criterion of rationality.

Practical rationality is defined in this framework as practical reasoning based on an agent's goals, the means at its disposal in its given situation, knowledge of its circumstances in that situation, its values (in the case of value-based practical reasoning), and its commitments to other agents in the communicative and social setting in which the agent is participating. It was shown in Chapter 5 that the commitment model is a better place to begin to analyze practical reasoning than the BDI model precisely because intentions can only be determined by using abductive reasoning. Such reasoning is often far from straightforward. It proceeds from a set of facts to choosing the best explanation of those facts as a hypothesis. Instead of being based on the mental notion of intention, the commitment model is based on the notion of a goal. Goals are less problematic to specify and can be set and agreed on at least partly by stipulation.

Goals can be abstract or they can be highly specific. When they are highly abstract, it can be difficult to know precisely what constitutes achievement of the goal, and that is why there is typically argumentation about the matter. For example, it can be very hard to define an abstract goal, like happiness or health, in a way that everyone will agree with. A close look has to be taken at the purpose of the definition. For example, if the term has to be defined legally – say, for the purpose of a contract – the definition may have to be at least partly stipulative. On the other hand, sometimes goals are relatively easy to define, especially if they are fairly specific. Consider the example of running a mile in 4 minutes or less, the goal of living to age 100, or the goal of graduating from the University of Windsor in 2014.

Goals can be stipulated by an agent, much in the way that definitions can be stipulated, for example in law. It may be extremely difficult to define a general concept in law, but this problem can sometimes be solved by setting down necessary conditional elements. For example, it may be very hard to offer a definition of the term 'murder' or the term 'contract' that is not open to question or revision in specific cases. Such legal terms are defeasible, meaning that they are subject to exceptions in particular cases. Also, the meaning of such terms can vary with jurisdictions, or from one legal system to another.

One way to partially define a general goal is to tie it to a more precisely formulated set of requirements that determine what counts as achieving the goal. The set of requirements can change over time as argumentation based on the goal has been met or not by particular cases leads to a more precise formulation of the goal for a specific purpose. An example can be used to show how this procedure works.

A team from the University of Toronto called AeroVelo won the Igor Sikorsky Human Powered Helicopter Competition on July 11, 2013. The goal of the competition was for a human-powered helicopter to achieve a flight of sixty seconds reaching an altitude of three meters (9.8 feet) with the center point of the aircraft hovering over a square area of ten meters by ten meters. This goal was formulated more precisely by setting a number of more specific requirements about the flight requirements, the crew, the ground conditions, and so forth that had to be met in order to win the contest. Selected subsets of these conditions are quoted[1] here for purposes of illustration. The requirements set below fall into three categories of goals: flight requirements, ground conditions, and crew requirements.

1. Flight Requirements

The flight requirements shall consist of hovering for one minute while maintaining flight within a 10-meter square. During this time, the lowest part of the machine shall exceed momentarily 3 meters above the ground.

The machine shall be in continuous flight from takeoff to landing, and at no time during the flight shall any part of the machine touch the ground.

2. Ground Conditions

All attempts, which shall include the takeoff, shall be made over approximately level ground (i.e., with a slope not exceeding 1 in 100 in any direction).

All attempts shall be made in still air, which shall be defined as a wind not exceeding a mean speed of approximately one meter per second (3.6 kilometers per hour, 2.24 miles per hour, 1.94 nautical miles per hour) over the period of flight.

3. Crew Requirements

The crew shall be those persons in the machine during takeoff and flight, and there shall be no limit set to their number.

No member of the crew shall be permitted to leave or enter the aircraft at any time during takeoff or flight.

Up to four handlers or ground crew shall be permitted to assist in stabilizing the machine during takeoff and landing, but in such a manner that they do not assist in accelerating or decelerating any part of the machine.

---

[1] https://vtol.org/awards-and-contests/human-powered-helicopter/hph-rules

Of course, the goal of any group of participants is to win the competition, but what counts as winning is determined by the set of requirements of the kinds indicated above. So when any group undertakes to design and fly a human-powered helicopter in order to win the competition, all of their actions in this endeavor need to be directed toward fulfilling this set of requirements. In effect, this set of requirements defines their ultimate goal. All the subgoals they set during the procedure of trying to achieve this ultimate goal are linked to actions and this connected sequence of subgoals and actions aims at achieving the ultimate goal. It is this sequence of practical reasoning that defines practical rationality as a normative structure.

The theory of practical reasoning in multi-agent deliberation summarized at the end of Chapter 6 postulated two levels of rationality. At the level of reasoning, rationality is defined in relation to a sequence of reasoning made up of a chain of inferences. In a chain of reasoning of this kind, the beginning points are the initial premises. The conclusion of one inference can also function as a premise in the next inference in the sequence so that reasoning is chained forward. Such a reasoning sequence can be visually represented by an argument diagram showing a graph with text boxes containing propositions and arrows representing inferences from propositions to propositions. The end point is the ultimate conclusion. This proposition, which sets the issue or question to be discussed, is set in place at the opening stage of a dialogue. At a second level, that of argumentation, rationality is defined in relation to how an argument (or other speech act, like the offering of an explanation or the asking of a question) was put forward in some goal-directed conversational exchange. This second level of rationality is the dialectical level. Traditional accounts of rationality have neglected the second level.

8.5 Practical Rationality and Reasoning

What is the connection between reasoning and rationality? And what is reasoning? It seems to me that there is a useful sort of reply to these questions, or at least a set of propositions that are compatible with current methods of applied logic. These propositions are summarized in the following ten points:

1. Rationality is based on reasoning.
2. Reasoning is a chaining together of inferences.
3. Practical reasoning is means-end goal-directed reasoning of agents, leading to actions.

4. There is some kind of reasoning other than practical reasoning.
5. Reasoning is used in arguments and explanations.
6. Reasoning is not the same as arguing (or as an argument).
7. Reasoning can be evaluated as correct or not by various logical methods and standards.
8. Deductive reasoning can be evaluated as valid or not by standards of deductive logic.
9. Formal fallacies are faults in reasoning.
10. Informal fallacies are dialectical faults in argumentation.

These points do not seem terribly controversial, but I am sure there are many philosophers who will disagree with some or perhaps even all of them. The last two are probably the most controversial. But if these ten points are regarded as provisional assumptions, they can be used as basis for discussing and exploring the concept of rationality.

An argument always involves two parties: a proponent and a respondent. They don't have to be two real people. You can argue with yourself by first advocating one side of an issue, and then looking for weaknesses in the side you advocate, or even advocating the other side by playing "devil's advocate." Reasoning, by contrast, does not have to involve two participants. A chaining together of a sequence of deductive inferences, for example, could quite rightly be called reasoning, even though it is just a sequence of propositions. But, of course, practical reasoning always requires an agent. To summarize this view of argument and reasoning, the relationship could be expressed as follows (Walton, 1990b). Reasoning is a chaining together of steps of inference. An argument is a conversational exchange between two parties in which the two parties reason with each other. So argumentation uses reasoning, and is based on reasoning. But reasoning is a context-free notion. It only involves a sequence of propositions. Argument is a dialectical notion. It is a matter of how reasoning is used for some purpose in a conversational exchange between two parties.

Practical reasoning, as described in the previous chapters, is carried out by an agent. An agent has goals, and has the capability to carry out actions in order to achieve these goals. This agent-centered notion of practical reasoning goes back to Aristotle's conception of *phronesis*, or practical wisdom. Aristotle sketched out many of the leading characteristics of practical reasoning in a highly evocative, if incomplete and fragmented form that has always been hard for scholars to interpret. Put in modern terms, practical reasoning can be defined as follows. Practical reasoning is a goal-directed, knowledge-based, action-guiding species of reasoning that meshes goals with possible alternative courses of action, in relation to an agent's knowledge of its given circumstances in a particular situation. Practical reasoning is carried out by an agent, an entity that is capable of intelligent action on the basis of observing its circumstances, including its own actions, using this information to guide its behaviors.

The account of practical rationality given by Searle (2001) fits the BDI framework that, with all kinds of variations, has been generally accepted by analytical philosophers since the second half of the twentieth century. In this account, rationality is based on reasons that support an agent's action where the reasons derive from the motivational causal state of the agent (the mainspring of the action). An agent's motivational state contains its desires, beliefs, and intentions, and the rationality of the agent's decision to carry out a particular action is to be sought in the linkage between the action and the motivational state that activated it. The theory of practical rationality presented in this book partly accommodates this account, but argues that there are so many unsolved perplexities in it that a better way to begin is with a simpler, if less initially powerful, commitment-based approach based on argumentation schemes and work forward from there. Most importantly, this approach has as its central components the two schemes for practical reasoning – the instrumental one and the value-based one – and the evaluation of them in the formal and computational model of rational deliberation presented in Chapter 6.

Practical rationality is a property of an intelligent agent with the capability of engaging in deliberative goal-directed action. Practical rationality needs to be defined in relation to the twenty-one characteristics of an intelligent agent postulated in Chapter 1 (Sections 3 and 10). How such a practical agent functions can be summarized as follows. An agent has goals and can also set goals that become commitments as it moves forward through a set of changing circumstances it knows or finds out about, and it decides what to do on this basis. It can remember its commitments and act on them (or not). It can carry out a sequence of ordered actions – for example, through a list of instructions on what to do – and organize the sequence into a hierarchy to fit general goals to specific actions. It is capable of carrying out actions that can change its external circumstances and is capable of monitoring the consequences of its actions and making error corrections by feedback. It can be aware of the normal and expected consequences of its actions by its capacity to understand scripts about the way things normally work in its environment. It must have the capability of communicating with other agents, and it can obtain information from them. It can even criticize or evaluate its own actions and those of other rational agents by asking critical questions about its own actions, goals, and values.

As it weaves its way through its external circumstances based on what it knows about them, and its goals, an agent draws conclusions from the data it has, based on the instrumental argumentation scheme for practical reasoning. But that is not the whole story of practical rationality. It also needs to guide its path of actions toward its goals by constantly asking critical questions about its own actions and goals, and taking the answers into account as it moves forward. This procedure of deliberation is part of practical reasoning, in the theory of deliberation dialogue set out in Chapter 6. In this theory, an intelligent agent using practical reasoning must draw premises from an open knowledge base that informs the argumentation stage of the procedure. The agent applies the practical reasoning scheme not only by utilizing information about its circumstances from its knowledge base, but also by deriving information by interacting with other intelligent agents, and even by continually questioning its own reasoning. It may also need to take values into account, and engage in value-based practical reasoning as it weighs its goals against the projected positive or negative consequences of its actions. It only reaches the closing stage of this procedure when the deliberations have been thorough enough to reach an intelligent, informed, and timely decision on what to do.

8.6 Practical Irrationality and Multi-agent Attributions of Goals

So far the work in this book has built models of practical reasoning in which practical reasoning is used to make rational decisions on how to arrive at good decisions on what is a prudent course of action. There has been very little concern about how practical reasoning can go wrong, or be used badly, in irrational deliberations that arrive at bad decisions. But this is an important aspect of this branch of study. We can't hope to do justice to it in this book, but it will be useful to offer some directions for research on it, based on the positive findings of the book.

According to a traditional philosophical view of irrationality expressed by the definition given in the *Oxford American Dictionary* (Ehrlich et al., 1979), 'irrational' means "not guided by reasoning" or "illogical." For example, suppose a person draws a conclusion from a set of premises that does not follow by deductive logic from those premises, as opposed to one that does. Or suppose a person draws a conclusion from a set of premises other than the conclusion that would follow inductively from it by the probability calculus. Or suppose a person adopts a position from which a logical contradiction can be derived by deductive reasoning. These are the kinds of cases where irrationality is determined by logical criteria, according to this traditional viewpoint (Brown, 1988). But these criteria do not help us to define practical irrationality.

The most widely discussed type of phenomenon associated with practical irrationality, called *akrasia* or weakness of will, occurs in cases where an agent sees a means that would carry out a goal he is committed to, but fails to act to implement that means, without any apparent good reason for this failure to act. Another type of phenomenon associated with practical irrationality is the kind of case where an agent has a goal, and attempts to carry it out, but even when these attempts lead to negative consequences that undermine the goal, the agent retains commitment to the goal. Even when it is shown that the actual consequences of the agent's attempts to fulfill the goal can be demonstrated factually to be inconsistent with the goals, the agent persists with trying to implement the goal. This kind of irrationality often occurs in multi-agent situations where the behavior that has been undertaken is not changed simply due to bureaucratic gridlock. In such cases we have a kind of practical inconsistency, but it is not an inconsistency between the agent's goals – that is, a conflict of goals. It could be a conflict between the carrying out of the agent's goal and the negative side effects produced by these actions that are found to run contrary to the goal.

An article in the *Economist* on America's poppy policy in Afghanistan,[2] concerning the growing of poppies used to make opium, described how America has spent more than $10 billion trying to suppress the opium trade. The article stated that in 2013 Afghan farmers planted 200,000 hectares with opium poppies, according to a UN source. The article stated that this is a new record, and supported this statement with a graph showing rates of poppy cultivation according to a UN source. The article then critically questioned the current American policy by quoting some remarks made in a program on National Public Radio:

> John Sopko, the American official whose job it is to oversee how Uncle Sam's money is spent in Afghanistan, told National Public Radio: "if the goal was to reduce cultivation, we failed. If the goal was to reduce opium production, we failed . . . . If the goal was to break that narco-trafficking nexus and the corrupting influence, we have failed."

[2] America, Afghanistan and Opium: Ten Billion Wasted, *The Economist*, April 12, 2014, 22.

Citing the opinion of a professor of economics at a prominent American university, the article offered the following explanation of why the current policy has enriched the Taliban. The current effort to pull up poppies and shut down opium labs has displaced production into Taliban-controlled areas, enriching America's enemies. Because America has suppressed cultivation in friendly areas the price of opium has gone up. A lot of the profits from opium cultivation have flowed to the Taliban. The article supported this claim by citing a UN estimate stating that the Taliban earned $100 million from opium profits in 2011 and 2012.

The argumentation in the article combines argument and explanation. It cites the argument of a professor of economics that displacing production into Taliban-controlled areas has had the effect of enriching America's enemies. This aspect of the article represents an attribution of an argument to an expert (an economist) and therefore it exemplifies use of argument from expert opinion. At the same time, the article presents an explanation of the sequence of events, based on sources reporting economic data about opium cultivation in Afghanistan. Argumentation and explanation are therefore combined in an interesting way.

The explanation of the sequence of events presented in the article can be represented by the script shown in Figure 8.1. This script is a very good example of a causal explanation. Each of the rounded text boxes represents a state of affairs and the arrows represent a transition from a cause to an effect in each instance. The sequence runs as follows. The current effort to pull up

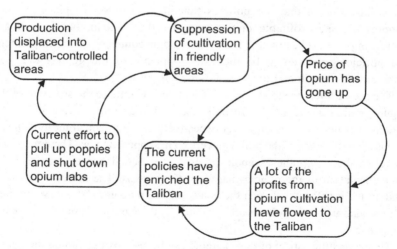

Figure 8.1: Script of the Sequence of Events in the Opium Example

poppies and shut down opium labs has caused production to be displaced into Taliban-controlled areas. This has had two effects. One is the suppression of cultivation in friendly areas. The other is displacement of production into Taliban-controlled areas. The suppression of cultivation in friendly areas has caused the price of opium to go up. The sequence of events shown in the script represents this series of economic causal transitions.

From an argumentation point of view, the overall argument presented in the article is based on practical reasoning and argument from negative consequences. The article is showing that the American policy is apparently not achieving the goals that American policymakers supposed it would. The article is probing into the intentions of the policymakers, and weighing these intentions against the actual outcomes of the policies that are set in place. The thrust of the argument is that these outcomes are running contrary to what presumably was the original intention of the policymakers. The intention was to try to suppress the opium trade that is so profitable to the Taliban in Afghanistan. At least this attribution of intention is a reasonable conjecture, even though we do not know the real intention of the American policymakers who formulated these policies and put them into effect. So, the problem is one of extrapolating from the factual data in the case report on what happened, and the economic data about the profitability of opium cultivation in Afghanistan, to derive a hypothesis about the original intentions of the policymakers. The thrust of the article argues that the implementation of these policies has led to outcomes that are directly opposed to the presumed intentions. The article essentially argues that the policies that have been set in place are not suppressing the profitable opium trade by the Taliban, but in fact are increasing it. In other words, the negative consequences of the implemented policies appeared to be the exact opposite of the goal(s) that can apparently be attributed to the policymakers.

The use of inference to the best explanation is central to the structure of the argumentation in the article. To build the central argument presented in the article, it is necessary to argue retrospectively to try to construct hypotheses about what the goals of the policymakers were supposed to be. The next step is to relate these hypotheses about goals to the actual consequences of the implementation of the policies based on these goals. The ultimate aim is to find an inconsistency between the goals and the outcomes, showing that outcomes contrary to the policies are exhibited by a factual account of what really happened.

The interesting aspect of this example can be seen by examining the quotation attributed to John Sopko in the extract given above. He puts forward three

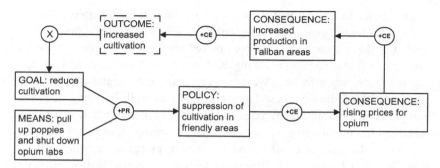

Figure 8.2: Policy Leads to Consequences Undermining the Goal

conditional propositions, each one of which attributes a hypothetical goal to the American policymakers. In each of the three instances it is argued that the policy failed to be implemented. The policy failed to reduce cultivation – it actually increased cultivation. The policy failed to reduce opium production – it actually increased opium production. The policy failed to break the narco-trafficking nexus and the corrupting influence that arose from cultivation of opium – it actually contributed to the growth of this nexus and corrupting influence.

A simplified account of the argumentation structure showing the negative consequences of the policy relevant to the first of the three hypothetical statements attributed to John Sopko is offered in Figure 8.2. On the left, the goal of reducing cultivation, along with the means taken (pulling up poppies and shutting down opium labs) are shown in two text boxes. It is shown how these two premises are used in an argument from practical reasoning that was presumably used by the policymakers to conclude to adopting their policy of suppression of cultivation in friendly areas. The notation +CE stands for a positive argument from cause to effect. The X notation in the one node stands for a conflict between a goal and an outcome of an action or policy that is the means to achieve the goal.

One consequence shown is the rising price of opium, which in turn leads to another consequence of increased production in Taliban areas. These two consequences are shown by the plus signs on the arrows. However, the second consequence of increased production in Taliban areas, as shown by the final arrow, is opposed to the goal of reducing cultivation. Instead of succeeding in reducing cultivation, the sequence of practical reasoning leading to the policy that was adopted has led to increased cultivation of opium. This sequence of reasoning graphically displays the inconsistency that the argumentation in the article is meant to bring out.

The reader will recall that Sopko, in the argument quoted above, did not just claim that the goal of reducing cultivation was a failure, if that was the goal. He also claimed that the goal of reducing opium production was a failure, and that the goal of breaking the narco-trafficking nexus and corrupting influence was a failure. We could reconstruct the argumentation with respect to the failure of these latter two goals as well, by using diagrams comparable to Figure 8.2. What is especially significant is that in all three instances the methodology of hypothetical reasoning from factual circumstances of the case to build hypotheses about an agent's presumed goals described in Chapter 5 are illustrated by this example. In this example, comparably to the examples studied in Chapter 5, argument and explanation interweaving goals and actions are combined. But instead of reasoning backward from facts to goals, this example shows factual information about consequences relating to hypotheses about an agent's goals.

When criticism such as the argument put forward in this example points out such a pragmatic inconsistency between goals and consequences of actions, it does not mean that the policy set in place by government agencies intended to reduce the cultivation of opium is practically irrational, or that the agencies that put this policy in place are practically irrational. These agencies and the policy they implemented could be correctly described as irrational, however, if the agent persisted in implementing them even though critics persuasively argued by offering evidence that the consequences of the implementation were in conflict with the supposed goal of the agent. Evidence of such persistence would be an indicator of practical irrationality. Lessons of these observations are important for helping us to better understand the concept of practical irrationality as more than some sort of logically narrow defect in thinking.

The model of intelligent deliberation proposed in Chapter 6 had as one of its most important aspects the requirement that an agent's practical reasoning should be informed by knowledge of its circumstances continually coming in from an open knowledge base. A rational agent making a decision to act or not in such a setting of deliberation dialogue needs to be continually open to new evidence coming in and being assessed during the argumentation stage. Another important requirement is that the closing stage should not be reached prematurely before all the evidence on the decision-making situation has been collected, taken into account, and properly evaluated. The kind of practical reasoning used in such a deliberation framework needs to be seen as a defeasible form of argumentation that is continually subject to assessment and correction by asking the appropriate critical questions. Practical reasoning employed with a closed knowledge base so that the agent fails to react properly to new information about its changing circumstances represents a severe defect of practical rationality. It is a thesis of this chapter that such a characteristic of engaging in practical reasoning with a "closed mind" represents an important kind of practical irrationality.

To give another example, suppose that an arguer commits herself to an inconsistency. She accepts proposition A, but then at some later point in her argumentation, she also accepts the negation of A. Does this make her argument irrational? According to the thesis put forward here, it does not. What makes her argument irrational or not is how she reacts when the other party in the dialogue points out that she is committed to an inconsistency. So, for example, if she retracts one of the propositions, or if she tries to explain that asserting A was not really what she meant to say, or gives some other reasonable response of this sort, these are all indicators of rationality. Not only can it be acceptable to change your mind in some instances, rationality can require you to do so. As shown in the previous chapters, practical reasoning is typically carried out in changing circumstances where a retraction of a previous commitment because of new incoming information is the rational thing to do. But suppose an agent does not respond with one of these reasonable kinds of retraction responses, and instead replies "I'm inconsistent – so what?" This is precisely the kind of case where her argument should be judged to be irrational. In other words, it is not just the inconsistency itself that makes her, or her argumentation, rational or irrational. Whether her argumentation should be judged to be irrational, according to the dialectical meaning of this term, depends on her response (or lack of appropriate response) when a critic points out that inconsistency and asks for a response.

In short, the view advocated here is that practical irrationality is at least partly a social concept, instead of being construed as a narrowly logical concept in the semantic sense of having to do with truth and falsity or consistency of statements (Tuomela, 2007). What matters in judging irrationality, according to the view argued for here, is how these statements were put forward, defended, and elaborated in response to questioning in a conversational exchange with a speech partner. This view is a pragmatic one, from the point of view of traditional logic, because it implies that the evaluation of argumentation needs to be partly a function of the use of a statement or argument in a conversational context. Judging an argument to be logically acceptable or deficient as a cognitive entity is no longer just a function of the truth-values of the propositions in it, or the semantic structure of whether the conclusion follows by logical entailment from the premises of the argument. It needs to be a pragmatic and contextual matter of how the argument was supposedly used for some purpose in a multi-agent conversational exchange between parties who are engaged in an orderly dialogue with each other.

8.7 Rationality and Fallacies

The view has already been defended that fallaciousness of arguments needs to be judged on the basis of how well an argument, or other move in argumentation, contributes to a goal-directed conversation between two (or more) parties (van Eemeren and Grootendorst, 1992; Walton, 1995). This thesis is not new, and has been widely argued for by a growing international and interdisciplinary group of scholars in the field of argumentation studies. What is new here is the attempt to extend this multi-agent dialectical viewpoint on argumentation to the analysis of the concepts of rationality and irrationality.

This analysis of irrationality reveals that rationality needs to be seen as a dialectical concept. According to the dialectical view of irrationality, a rational agent does bring his own positions and interests to an argument, but that is not in itself bad, or any indicator of irrationality. What is the indicator of irrationality (and fallaciousness) is how that agent reacts when his interests and positions are pointed out by another agent, and then used to raise questions and criticisms concerning his arguments. If he reacts in a closed manner by shielding off the criticisms, instead of properly replying to them, in many cases such a sequence of moves in a dialogue is the most serious and telling evidence of irrationality. Irrationality can be identified with the stance of the dogmatic or even fanatical arguer who is closed to critical questions and counter-arguments, in advance of these questions and counter-arguments even being posed. Irrationality, in the dialectical view, needs to be defined by how an arguer reacts in a conversational sequence of argumentative moves, following on from criticism.

Rationality is closely connected to the concept of fallacy. The theory of rationality put forward in Sections 1–5 of this chapter suggests that rationality is much weaker than the traditional epistemic view has taken it to be. On the fallibilistic view, reasoning is not only susceptible to error, but constantly prone to it. Hence, one of the most important characteristics of rationality is the awareness of the likelihood of error, the recognition of the constant need to search for errors, and a willingness to correct them. Reasoning requires a vigilance to try to avoid mistakes.

Both rationality and fallacy are dialectical concepts, and both are fundamental concepts for informal logic. But one must be careful not to identify the two concepts too closely, by adopting the position that irrationality may simply be defined as the committing of (logical) fallacies. There are various reasons why equating irrationality with the committing of fallacies won't work.

Consider, for example, the informal fallacy of the *argumentum ad baculum*. Suppose, in a typical kind of case, that two parties are having an argument, and one makes a credible threat to the other. Using such a threat in the course of an argument could be an instance of the *ad baculum* fallacy. But would the making of the threat be irrational? Well, the answer is, not necessarily. In fact, the making of the threat by the one party could be rational, in the sense that it effectively promotes her self-interest. From a prudential or practical point of view, the threat move could be rational. It could get her what she wants, whatever that is. But surely, in another sense, the making of the threat was irrational, if it was a kind of interruption or blocking of the dialogue the two parties were having. Suppose, for example, that the dialogue was a critical discussion of some philosophical issue. The threat would have no place in contributing to such a conversation. It is inappropriate and, in that context, could be said to be fallacious. What we see, in such a case, is that there are two distinct meanings of the term 'rational.' One refers to prudential rationality – getting what you want, or promoting your own self-interest. The other is a kind of rationality that has to do with discussing an issue by bringing forward arguments and criticizing them. What is important here is giving reasons to support your expressed view. The making of a threat against the other party is not a way of doing this. It is materially irrelevant, in that it does not give any reason to accept or reject a stated view on the basis of evidence for or against it. Instead, it gives the speaker a prudential reason for backing off.

In such a case, the committing of the *ad baculum* fallacy is in one sense irrational. But in another, prudential sense, it is a rational move. We must conclude, then, that being irrational is not necessarily the same thing as committing a fallacy. But what else should we conclude from this puzzling kind of case? Does it mean that the same argument can be both rational and irrational? Can the dialectical view of rationality accommodate or explain this apparent contradiction?

The dialectical view of rationality deals with the problem by allowing two points to be made, and by reconciling them. One point is that the use of the threat was rational in a prudential sense. The other is that making the threat was irrational in the sense that it was irrelevant to the critical discussion, and was not a genuine contribution to that discussion. What we have to look at here is that the making of a threat needs to be evaluated within two different conversational contexts. Looked at within the dialectical framework of the critical discussion making the threat is an *ad baculum* fallacy. It does not contribute to realizing the goal of that type of conversation. From that perspective, it is "irrational," or, at least, goes against the social framework of what defines rationality in that context. But from a point of view of maximizing narrow self-interest, the making of the threat was rational, in a different sense. Within the conversational framework of interest-based bargaining or negotiation dialogue, the *ad baculum* move is 'rational.' Here the term 'rational' has two different senses, depending on the context of the conversation. It depends on how the threat was being used for some purpose in a conversational exchange in which two parties were supposedly taking part.

In this kind of problematic case, the dialectical view of rationality explains the apparent contradiction very well. Each meaning of the term 'rational' is seen as working within a dialectical context of dialogue. So whether or not the threat is judged to be rational or irrational depends on what type of dialogue the participants in the argument were supposedly taking part in. If it was a critical discussion, the *ad baculum* move was fallacious and could be seen as a kind of obstacle to rationality, in the sense of being an obstacle to the continuance of the dialogue toward its goal. As expressed by the conversational principle of Grice (1975), participants in a conversation should make the kinds of moves that contribute to the moving forward of the conversation toward its proper goal, and be appropriate for the stage the conversation is now in. In this conversational sense, the *ad baculum* move was inappropriate, and did not conform to the standards of rationality appropriate for the critical discussion type of dialogue. But on the other hand, if the conversation were to be viewed as a bargaining session over some disputed interests, the *ad baculum* move can be seen as quite rational, in the sense that it is just another bargaining move. The other party in the conversation could react by making a counter-threat, by calling the other party's bluff, or by making some other kind of reply that is appropriate in a negotiation session.

To sum up, from this simple example, and many others like it that could be given, two main conclusions follow. One is that irrationality is not necessarily the same thing as fallaciousness. The other is that the dialectical account of fallacy shows promise of dealing very well with problems and apparent contradictions in the concept of rationality. What should define irrationality is not just faulty reasoning, but also disruptions of the progress of a regulated collaborative conversation that the given argument or other move was supposed to be part of. The rationality resides in the reasoning, but not just in the reasoning as a set of premises and conclusions (propositions). It resides in how that reasoning was used for some purpose in a conversational exchange between two parties.

It is appropriate to conclude this section by summarizing the seven characteristics of practical irrationality that have been discovered:

- Practical irrationality is more than mere weakness of will, where an agent fails to bring about a means necessary to achieving its goal; nor is it a purely inferential failure.
- It is a dynamic failure best identified and understood in a framework of deliberation in which a rational agent needs to balance the consequences of its actions against its goals.
- During this dynamic procedure, a rational agent needs to be aware of or to find conflicts between its goals, and between them and the known consequences of attempting to implement its goals by taking action.
- An irrational agent may jump too quickly to a conclusion to take action without properly assessing the arguments bearing on the decision, or it may unwisely delay by continuing to examine the pros and cons when there is a practical need to take timely action.
- Engaging in practical reasoning with a "closed mind" by failing to make revisions from an open knowledge base during the argumentation stage is an important factor in judging whether practical irrationality is exhibited in a given case.
- An agent acts in a practically irrational manner if it has been made aware of practical conflicts between its goals and negative consequences of implementing them, and yet it refuses to make the required corrections and change it current actions or policies.
- More generally, practical irrationality should be determined by multi-agent criteria, in a setting such as a deliberation dialogue that has an opening, stage, an argumentation stage, and a closing stage.

8.8 Dialectical Frameworks of Practical Rationality

According to Chapter 6, practical reasoning is used in various types of conversational exchanges called dialogues, but the type of dialogue in which practical reasoning is most typically used in everyday conversations is that of rational deliberation. Deliberation, in this view, arises out of a need to take action in a given situation, and the purpose of the deliberation is to determine the right, or the most prudent, course of action in the situation. Aristotle's account of deliberation, especially in the *Nicomachean Ethics*, at 1112a30 and following, describes its main characteristics very well. But although Aristotle was the founder of formal dialectic (Krabbe, 2013) and he defined several types of dialogue in which arguments are used, he did not include deliberation as one of these types. In *On Sophistical Refutations* (9165a38–165b12), he distinguished four kinds of arguments used in discussion: didactic, dialectical, examination, and contentious. In the *Topics* (100a25–100b23) he also distinguished between two kinds of reasoning in a discussion called demonstration and dialectical reasoning. But he does not mention deliberation in either of these classifications. The view put forward in the previous chapters is not Aristotelian. This view portrays deliberation as a distinctive type of dialogue or discussion framework in which argumentation is used for some conversational purpose.

Can the practical reasoning used in the printer example be properly seen as part of a deliberation dialogue? In this example, Brian had the problem that a black line appeared down the middle of the page of a scanned document produced by his printer. He took a series of steps that resulted in his solving the problem, after some study of the problem. It is more natural to see the reasoning in the printer example as part of a problem-solving procedure rather than being part of a deliberation dialogue used for making a choice on what to do. The printer example asks the question of how to do something, whereas the other examples ask the question of what to do in a situation requiring a choice on how to proceed. These observations are basically correct, but an answer about what conclusions to draw from them can be given.

The answer to this question is that for the purposes of the theory put forward in this book, a problem-solving sequence of this sort can be classified as a deliberation dialogue. Such a way of proceeding may seem odd at first, given that the two other examples (the real estate example and the town hall meeting example) appear to be different in that both are clearly dialogues aimed at making a choice on what to do in a situation requiring action. But if you look more closely at the details of the printer example, it is possible to say that what Brian is doing is trying to take action, and that the problem he confronts is one of making a choice about what to do. First of all, when he confronts the problem, he needs to decide whether to take the printer to a computer repair site, whether to do nothing at all and just live with the black line on his documents, or whether to try to fix it himself. After a while, let's say, he gets tired of seeing the black line on his documents, but keeps the choice of going to the computer repair site as his back-up choice. First he will go down the avenue of trying to fix the printer himself. He is not sure whether this is possible, but he knows that he can get useful advice from Google, from his experiences in the past, so he sets down the path of trying to fix it himself by first looking for advice on Google. Looked at this way, we can see that decision-making is involved in the sequence of practical reasoning that Brian moves forward with. If this doesn't work, he can always take the printer to be repaired.

Next, we need to see that in both the real estate example and the town hall meeting example, if we were to analyze the argumentation using the sequence of practical reasoning, it is possible to see that the proposals put forward by Bob and Alice, and then critically analyzed by both of them, are comparable to the hypotheses that Brian sets up in the printer example as assumptions about the best way to proceed. In the real estate example and the town hall meeting example there is much more focus on the ultimate outcomes in the decisions to be made. In the printer example, the three options of whether to fix the printer, do nothing, or take it to the repair site are present initially, but then disappear into the background as Brian only pursues the one choice and ultimately found the action that works best. He does consider the other two possible courses of action at the beginning, but after that nothing is really said about them. Brian's method could be described as trial and error. He is not an expert on fixing printers, but he moves forward one step at a time, hoping that by following the instructions he will ultimately fulfill his goal of removing the black line.

Based on these observations about the similarities between the printer example and the other two examples, despite their differences, a better case can be made for classifying all three of them under the general category of deliberation dialogues. We can use the term 'deliberation dialogue' as the most general category to mark this type of dialogue, and then classify the problem-solving type of procedure as a subcategory of deliberation dialogue. This method of classification may seem a little artificial, but as a technical device, it is a useful way of classifying this general type of setting in which practical reasoning typically takes place.

An aspect of the printer example that can now be commented on, given what was found out about explanations in Chapter 4, is that this case involves explanation as well as argument. When Brian searched for information on the Internet, he found a support page for his printer that contains a troubleshooting guide. As shown in Chapter 6, Section 1, the guide gave a series of five main instructions to solve the problem. This series of instructions can be seen as an explanation to someone who has this particular problem with this type of printer, telling that person how to do something – namely, to solve the problem by doing something that will eliminate the black line. In other words, the message communicated to Brian by the Samsung website is an explanation. The explanation tells Brian how to fix the printer.

During the next stage of his practical reasoning procedure, Brian tried to apply the sequence of instructions given in the explanation. This project turned out to be non-trivial, and involved considerable trial and error. At first Brian could not get the plastic piece covering the small strip of glass to come away from the larger plate of glass. He had to tug and pull the edge of the plastic piece in different directions. Finally, he was able to remove it. He tried cleaning the plastic to remove the black mark, but that did not work either, and he had to take steps to struggle with that problem. He asked his wife Anna about it and she helped him remove the black mark. This whole trial and error process, in which Brian tries to carry out the instructions but confronts various difficulties and manages to cope with them, can be seen as a sequence of practical reasoning.

In other words, in the printer example there is a shift from an initial explanation phase to a secondary phase in which Brian acts on the explanation by trying to apply it to the specific circumstances that he confronts as he observes the parts of the printer and experiments in the way explained by the instructions. So, in this case, just as we found in the cases of practical reasoning in health product ads studied in Chapter 2, both argument and explanation are involved. As Brian goes through the sequence of practical reasoning in which he experiments with ways of trying to follow the instructions to solve this problem, he is engaging in a process that can properly be called argumentation, even though he can be described as a solitary reasoner who is working through the solutions to the problems himself. Of course, he is not entirely alone, because he is following the advice given from the manufacturer's website and he has to seek the help of Anna, and therefore has to explain at least part of the problem to her so that she can engage in the kind of practical reasoning required to solve that part of the problem. As we look over all the details of the case and how they fit together, it is possible to see in it how there is a shift from an initial explanation to a subsequent sequence of argumentation in which Brian tries out various hypotheses that he formulates along the way.

8.9 The Dialectical Model of Rationality

The view advocated in this chapter is that irrationality is determined not exclusively by purely abstract logical criteria relating to the deductive validity of arguments, or by a person's being logically inconsistent, or by a person's departing from the probability calculus. A second thesis of this chapter is that practical irrationality is partly determined by conflicts between goals attributed to an agent or conflicts between such goals and negative consequences of implementing them that the agent has been made aware of. It is a third thesis of this chapter that practical irrationality should also be determined partly by multi-agent criteria, relating to a person's dialectical argumentation in a conversational exchange with another party.

To deepen the distinction between practical and epistemic rationality, it is necessary to go back to Table 2.1, where a dialogue typology was presented showing the characteristics of seven basic types of dialogue. The seven types of dialogue are the inquiry, the discovery dialogue, the negotiation dialogue, the persuasion dialogue, the information-seeking dialogue, the deliberation and the eristic type of dialogue. While practical reasoning is often encountered in the six types of dialogue other than the deliberation, there tends to be a complex embedding in which deliberation is contained, in some way, in the other types of dialogue.

The type of dialogue that most clearly embodies the concept of epistemic rationality is the inquiry dialogue. To take part in this type of dialogue, a group of investigators begin by identifying a proposition to be proved or disproved, and a standard of proof that can be set before the investigations begin to determine what counts as a successful proof or disproof. Generally, the standard of proof set for an inquiry is high. For example, in the public inquiry into an air crash disaster, it will have to be proved to a high standard that there was some specific cause of the disaster that can be identified – for example, pilot error or a design failure in the aircraft. At the next stage of the inquiry the participants organize the evidence and collect as much of it as possible during the constraints of time and resources that they have at their disposal. When they reach the argumentation stage, they draw their conclusions in an orderly way, and carefully evaluate the pros and cons of any hypothesis put forward. Clearly, therefore, the goal of the inquiry as a general type of dialogue is to prove (to a designated standard) that a particular proposition is true or false, or if neither of these objectives can be achieved, to show that the investigation has so thoroughly evaluated all the existing evidence that it has shown that this evidence is insufficient to prove whether the designated proposition is true or false.

CAS can be extended to represent a procedural view of inquiry in which evidence is marshaled to support or defeat claims to knowledge. The model is a sequence of moves in a collaborative group inquiry in which parties take turns making assertions about what is known or not known, putting forward evidence to support them, and subjecting these moves to criticisms. It has been shown in this book how this model of evaluating evidence in an inquiry needs to be based on a defeasible logic using forms of argument that admit of exceptions. It has been contended that reasoning from absence of knowledge is as important to inquiry as positive reasoning from evidence to knowledge. The philosophical conflict between this view of reasoning about knowledge and the veristic view has been explored by airing objections and replies on both sides.

In general, the relationship between knowledge and evidence has five components. The first component is the ultimate conclusion to be proved, the proposition that is claimed to have the status of knowledge. The second is the body of data that is being put forward as the basis for drawing inferences from the data. The third is the marshaling, or collecting together, of the data and conclusions drawn from them that are relevant to support the claim that this proposition can be classified as knowledge. This is the body (or mass) of evidence. The fourth is the chain of reasoning that provides the argumentation, or justification as it might equivalently be called, proving the ultimate proposition from the mass of evidence. The fifth is the standard of proof that this chain of reasoning has to meet in order to prove the ultimate conclusion. Evidence comes to be knowledge through a dialogue procedure called an inquiry, which can be modeled as a dialogue system.

The argumentation stage A of a dialogue is made up of a sequence of moves, where each move M is an ordered pair $<SpA, Con>$, where A is the content of the move and SpA is a speech act representing the type of move whereby A was put forward in D. For example, there is a speech act for making a claim, or assertion as it can equivalently be called. The speaker can say 'I assert proposition A,' and the commitment rule for assertions requires that proposition A be inserted into the speaker's commitment set. Generally, there is a rule regarding burden of proof such that whenever a speaker puts forward a speech act of this sort, and the hearer challenges it, thereby requiring the speaker to back up his claim with some evidence, the speaker must either provide the appropriate evidence or give up his claim. It is a problem in formal dialogue systems that this rule does not always apply to all assertions. Sometimes a participant may assert a statement hypothetically, even though he can't presently prove it. However, if the speaker makes a move claiming that he knows proposition A, then he not only has to give evidence to back up this claim, but the evidence has to meet a standard of proof that is high enough to sustain a claim to knowledge. In dialogue systems, the way to distinguish between knowledge claims and weaker kinds of claims that require less strong supporting arguments to back them up when they are challenged is to use speech acts for different kinds of claims. Each type of claim when made in a dialogue has a standard of proof attached to proving it. A knowledge claim has a higher standard of proof than a claim made as a hypothesis.

It has been shown in this book, through many examples, how the use of practical reasoning in deliberation dialogue represents the paradigm of practical rationality. But complications have also been observed in some detail in Chapter 2, where examples for commercial advertisements for medications clearly exhibited the structure of practical reasoning. In such cases, it was observed that the framework of dialogue in which the practical reasoning was used was basically a persuasion type of dialogue where the advertiser of the product had the goal of trying to get the reader of the ad to buy the product. The advertiser was offering reasons for the conclusion that the reader should find it a good idea to buy this product because it would solve some practical problem that the reader (the target audience) presumably has. But a case of this sort is more complicated than just being an instance of persuasion dialogue. It is also a case of multi-agent practical reasoning, because the reader of the ad may be presumed to be making a decision about how to try to solve his medical problem, and the writer of the ad, by trying to reconstruct what he thinks the practical reasoning of the reader is likely to be, is trying to place his persuasion attempt within that communicative framework. In such a case there is an embedding of one type of dialogue into another. Similarly, in Chapter 5, it was shown how there are complex embeddings of arguments into explanations, and explanations into arguments.

8.10 Concluding Remarks on Rationality

Drawing a clear and precise distinction between practical and epistemic rationality at the ground level of actual use of practical reasoning in a given case is rarely a straightforward exercise. In practice, in cases that are analyzed by the normative standards proposed here, it may not be easy to determine whether an argument should be assessed by the standards of practical rationality or by the standards of epistemic rationality. The reason is basically that practical reasoning is based not only on goals, but also on the agent's knowledge of its circumstances. This latter kind of knowledge is factual, and therefore evaluating it as knowledge needs to be based on epistemic rationality. The agent's knowledge of its circumstances is fallible, because its circumstances tend to be constantly changing.

Because of their dependency on factual knowledge of the circumstances, pro and contra arguments in deliberation have to be continually re-evaluated as new evidence about the situation comes in. For these reasons it is common for there to be a shift between practical rationality and epistemic rationality, and there is nothing wrong with that, even though in some cases confusing the two types of rationality can lead to errors. Despite these complexities, for purposes of moving the theory forward and showing what direction of research would be useful to further study and support it, some general remarks are in order.

Distinguishing between persuasion and deliberation dialogues is often confounded by borderline cases where it appears to be difficult to decide how to categorize a particular argument or discussion. For example, if you look at debate digest articles taken from Debatepedia, you can see that issues such as the following are typical questions for discussion (Atkinson et al., 2013, 2). Should there be a ban on sales of violent video games to minors? Should colleges ban fraternities? Should governments legalize all drugs? Should public schools be allowed to teach creationism alongside evolution as part of their science curriculum? The debates on these questions that can be found in Debatepedia at first appear to be deliberation dialogues because the debate concerns the choice between alternative courses of action. The example from *The Economist* in this chapter also shows how deliberation and persuasion can be mixed in with each other.

As noted in Atkinson et al. (2013, 2), the debaters who discuss issues on the Debatepedia website are not in a position themselves to take action to, for example, ban fraternities or the sale of violent videogames to minors. Hence, the type of discussion typified by these examples is classified by Atkinson et al. as falling into the category of persuasion over action. To solve the problem of distinguishing between deliberation dialogue and dialogues that should be properly categorized as persuasion over action dialogues, Atkinson et al. (2013) drew attention to differences in the speech acts used in the two types of dialogue and set out a number of points of contrast between the two types of dialogue. The two types of dialogue often look alike because they very often use the same kinds of arguments, but one can see differences – for example, in how information is used in different ways in the two types of dialogue. In a persuasion dialogue one party is expected to supply information to answer the questions of the other party, and this information is then used to supply premises for arguments used to persuade the first party that some designated proposition is true or false. In deliberation dialogue, all the concerned parties freely supply and request relevant information, and the aim is to reach a collective decision about what to do in a situation requiring action.

Closer study of the characteristics of the two types of dialogue has revealed examples showing that the adversarial aspect is different in them. The ongoing example used in Atkinson et al. (2013) was a case where participants in a conference had to make a decision about which restaurant to go to for dinner when their workshop was over. This discussion was clearly a deliberation about where to go for dinner, but it often shifted to information-seeking or persuasion dialogue intervals. Even so, it could be identified when such a shift took place because of the characteristics of the different types of dialogue. One such difference is that a persuasion dialogue is more adversarial in nature, even though the success of such a dialogue requires basic agreement about common knowledge and a willingness to follow cooperative rules, such as the rule not to wander off topic, so forth. The deliberation dialogue is much less adversarial, because it presumes that the participants will often have to sacrifice their own individual interests and commitments as a basis of agreement to move forward in a collective decision-making format where the collective interests and needs of the group have to be given priority.

The persuasion dialogue fits the framework of epistemic rationality because the ultimate aim of this type of dialogue is to resolve a conflict of opinions by showing that one proposition is true while the opposed proposition or claim is false, or at least can be subject to sufficient doubt to disqualify it as being provably true.

The information-seeking type of dialogue appears to be similar to the persuasion dialogue and the inquiry dialogue in that its aim is partly one of trying to determine, based on evidence, whether a particular proposition is true or not. However, the standard of proof is not generally so high in an information-seeking dialogue. It needs to be emphasized, however, that the aim of an information-seeking dialogue is not to collect just any kind of data, but to collect reliable data that can be documented as coming from a reliable source. Hence, there is a concern in information-seeking dialogue about critically questioning supporting evidence offered to show that a claim is true, or using counter-arguments to show that a claim may not be true. For this reason the information-seeking type of dialogue can arguably be categorized as fitting the framework of epistemic rationality.

The inquiry dialogue is the only procedural model that can be used to prove or disprove, to the standard of proof appropriate for the field of inquiry, that a proposition should be classified as part of scientific knowledge (Black and Hunter, 2007). The inquiry represents the paradigm of epistemic rationality. However, it was shown in this book that in a deliberation on what to do, for practical purposes, the choice typically needs to be arrived at on a basis of argumentation from expert opinion. Think of the case of Brian and his printer. To arrive at selecting the best proposal in a deliberation dialogue, however, the practical reasoners typically need to examine such expert opinions with care by asking the right critical questions. They do not have the time or resources to become experts themselves. Hence, it is typical to have embeddings of one type of dialogue within another. The capability of managing such dialectical shifts is another aspect of rationality

Negotiation dialogue is about conflicts of interest in the process of bargaining leading to the goal of settling the issue in a way so that both parties can at least get part of what they want out of the agreement that is reached. It is definitely not a truth seeking type of dialogue that fits into the epistemic category, even though it can be interspersed with intervals of persuasion dialogue concerning matters of truth and falsity of propositions. The eristic type of dialogue is comparable to negotiation in this regard. Although it is sometimes interspersed with arguments that appear to be aiming at finding the truth of the matter being discussed, in its ultimate goal of revealing the deeper feelings of the participants, there is little relationship to epistemic concerns.

What will seem most radical in the approach of this book is the idea that arguments, explanations, or other kinds of moves made in argumentation should be viewed as reasonable, deficient, questionable, open to criticism, irrational, or fallacious at two levels. At the first level, such a move needs to evaluated as an instance of good reasoning or not by the standards for good reasoning provided, for example, using the argumentation scheme for practical reasoning. At the second level, it needs to be evaluated in the context of a multi-agent communication, on the basis of whether it contributes to a conventional type of goal-directed conversation that has goals and protocols that can be identified. Adding such a multi-agent conversational level of argument evaluation to the more familiar inferential level of logic has opened the way to providing a new procedural model of rationality that has proved to be useful for applying logic to cases of argumentation and explanation in given texts of discourse. This procedural approach to rationality has been shown in this book to have important implications concerning the meaning of the terms 'rationality' and 'irrationality' in philosophy.

While clearly this approach can solve significant problems about practical rationality, it has also posed problems that have not yet been solved. What can be done, at this point, is to make a general statement in the form of a hypothesis on how to proceed by taking a certain approach to rationality. Real arguments often contain deceptions, fallacies, intentional ambiguities, and shifts from one type of dialogue to another – for example, problematic shifts from deliberation dialogue and negotiation dialogue or persuasion dialogue. A real argument, as used in a particular case, in many instances may not be conclusively judged, using the methods applied in this book, as absolutely correct, deficient, or fallacious. From this viewpoint, the best type of evaluation that can reasonably be given in such cases is a conditional evaluation based on what the argument analyst can take the speaker to have meant, judging by the evidence furnished by the text and context of the case and depending on whether the dialogue has reached the closing stage. It is this dialectical approach that has been taken in this book. On it, an argument or an explanation is not only a set of statements connected in a chain of reasoning. An important factor in its evaluation is the determination of where the reasoning has supposedly been used in relation to some conversational goal that can be presumed to apply. The argument analyst must ask what the reasoning is being used for. The argument needs to be judged at this procedural level as a speech act that contributes collaboratively (Grice, 1975) to a conventional type of dialogue in a multi-agent communication. The argumentation scheme for practical reasoning has been centrally important in guiding this investigation of rationality, and in particular in fitting practical rationality together with epistemic rationality, but fitting this scheme into deliberation dialogue, and to other types of dialogue that can be embedded into deliberation dialogue, has also proved to be essential.

Bibliography

Aakhus, M. (2006). The Act and Activity of Proposing in Deliberation. In P. Riley (ed.), *Engaging Argument: Selected Papers from the 2005 National Communication Association Summer Conference on Argumentation*. Washington, DC: National Communication Association, 402–408.

Achinstein P. (1983). *The Nature of Explanation*. New York, Oxford University Press.

Anscombe, E. (1957). *Intention*. Oxford: Blackwell.

Aristotle (1912). *Topics*. In *The Works of Aristotle Translated into English*, ed. W. D. Ross. Oxford: Oxford University Press.

Aristotle (1939). *Topics*. Trans. E. S. Forster, Loeb Classical Library, Cambridge, MA: Harvard University Press.

Aristotle (1955). *On Sophistical Refutations*. Trans. E. S. Forster, Loeb Classical Library, Cambridge, MA: Harvard University Press.

Aristotle (1968). *Nicomachean Ethics*. Trans. H. Rackham, Loeb Classical Library, Cambridge, MA: Harvard University Press.

Atkinson, K. and Bench-Capon, T. J. M. (2007). Practical Reasoning as Presumptive Argumentation Using Action Based Alternating Transition Systems, *Artificial Intelligence*, 171, 855–874.

Atkinson, K. and Bench-Capon, T. J. M. (2008). Addressing Moral Problems through Practical Reasoning, *Journal of Applied Logic*, 6, 135–151.

Atkinson, K., Bench-Capon, T. J. M., and McBurney, P. (2004a). Justifying Practical Reasoning, *Proceedings of the Fourth International Workshop on Computational Models of Natural Argument* (CMNA 2004), ECAI 2004, Valencia, Spain, 87–90.

Atkinson, K., Bench-Capon, T. J. M., and McBurney, P. (2004b). PARMENIDES: Facilitating Democratic Debate, *Electronic Government*, ed. R. Traunmuller, Lecture Notes in Computer Science (LNCS), 3183. Third International Conference on eGovernment (EGOV 2004), DEXA 2004. Berlin: Springer.

Atkinson, K., Bench-Capon, T. J. M., and McBurney, P. (2004c). Persuasive Political Argument, *Proceedings of the Fifth International Workshop on Computational Models of Natural Argument* (CMNA 2005), ed. F. Grasso, C. Reed, and R. Kibble, Edinburgh, 2005, 44–51.

Atkinson, K., Bench-Capon, T. J. M., and McBurney, P. (2006). Computational Representation of Practical Argument, *Synthese*, 152(2), 157–206.

Atkinson, K., Bench-Capon, T. J. M., and Walton, D. (2013). Distinctive Features of Persuasion and Deliberation Dialogues, *Argument and Computation*, 4(2), 2013, 105–127.

Audi, R. (1989). *Practical Reasoning*. London: Routledge.

Bartley, W. (1962). *The Retreat to Commitment*. New York: Alfred A. Knopf.

Bench-Capon, T. J. M. (2003a). Persuasion in Practical Argument Using Value-based Argumentation Frameworks, *Journal of Logic and Computation*, 13, 429–448.

Bench-Capon, T. J. M. (2003b). Agreeing to Differ: Modelling Persuasive Dialogue between Parties without a Consensus about Values, *Informal Logic*, 22, 231–245.

Bench-Capon, T. J. M. and Atkinson, K. (2009). Abstract Argumentation and Values. *Argumentation and Artificial Intelligence*. Ed. I. Rahwan and G. Simari, Berlin: Springer, 45–64.

Bex, F. J. (2011). *Arguments, Stories and Criminal Evidence: A Formal Hybrid Theory*. Dordrecht: Springer.

Bex, F. J., Bench-Capon, T. J. M., and Atkinson K. (2009). Did He Jump or Was He Pushed?, *Artificial Intelligence and Law*, 17, 79–99.

Bex, F. J. and Budzynska, K. (2010). Argumentation and Explanation in the Context of Dialogue, *Proceedings of 10th International Conference on Computational Models of Natural Argument*, 1–4: www.florisbex.com/papers/CMNA10.pdf.

Bex, F. J. and Walton, D. (2012). Burdens and Standards of Proof for Inference to the Best Explanation: Three Case Studies, *Law, Probability and Risk*, 11(2–3), 113–133.

Bex, F. J. and Walton, D. (2013). Combining Explanation and Argumentation in Dialogue, *Proceedings of the Workshop on Computational Models of Argument*. Berlin: Springer.

Birdsell, D. S. and Groarke, L. (1996). Toward a Theory of Visual Argument, *Argumentation and Advocacy*, 33, 1–10.

Black, E. and Hunter, A. (2007). A Generative Inquiry Dialogue System, *Sixth International Joint Conference on Autonomous Agents and Multi-agent Systems*, ed. M. Huhns and O. Shehory, 1010–1017.

Black, E. and Hunter, A. (2009). An Inquiry Dialogue System. *Autonomous Agents and Multi-Agent Systems*, 19(2):173–209. Springer. DOI 10.1007/s10458-008-9074-5

Bratman, M. (1987). *Intentions, Plans, and Practical Reason*. Cambridge, MA: Harvard University Press.

Bratman, M. (1992). Shared Cooperative Activity, *The Philosophical Review*, 101(2), 327–341.

Bratman, M. (2014). *Shared Agency*. Oxford: Oxford University Press.

Bratman, M., Israel D., and Pollack, M. (1988). Plans and Resource-bounded Practical Reasoning, *Computational Intelligence*, 4, 349–355.

Brown, H. (1988). *Rationality*. London: Routledge.

Burke, M. (1985). Unstated Premises, *Informal Logic*, 7, 107–118.

Calfee, J. E. (2002). Public Policy Issues in Direct-to-Consumer Advertising of Prescription Drugs, *Journal of Public Policy and Marketing*, 21(2), 174–193.

Cassens, J. and Kofod-Petersen, A. (2007). Designing Explanation-Aware Systems: The Quest for Explanation Patterns, *Explanation-Aware Computing: Papers from the 2007 AAAI Workshop*, Technical Report WS-07-06. Menlo Park, CA: AAAI Press, 20–27.

Cawsey, A. (1992). *Explanation and Interaction: The Computer Generation of Explanatory Dialogues*. Cambridge, MA: MIT Press, 1992.

Clarke, D. S. (1985). *Practical Inferences*. London: Routledge and Kegan Paul.

Collingwood, R. (1946). *The Idea of History*. Oxford: Oxford University Press.

Cooke, E. F. (2006). *Peirce's Pragmatic Theory of Inquiry*. London: Continuum.

Copi, I. M. and Cohen, C. (1990). *Introduction to Logic*. 8th edn. New York: Macmillan.

Copi, I. M. and Cohen, C. (2005). *Introduction to Logic*. 12th edn. Upper Saddle River, NJ: Pearson Educational.

Dragoni, A. F., Giorgini, P., and Serafini, L. (2002). Mental States Recognition from Communication, *Journal of Logic and Computation*, 12(1), 119–136.

Dray, W. (1964). *Philosophy of History*. Englewood Cliffs, NJ: Prentice Hall.

Dung, P. (1995). On the Acceptability of Arguments and Its Fundamental Role in Nonmonotonic Reasoning, Logic Programming and n-Person Games. *Artificial Intelligence*, 77(2), 321–357.

Dunne, P. E., Doutre, S., and Bench-Capon, T. J. M. (2005). Discovering Inconsistency through Examination Dialogues. *Proceedings IJCAI-05*, Edinburgh, 1560–1561.

Ehrlich, E., Flexner, S., Carruth, G., and Hawkins, J. (1980). *Oxford American Dictionary*. New York: Oxford University Press.

Engel, P. (ed.) (2000). *Believing and Accepting*. Dordrecht: Kluwer.

Ennis, R. (1982). Identifying Implicit Assumptions, *Synthese*, 51, 61–86.

Ehrlich, E., Berg Flexner, S., Carruth, G., and Hawkins, J. M. (eds.) (1979). *The Oxford American Dictionary*. Oxford: Oxford University Press.

Garner, B. (2009). *Black's Law Dictionary*, 9th ed. St Paul: Thomson Reuters.

Gilbert, M. (1990). Walking Together: A Paradigmatic Social Phenomena, *Midwest Studies in Philosophy*, 15, 1–14.

Girle, R. Hitchcock, D., McBurney, P., and Verheij, B. (2003). Decision Support for Practical Reasoning: A Theoretical and Computational Perspective, in *Argumentation Machines: New Frontiers in Argument and Computation*, ed. C. Reed and T. Norman. Dordrecht: Kluwer, 58–84.

Gordon, D. and Niznik, J. (eds.) (1998). *Criticism and Defense of Rationality in Contemporary Philosophy*. Amsterdam, Rodopi.

Gordon, T. F. (2010). The Carneades Argumentation Support System, in *Dialectics, Dialogue and Argumentation*, ed. C. Reed and C. W. Tindale. London: College Publications.

Gordon, T. F. and Karacapilidis, N. I. (1997). The Zeno Argumentation Framework. In *Proceedings of 6th International Conference on AI and Law (ICAIL-1997)*. New York: ACM Press, 10–18.

Gordon, T. F. and Richter, G. (2002). Discourse Support Systems for Deliberative Democracy, in *eGovernment: State of the Art and Perspectives (EGOV)*, ed. Roland Traunmuller and Lalus Lenk, Aix-en-Provence: Springer Verlag, 248–255.

Gordon T. F. and Walton, D. (2006). The Carneades Argumentation Framework, in *Computational Models of Argument: Proceedings of COMMA 2006*, ed. P. E. Dunne and T. J. M. Bench-Capon. Amsterdam: IOS Press, 195–207.

Gordon, T. F. and Walton, D. (2009). Proof Burdens and Standards, in *Argumentation in Artificial Intelligence*, ed. I. Rahwan and G. Simari. Berlin: Springer, 239–260.

Gordon, T. F., Prakken, H., and Walton, D. 2007. The Carneades Model of Argument and Burden of Proof, *Artificial Intelligence*, 171, 875–896.

Gough, J. and Tindale, C. (1985). Hidden or Missing Premises, *Informal Logic*, 7, 99–106.

Grice, H. P. (1975). Logic and Conversation, in *Syntax and Semantics*, vol. 3, ed. P. Cole and J. L. Morgan. New York: Academic Press, 1975, 43–58.

Groarke, L. (2009). Informal Logic, in *Stanford Encyclopedia of Philosophy*, ed. Edward N. Zalta: http://plato.stanford.edu/entries/logic-informal

Hamblin, C. L. (1970). *Fallacies*. London: Methuen, 1970.

Hamblin, C. L. (1971). Mathematical Models of Dialogue, *Theoria*, 37, 130–155.

Hannon, M. (2014). Fallibilism and the Value of Knowledge, *Synthese*, 191(6), 1119–1146.

Hare, R. M. (1971). *Practical Inferences*. London: Macmillan, 1971.

Hempel, C. (1965). Aspects of Scientific Explanation, in C. Hempel, *Aspects of Scientific Explanation and Other Essays in the Philosophy of Science*. New York: Free Press, 331–496.

Hitchcock, D. (1985). Enthymematic Arguments, *Informal Logic*, 7, 83–97.

Hitchcock, D. (1991). Some principles of rational mutual inquiry. In F. van Eemeren, R. Grootendorst, J. A. Blair, and C. A. Willard (eds.), *Proceedings of the Second International Conference on Argumentation*, 236–243. Amsterdam: SICSAT: International Society for the Study of Argumentation.

Hitchcock, D. (2002). Pollock on Practical Reasoning, *Informal Logic*, 22, 247–256.

Hitchcock, D., McBurney, P., and Parsons, S. (2001). A Framework for Deliberation Dialogues, Proceedings of the 4th OSSA (Ontario Society for the Study of Argumentation) Conference, 2001, 1–24. www.humanities.mcmaster.ca/~hitchckd/deliberationdialogues.pdf

Horty, J. and Belnap, N. (1995). The Deliberative Stit: A Study of Action, Omission, Ability and Obligation, *Journal of Philosophical Logic*, 24, 1995, 583–644.

Jonsen, A. R. and Toulmin, S. (1988). *The Abuse of Casuistry: A History of Moral Reasoning*. Berkeley: University of California Press.

Josephson, J. R. and Josephson, S. G. (1994). *Abductive Inference: Computation, Philosophy, Technology*. New York: Cambridge University Press.

Kauffeld, F. J. (1995). The Persuasive Force of Arguments on Behalf of Proposals, Amsterdam, SicSat, Analysis and Evaluation. In *Proceedings of the Third ISSA Conference on Argumentation*, Vol. 2.

Kauffeld, F. J. (1998). Presumptions and the Distribution of Argumentative Burdens in Acts of Proposing and Accusing, *Argumentation*, 12, 245–266.

Kok, E., Meyer, J., Prakken, H., and Vreeswijk, G. (2010). A Formal Argumentation Framework for Deliberation Dialogues, in *Proceedings of the 7th International Workshop on Argumentation in Multi-Agent Systems*, P. McBurney, I. Rahwan, and S. Parsons (eds.). Berlin: Springer, 73–90.

Krabbe, E. C. W. (2013). Topical Roots of Formal Dialectic, *Argumentation*, 27(1), 71–87.

Kukafka, R. (2005). Tailored Health Communication, in *Consumer Health Informatics: Informing Consumers and Improving Health Care*, ed. D. Lewis, G. Eysenbach, Z. Stavri, and H. Jimison, New York: Springer, 22–33.

Lascher, E. L. (1999). *The Politics of Automobile Insurance Reform: Ideas, Institutions, and Public Policy in North America*. Washington, DC: Georgetown University Press.

Leake, D. B. (1992). *Evaluating Explanations*. Hillsdale, NJ: Erlbaum.

Leonard, D. P. (2001). Character and Motive in Evidence Law, *Loyola of Los Angeles Law Review*, 34, 439–536.

Lexchin, J. and Mintzes, B. (2002). Direct-to-Consumer Advertising of Prescription Drugs: The Evidence Says No, *Journal of Public Policy & Marketing*, 21(2), 194–201.

McBurney, P., Hitchcock, D., and Parsons, S. (2007). The Eightfold Way of Deliberation Dialogue, *International Journal of Intelligent Systems*, 22, 95–132.

Moore, J. D. (1995). *Participating in Explanatory Dialogues*. Cambridge, MA: MIT Press, 1995.

Moulin, B., Irandoust, H., Belanger, M., and Desbordes, G. (2002). Explanation and Argumentation Capabilities, *Artificial Intelligence Review*, 17, 169–222.

Paglieri, F. and Castelfranchi, C. (2005). Arguments as Belief Structures, in *The Uses of Argument: Proceedings of a Conference at McMaster University*, ed. D. Hitchcock and D. Farr, Ontario Society for the Study of Argumentation, 356–367.

Panzarasa P., Jennings N. R., and Norman T. J. (2002). Formalizing Collaborative Decision-making and Practical Reasoning in Multi-agent Systems. *Journal of Logic and Computation*, 12(1), 55–117.

Peirce, C. S. (1931). *Collected Papers*. Edited by C. Hartshorne and P. Weiss. Cambridge: Harvard University Press.

Peirce, S. (1984). *Writings of Charles S. Peirce*, vol. 2. Edited by E. C. Moore. Bloomington: Indiana University Press.

Pennington, N. and Hastie, R. (1993). The Story Model for Juror Decision Making, in *Inside the Juror: The Psychology of Juror Decision Making*, ed. R. Hastie. Cambridge: Cambridge University Press, 192–221.

Pollock, J. L. (1995). *Cognitive Carpentry*. Cambridge, MA: The MIT Press.

Popper, K. (1963). *Conjectures and Refutations: The Growth of Scientific Knowledge*. Routledge: London.

Prakken, H. (2006), Formal Systems for Persuasion Dialogue, *The Knowledge Engineering Review*, 21, 163–188.

Prakken, H. (2010). An Abstract Framework for Argumentation with Structured Arguments, *Argument and Computation*, 1(2), 93–124.

Prakken, H. (2011). An Overview of Formal Models of Argumentation and Their Application in Philosophy, *Studies in Logic*, 4(1), 65–86.

Rahwan, I. and Amgoud, L. (2006). An Argumentation-based Approach for Practical Reasoning. *Proceedings of the 5th International Joint Conference on Autonomous Agents and Multiagent Systems (AAMAS)*, Hakodate, Japan and New York: ACM Press, 347–354.

Reed, C. and Rowe, G. (2002). Araucaria: Software for Puzzles in Argument Diagramming and XML. *Technical Report*, Department of Applied Computing, University of Dundee.

Reed, C. and Norman, T. J. (2003). *Argumentation Machines: New Frontiers in Argument and Computation*. Dordrecht: Kluwer.

Reed, C. and Rowe, G. (2004). Araucaria: Software for Argument Analysis, Diagramming and Representation, *International Journal of AI Tools*, 14(3–4), 961–980. Retrieved from http://araucaria.computing.dundee.ac.uk/doku.php.

Reiter, R. (1980). A Logic for Default Reasoning. *Artificial Intelligence*, 13(1–2), 81–132.

Rescher, N. (1966). Practical Reasoning and Values, *The Philosophical Quarterly*, 16(63), 121–136.

Rescher, N. (1988). *Rationality*. Oxford: Clarendon Press.

Rescher, N. (2003). *Epistemology: An Introduction to the Theory of Knowledge*. Albany: Sate University of New York Press.

Rubinelli, S. (2005). Ask Your Doctor: Argumentation in Advertising of Prescription Medicines, *Studies in Communication Sciences*, 5(2), 75–98.

Rubinelli, S., Nakamoto, K., and Schulz, P. K. (2007). Reading Direct-to-Consumer Advertising of Prescription Medicine: A Qualitative Study from Argumentation Theory on Its Dialectical and Rhetorical Features, in *Proceedings of the Sixth Conference of the International Society for the Study of Argumentation*, ed. Frans van Eemeren et al., Amsterdam SicSat, 1211–1215.

Rubinelli, S., Nakamoto, K., and Schulz, P. K. (2008). The Rabbit in the Hat: Dubious Argumentation and the Persuasive Effects of Prescription Drug Advertising, *Communication & Medicine*, 5 (1), 49–58.

Russell, S. J. and Norvig, P. (1995). *Artificial Intelligence: A Modern Approach*. Upper Saddle River, NJ: Prentice Hall.

Sartor, G. (2005). *Legal Reasoning: A Cognitive Approach to the Law*. Springer: Berlin.

Schank, R. C. (1986). *Explanation Patterns: Understanding Mechanically and Creatively*. Hillsdale, NJ: Erlbaum.

Schank, R. C. and Abelson, R. P. (1977). *Scripts, Plans, Goals and Understanding*. Hillsdale, NJ: Erlbaum.

Schank, R. C. and Riesback, C. K. (1981). *Inside Computer Understanding*. Hillsdale, NJ: Erlbaum.

Schank, R. C., Kass, A., and Riesbeck, C. K. (1994). *Inside Case-Based Explanation*. Hillsdale, NJ: Erlbaum, 1994.

Scheuer, O., Loll, F., Pinkwart, N., and McLaren, B. M. (2009). Computer-Supported Argumentation: A Review of the State of the Art, *International Journal of Computer-Supported Collaborative Learning*, 5(1), 1–67.

Scriven, M. (1976) *Reasoning*. New York: McGraw-Hill.

Searle, J. (1990). Collective Intentions and Actions, in *Intentions in Communication*. Cambridge: MIT Press, 401–415.

Searle, J. (2001). *Rationality in Action*. Cambridge, MA: The MIT Press.

Segerberg, K. (1984). Towards an Exact Philosophy of Action, *Topoi*, 3, 75–83.

Simon, H. (1981). *The Sciences of the Artificial*. Cambridge, MA: The MIT Press.

Slade, C. (2003). Seeing Reasons: Visual Argumentation in Advertisements, *Argumentation*, 17, 145–160.

Thorsrud, H. (2002). Cicero on His Academic Predecessors: The Fallibilism of Arcesilaus and Carneades, *Journal of the History of Philosophy*, 40, 1–18.

Toniolo, A. (2013). *Models of Argument for Deliberative Dialogue in Complex Domains*. PhD Thesis, University of Aberdeen.

Toniolo, A., Norman, T. J., and Sycara, K. (2012). An Empirical Study of Argumentation Schemes for Deliberative Dialogue. In L. De Raedt, C. Bessiere, D. Dubois, P. Doherty, P. Frasconi, F. Heintz, and P. Lucas (eds.), *ECAI 2012: 20th European Conference on Artificial Intelligence. Frontiers in Artificial Intelligence and Applications*, IOS Press, vol. 242, 756–761.

Toniolo, A., Norman, T., and Sycara K. (2013). An Empirical Study of Argumentation Schemes for Deliberative Dialogue, in *Computational Models of Natural Argument*. Berlin: Springer.

Trout, J. D. (2002). Scientific Explanation and the Sense of Understanding, *Philosophy of Science*, 69 (2), 212–233.

Tuomela, R. (2007). *The Philosophy of Sociality: The Shared Point of View*. Oxford: Oxford University Press, 2007.

Tuomela, R. (2013). *Social Ontology: Collective Intentionality and Group Agents*. Oxford: Oxford University Press.

Tuomela, R. and Miller, K. (1988). We-Intentions, *Philosophical Studies*, 53, 367–389.

Van Eemeren, F. H. (2010). *Strategic Maneuvering in Argumentative Discourse*. Amsterdam: Benjamins.

Van Eemeren, F. H. and Grootendorst, R. (1984). *Speech Acts in Communicative Discussions*. Dordrecht: Foris.

Van Eemeren, F. H. and Grootendorst, R. (1992). *Argumentation, Communication and Fallacies*. Hillsdale, NJ: Lawrence Erlbaum Associates.

Van Eemeren, F. H. and Grootendorst, R. (2004). *A Systematic Theory of Argumentation*. Cambridge: Cambridge University Press.

Van Gijzel, B. and Prakken, H. (2012). Relating Carneades with Abstract Argumentation via the ASPIC+ Framework for Structured Argumentation, *Argument and Computation*, 3(1), 21–47.

Verheij, B. (2003a). DefLog: on the Logical Interpretation of Prima Facie Justified Assumptions, *Journal of Logic and Computation*, 13(3), 319–346.

Verheij, B. (2003b). Dialectical Argumentation with Argumentation Schemes: An Approach to Legal Logic, *Artificial Intelligence and Law*, 11, 167–195.

Verheij, B. (2005). *Virtual Arguments. On the Design of Argument Assistants for Lawyers and Other Arguers*. The Hague: TMC Asser Press.

Verheij, B. (2007). Argumentation Support Software: Boxes-and-arrows and Beyond, *Law, Probability and Risk*, 6, 187–208.

Von Wright, G. H. (1963). Practical Inference, *The Philosophical Review*, 72, 159–179.

Von Wright, G. H. (1972). On So-Called Practical Inference, *Acta Sociologica*, 15, 39–53.

Wagenaar, W. A., van Koppen, P. J., and Crombag, H. F. M. (1993). *Anchored Narratives: The Psychology of Criminal Evidence*. Hertfordshire: Harvester Wheatsheaf.

Wallace, R. J. (2014). Practical Reason, *The Stanford Encyclopedia of Philosophy* E. N. Zalta (ed.): http://plato.stanford.edu/entries/practical-reason/

Walton, D. (1990a). *Practical Reasoning: Goal-Driven, Knowledge-Based, Action-Guiding Argumentation*. Savage, MD: Rowman & Littlefield.

Walton, D. (1990b). What Is Reasoning? What Is an Argument?, *Journal of Philosophy*, 87, 399–419.

Walton, D. (1995). *A Pragmatic Theory of Fallacy*. Tuscaloosa and London: The University of Alabama Press.

Walton, D. (1996). *Argumentation Schemes for Presumptive Reasoning*. Mahwah, NJ: Erlbaum.

Walton, D. (1997a). *Actions and Inconsistency: The Closure Problem of Practical Reasoning*, in *Contemporary Action Theory*, Vol. 1. ed. G. Holmstrom-Hintikka and R. Tuomela. Dordrecht: Kluwer, 159–175.

Walton, D. (1997b). *Appeal to Expert Opinion: Arguments from Authority*. University Park, PA: Penn State Press.

Walton, D. (1998a). *The New Dialectic*. Toronto: University of Toronto Press.

Walton, D. (1998b). *Ad Hominem Arguments*. Tuscaloosa: University of Alabama Press.

Walton, D. (2004a). *Abductive Reasoning*. Tuscaloosa: University of Alabama Press.

Walton, D. (2004b). *Relevance in Argumentation*. Mahwah, NJ: Erlbaum.

Walton, D. (2004c). A New Dialectical Theory of Explanation, *Philosophical Explorations*, 7, 71–89.

Walton, D. (2005). How to Make and Defend a Proposal in Deliberation Dialogue, *Artificial Intelligence and Law*, 14, 177–239.

Walton, D. (2006). *Fundamentals of Critical Argumentation*. Cambridge: Cambridge University Press.

Walton, D. (2007a). Evaluating Practical Reasoning, *Synthese*, 157, 197–240.

Walton, D. (2007b). Dialogical Models of Explanation, *Explanation-Aware Computing: Papers from the 2007 AAAI Workshop*, Association for the Advancement of Artificial Intelligence, Technical Report WS-07-06, Menlo Park, CA: AAAI Press, 1–9.

Walton, D. (2008). Three Bases for the Enthymeme: A Dialectical Theory, *Journal of Applied Logic*, 6, 361–379.

Walton, D. (2011a). Teleological Argumentation to and from Motives, *Law, Probability and Risk*, 10, 203–223.

Walton, D. (2011b). A Dialogue System Specification for Explanation, *Synthese*, 182(3), 349–374.

Walton, D. (2011c). An Argumentation Model of Deliberative Decision-Making, in *Technologies for Supporting Reasoning Communities and Collaborative Decision Making: Cooperative Approaches*, ed. J. Yearwood and A. Stranieri, Hershey, Pa., IGI Global, 1–17.

Walton, D. (2011d). Reasoning about Knowledge Using Defeasible Logic, *Argument and Computation*, 2(2–3), 131–155.

Walton, D. and Krabbe, E. (1995). *Commitment in Dialogue*, Albany: State University of New York Press.

Walton, D. and Reed, C. (2005). Argumentation Schemes and Enthymemes, *Synthese*, 145, 339–370.

Walton, D., Reed, C., and Macagno, F. (2008). *Argumentation Schemes*. Cambridge: Cambridge University Press.

Walton, D. and Schafer, B. (2006). Arthur, George and the Mystery of the Missing Motive: Towards a Theory of Evidentiary Reasoning about Motives, *International Commentary on Evidence*, 4(2), 1–47.

Walton, D. and Zhang, N. (2013). The Epistemology of Scientific Evidence, *Artificial Intelligence and Law*, 21, 173–219.

Walton, D., Norman, T. J., and Toniolo, A. (2015). Missing Phases of Deliberation Dialogue for Real Applications, in *Lecture Notes in Computer Science*, Berlin: Springer, 1–20. http://www.dougwalton.ca/papers%20in%20pdf/14ArgMAS.pdf

Wigmore, J. H. (1931). *The Principles of Judicial Proof*, 2nd ed. Boston: Little, Brown and Company.

Wigmore, J. H. (1935). *A Student's Textbook of the Law of Evidence*. Chicago: The Foundation Press.

Wigmore, J. H. (1940). *Evidence in Trials at Common Law.* Boston: Little, Brown & Co.

Wilson, B. R. (1970). *Rationality.* New York: Harper and Row.

Wooldridge, M. (2000). *Reasoning about Rational Agents.* Cambridge, MA: The MIT Press.

Wooldridge, M. (2002). *An Introduction to MultiAgent Systems.* Chichester: Wiley.

Wooldridge, M. and Jennings, N. (1995). Intelligent Agents: Theory and Practice, *The Knowledge Engineering Review*, 10, 115–152.

Index